HOW GLOBAL CURRENCIES WORK

How Global Currencies Work

Past, Present, and Future

Barry Eichengreen

Arnaud Mehl

Livia Chiţu

PRINCETON UNIVERSITY PRESS

PRINCETON AND OXFORD

Copyright © 2018 by Princeton University Press

Published by Princeton University Press,
41 William Street, Princeton, New Jersey 08540

In the United Kingdom: Princeton University Press,
6 Oxford Street, Woodstock, Oxfordshire OX20 1TR

press.princeton.edu

Cover image courtesy of Shutterstock

First paperback printing, 2019

Paper ISBN 978-0-691-19186-7

Cloth ISBN 978-0-691-17700-7
Library of Congress Control Number 2017946118

British Library Cataloging-in-Publication Data is available

This book has been composed in Adobe Text Pro and Gotham

Printed on acid-free paper. ∞

Printed in the United States of America

CONTENTS

List of Tables   vii

List of Figures   ix

Acknowledgments   xiii

1   Introduction   1

2   The Origins of Foreign Balances   16

3   From Jekyll Island to Genoa   30

4   Reserve Currencies in the 1920s and 1930s   42

5   The Role of Currencies in Financing International Trade   58

6   Evidence from International Bond Markets   84

7   Reserve Currency Competition in the Second Half
      of the Twentieth Century   116

8   The Retreat of Sterling   145

9   The Rise and Fall of the Yen   158

10   The Euro as Second in Command   170

11   Prospects for the Renminbi   181

12   Conclusion   195

Notes   201

References   227

Index   245

TABLES

4.1. Coverage of Data on Reserve Currency Composition   46

5.1. German and British Overseas Banks in Latin
America: 1913 vs. 1921   72

5.2. Determinants of Banks' Acceptances   74

5.3. Determinants of Banks' Acceptances, Including
Federal Reserve's Own Market-Making Activities   75

5.4. Determinants of Banks' Acceptances, Including
Federal Reserve's Own Market-Making Activities
and Holdings on Foreign Account   76

5.5. Robustness: With Fed-Commercial Spread
Replacing Fed Holdings   77

5.6. Robustness: Using Log Market Share as
Dependent Variable   78

6.1. Determinants of Currency Shares: Baseline
Model Estimates   102

6.A1. Determinants of Currency Shares: Estimates Using
Alternative Estimation Methods   108

6.A2. Determinants of Currency Shares: Additional
Sensitivity Tests   110

6.A3. Determinants of Currency Shares: Treatments
for Endogeneity   113

6.A4. Determinants of Currency Shares: Estimates
Including Commonwealth Countries   114

6.A5. Determinants of Currency Shares: Estimates in
Relative Terms 115

7.1. Demand for Reserves: Basic Estimates 125

7.2. Demand for Reserves: Country-Level Estimates 130

7.3. Demand for Reserves: Estimates with Policy
Measures 131

7.A. Overview of Policy Measures to Support/
Discourage International Currency Use, 1947–2013 136

10.1. Selected Indicators of the International Use of the
Euro, 1998–2015 176

FIGURES

1.1. Shares of Currencies in Known Reserves, 1899   7

1.2. Shares of Currencies in Known Reserves, 1913   7

2.1. Diffusion of Monetary Denominations circa 1900   25

4.1. Aggregate Foreign Currency Holdings
      (16 countries), 1929   47

4.2. Fraction of Reserves in Third Currencies, 1919–1939   48

4.3. French Foreign Exchange and
      Gold Reserves, 1928–1939   49

4.4. Currency Composition of Reserves for Four
      Countries, 1920–1936   51

4.5. "G9" Exchange Reserves (Czechoslovakia,
      Denmark, Finland, Italy, Japan, Norway, Portugal,
      Spain, and Switzerland), 1923–1933   51

4.6. Non-English-Speaking Sterling Area Exchange
      Reserves, 1917–1934   53

4.7. Gold Bloc Exchange Reserves (excluding France),
      1920–1938   54

4.8. Latin American Exchange Reserves (Chile and
      Colombia), 1926–1938   55

4.9. Central European Exchange Reserves (Romania,
      Austria, and Czechoslovakia), 1923–1937   55

5.1. London and New York Money Market
      Rates, 1900–1939   64

5.2. Dollar and Sterling Acceptances, 1927–1937   65

5.3. Spreads between Official and Market Rates in
London and New York, 1917–1939   66

5.4. Total Outstanding Acceptances and Amounts Held
by the Federal Reserve Board, Own Account or for
Account of Foreign Correspondents, 1917–1939   66

5.5. Share of the Fed in the Acceptance Market and
Relative Interest Rates, 1917–1937   69

5.6. Bank of England Rediscount Rate and Open Market
Rate, 1900–1939   70

6.1. Number of Countries Reporting Data, 1914–1944   87

6.2. Global Foreign Public Debt, 1914–1945   88

6.3. Global Foreign Public Debt in U.S. Dollars—
Main Debtors, 1929   89

6.4. Global Foreign Public Debt in Sterling—
Main Debtors, 1929   90

6.5a. Global Foreign Public Debt—Full Sample, 1914–1944   92

6.5b. Global Foreign Public Debt—Excluding
Commonwealth Countries, 1914–1944   93

6.5c. Global Foreign Public Debt—Excluding
Commonwealth Countries, Arithmetic
Averages, 1914–1946   94

6.6. Global Foreign Public Debt—Alternative Methods
of Calculating Currency Shares, 1914–1944   95

6.7. Share of U.S. Dollar/Sterling Debt in Foreign Public
Debt—Breakdown by Country, 1914–1944   98

6.8. Estimated Contributions (Including Inertia Effects)
to Change in the Share of the U.S. Dollar in Global
Foreign Public Debt, between 1918 and 1932   104

6.9. Estimated Contributions (Including Inertia Effects)
to Change in the Share of Sterling in Global Foreign
Public Debt, between 1918 and 1932   105

6.10. Estimated Contributions (Including Inertia Effects) to Change in the Share of the U.S. Dollar in Global Foreign Public Debt, between 1932 and 1939   106

7.1. Currency Composition of Globally Disclosed Foreign Exchange Reserves, 1947–2015   119

7.2. Currency Composition of Globally Disclosed Foreign Exchange Reserves at Constant Exchange Rates, 1947–2015   120

7.3. Currency Concentration of Globally Disclosed Foreign Exchange Reserves, 1947–2013   121

7.4. Time-Varying Structural Break Tests   128

10.1. Comparison of the Dollar and the Euro   175

11.1. Bond Markets and GDP per Capita at Purchasing Power Parity, 2014   187

11.2. Equity Market Capitalization and GDP per Capita at Purchasing Power Parity, 2012   188

12.1. Currency Composition of Globally Disclosed Foreign Exchange Reserves, 1899–2015   196

ACKNOWLEDGMENTS

Many persons have contributed to this manuscript over its long gestation. By far the most important contributor, as will be evident from the material that follows, is Marc Flandreau. Marc was a coauthor of the journal articles that were forerunners to Chapters 4 and 5. His comments led us to fundamentally rethink the organization and content of Chapter 2. His contribution to this project cannot be overstated. It would not exist without his input. Marc's imprint on the final product will be clear to even the most casual reader.

We are grateful in addition to many friends and colleagues who commented on earlier drafts and on portions of the final manuscript. Attempting to list them risks offending by omission, since so many people have offered constructive feedback in seminars and over meals and coffee, spread over a period of years. Still, we would be remiss if we did not acknowledge the helpful comments of the following: Olivier Accominotti, Leszek Balcerowicz, Agnès Bénassy-Quéré, Matthieu Bussière, Menzie Chinn, Charles Engel, Kristin Forbes, Jeffrey Frankel, Jeffry Frieden, Norbert Gaillard, Pierre-Olivier Gourinchas, Pierre-Cyrille Hautcœur, John James, Robert Keohane, Philip Lane, Matteo Maggiori, Christopher Meissner, Ugo Panizza, Richard Portes, Angela Redish, Hélène Rey, and Thomas Willett.

Comments were also provided by seminar and conference participants at the following institutions: the American Economic Association annual meetings; the Asian Development Bank; Australian National University; the Bank for International Settlements; Clapes at the Catholic University of Santiago; Claremont McKenna College; the European Central Bank; the Fundación Areces (Madrid); Harvard University; Norges Bank; Stanford University; Tsinghua

University; the University of Southern California; the University of Cambridge; and the University of California at Berkeley, Los Angeles, and Riverside. We are also indebted to the two anonymous referees of Princeton University Press and to our editors, Joe Jackson and Peter Dougherty.

A contribution of this project is new data, some from the archives of central banks and other institutions, others drawn from obscure and well-known published sources. In assembling these data, we relied on the hard work and goodwill of graduate student researchers, librarians, archivists, friends, and officials in a large number of different countries. (In some cases, the individuals in question qualify under more than one of the aforementioned five headings.) We can't count the number of times we were told that "the information you're looking for no longer exists" or "we have those balance sheets from the 1920s that you're asking about, but you can't see them," only for the material to miraculously appear following intervention from the highest level (where, in monetary history, intervention from the highest level means a phone call from the central bank governor). For assistance with collecting data we are grateful to Olivier Accominotti, Leif Alendal, Walter Antonowicz, Gopalan Balachandran, Elizabeta Blejan, David Merchan Cardénas, Mauricio Cardenas, Pedro Carvalho, Filippo Cesrano, Vittorio Corbo, Jose DeGregorio, Oyvind Eitrheim, Rui Pedro Esteves, Peter Federer, Patrick Halbeisen, Mirako Hatase, Thomas Holub, Vappu Ikonen, Lars Jonung, Hans Kryger Larsen, Hassan Malik, Bernhard Mussak, Pilar Noguès Marco, Carry van Renslaar, Riad Rezzik, David Schindlower, Virgil Stoenescu, Trevin Stratton, and Pierre Turgeon. We are grateful for careful copyediting by Cyd Westmoreland.

Financial support for portions of this research was provided by the National Science Foundation, the France-Berkeley Fund, and the Committee on Research and Clausen Center for International Business and Policy, both of the University of California at Berkeley.

Finally, we acknowledge with thanks the permission of the following, where needed, to reproduce previously published material.

Note that all the material included in this book has been substantially reformatted and revised compared to these prior publications.

Chapter 2. Marc Flandreau and Clemens Jobst (2009), "The Empirics of International Currencies: Network Externalities, History and Persistence," *Economic Journal* 119, pp. 643–664.

Chapter 4. Barry Eichengreen and Marc Flandreau (2009), "The Rise and Fall of the Dollar (Or When Did the Dollar Replace Sterling as the Leading International Currency?)," *European Review of Economic History* 13, pp. 377–411.

Chapter 5. Barry Eichengreen and Marc Flandreau (2012), "The Federal Reserve, the Bank of England and the Rise of the Dollar as an International Currency 1914–39," *Open Economies Review* 23, pp. 57–87.

Chapter 6. Livia Chiţu, Barry Eichengreen, and Arnaud Mehl (2014), "When Did the Dollar Overtake Sterling as the Leading International Currency? Evidence from the Bond Markets," *Journal of Development Economics* 111, pp. 225–245.

Chapter 7. Barry Eichengreen, Livia Chiţu, and Arnaud Mehl (2016), "Stability or Upheaval? The Currency Composition of International Reserves in the Long Run," *IMF Economic Review* 64, pp. 354–380.

Chapter 10. Portions from Arnaud Mehl (2015), "L'euro sur la scène internationale après la crise financière et celle de la dette, " *Revue d'économie financière* 119(3), pp. 55–68.

Chapter 11. Portions from Barry Eichengreen (2013), "Number One Country, Number One Currency?" *World Economy* 36, pp. 363–374.

The views expressed in this book are those of the authors and do not necessarily reflect those of the European Central Bank or the Eurosystem. They should not be reported as such.

HOW GLOBAL CURRENCIES WORK

1

Introduction

In both scholarly narratives and popular histories, the dynamics of the global economy are portrayed in terms of the rise and fall of great powers.[1] The economic historian Angus Maddison, in his influential synthesis, characterized the dynamics of global growth in terms of the gap between the technological leader and its followers. The identity of the lead country may change, but technical progress in the leader always defines the limits of the possible. The task for other countries is not to expand that frontier but to follow the leader and close the technology gap.[2] Charles Kindleberger emphasized stability as well as growth, but like Maddison, he described global dynamics in terms of the changing identity but unchanging importance of the lead economy. In Kindleberger's analysis, only the leading power had the capacity to stabilize the international system. It was therefore in periods of transition, when economic leadership passed from one country to another, that risks to stability were greatest.[3]

More concretely, these stories are told in terms of British hegemony in the nineteenth century, when Great Britain as the first industrial nation defined the technological frontier, and the country helped stabilize the global system by lending countercyclically—exporting capital when other economies suffered downturns—and by maintaining an open market for the goods of distressed foreign producers. They are told in terms of American hegemony in the twentieth century, when the power of the United States was effectively institutionalized in what is sometimes referred to as the Bretton Woods–GATT System.[4] Extrapolating into the future, they will be told in terms of Chinese hegemony in the twenty-first.

Monetary historians view the same history through the lens of currencies. The nineteenth-century international economy—the era of the international gold standard, also sometimes called "the first age of financial globalization"—was dominated by the pound sterling. The Bank of England, its issuer, was conductor of the international orchestra.[5] Britain's status as leading foreign lender and home to the world's deepest financial markets gave its central bank unmatched influence over the operation of the international monetary and financial system. Britain's colonial trade, with India in particular, cushioned its balance of payments and eased adjustment in international financial markets.

Sterling, it is said, had no consequential rivals as an international and reserve currency in this period. London had no equals as an international financial center. The Bank of England had more influence over capital flows, exchange rates, and related financial matters than did any other central bank.

Paralleling these narratives of British economic and financial dominance in the nineteenth century, analogous stories are told about the twentieth-century international economy, or at least the international economy of the second half of the century. Once the torch of leadership was passed, international monetary and financial relations were dominated by the United States and the U.S. dollar. The dollar was the only freely available and widely accepted national currency in the Bretton Woods international monetary system, under which the greenback was pegged to gold while other currencies were effectively pegged to the dollar. Only the United States possessed deep and liquid financial markets on which its currency could be freely bought and sold and used by traders around the world, together with the economic, financial, and military strength to guarantee that its markets would remain open to other countries.

Moreover, what was true in the third quarter of the twentieth century—the heyday of Bretton Woods—was still true in the fourth, even though the Bretton Woods par value system was no more. Through the end of the twentieth century and longer, the dollar remained the dominant international and reserve currency. International monetary economists like Milton Gilbert and Ronald McKinnon referred to the monetary arrangements of the third and fourth quarters of the twentieth century, revealingly, not as the Bretton Woods and post–Bretton Woods periods but as the era of the "gold-dollar system" and the "dollar standard," respectively.[6]

The dominance of the dollar gave the Federal Reserve System singular leverage over global financial conditions. That leverage evidently persists to this day, as reflected in the close attention paid to the impact of Fed policy on international financial conditions and the complaints of policy makers about the implications for their countries of U.S. monetary easing and tightening.[7]

Looking to the future, the same stories of political, economic, and monetary dominance are now told in terms of Chinese hegemony. The twenty-first century global economy, it is suggested, will be organized around the Chinese renminbi and regulated by the People's Bank of China. China's immensely large population all but guarantees that the country will overtake the United States as the single largest economy, just as the U.S. overtook Britain in the late nineteenth century.[8] The renminbi will then overtake the dollar as the dominant international currency, for the same reasons that the dollar overtook sterling. Or so it is said by those who foresee this as the Chinese century, much as its predecessor was the American century.[9]

The Traditional View

This traditional view, that economic dominance and monetary dominance go together, flows from models with strong network externalities, so that first-mover advantage matters, and when those externalities are sufficiently powerful that the result is "winner takes all."[10] In these models, it pays when transacting across borders to use the same currency used by others transacting across borders.

Network returns are strongly increasing, in other words. Expressing the price of one's exports in the same currency as other exporters enables customers to easily compare prices and facilitates the efforts of entrants to break into international markets. Since intermediate inputs, when sourced from abroad, will similarly be priced and invoiced in the dominant international currency, a firm will prefer to express the prices of its exports in that same currency, thus preventing its costs from fluctuating relative to its revenues when the exchange rate changes.

Likewise, denominating one's debt securities in the same currency as other issuers enables investors to readily compare returns and makes it easier for new issuers to secure loans on international capital markets. Borrowing costs will be lowest in the deepest and most liquid financial market, which possesses its depth and liquidity because it is the market to which importers and exporters turn for trade finance. The country with the deepest and most liquid financial market will similarly be attractive as a place for investors from other countries to hold their foreign balances, since investors value the ability to buy and sell without moving prices. Thus, not only private investors seeking to diversify their portfolios but also central banks and governments, when deciding on the composition of their foreign reserves, will be drawn to the currency of the country with the deepest and most liquid financial markets—in other words, the same currency to which other investors are drawn.

For all these reasons, a single national unit will tend to dominate as the international unit of account, means of payment, and store of value. When those network increasing returns are sufficiently strong, international currency status will resemble a natural monopoly. There will be room in the world for only one true international currency. In the past this was sterling. Now it is the U.S. dollar. In the future it will be the renminbi.

These models imply, further, that the currency of the country that is the leading commercial and financial power is the natural candidate for this dominant status. As a large economy, it will have extensive international trade and financial links. It will have well-developed financial markets. Its residents being accustomed to transacting in their own currency, its national unit will have a relatively large "installed base," in the language of network economics.[11] Exporters and investors in other countries will consequently be drawn to the currency in question for transactions with residents of the lead economy. The currency of the leading economic power will thus have an intrinsic advantage in the competition for international currency status. This plausibly explains how sterling emerged as a global currency in the nineteenth century and how the dollar assumed this position in the twentieth.[12]

Models with network effects can also be models in which persistence is strong. In the limit, there may be "lock-in"—once an arrangement is in place, it will persist indefinitely.[13] Once market participants have settled on a technology—in this context, on a monetary and financial technology (call it an international currency)—they will have no incentive to contemplate alternatives. Transacting using a different technology or platform not also used by members of one's network will be prohibitively costly. In the international monetary and financial sphere, currencies other than the dominant unit will not possess the same attractions for individuals, banks, firms, and governments engaged in cross-border transactions. The prices of goods and financial instruments invoiced in other currencies will not be as easily compared. Settlements will not be as predictable. Investments will not be as liquid. Other currencies will not possess the same transparency, predictability, and liquidity, precisely because they are not the currencies that dominate international transactions. And since individuals, banks, firms, and governments make decisions in a decentralized fashion, there will be no mechanism for coordinating a large-scale shift from one international monetary and financial standard to another.[14]

It follows that international currency status will display inertia. It will persist even after the conditions making for the emergence and dominance of a particular national unit no longer prevail to the same extent. That currency will remain locked in unless a significant shock causes agents to abandon established practice and coordinate a shift from one equilibrium (from the common use of one international currency) to another. This explains, it is said, why sterling remained the dominant international currency well into the twentieth century, long after Great Britain had been surpassed in economic size and financial power by the United States. It explains why the shock of World War II was required for sterling to finally be supplanted by the dollar. These conjectures have obvious implications for how long the dollar is likely to remain the dominant international currency and what kind of shocks may be required for it to be supplanted by the renminbi.

The New View

This traditional view of international currency status is based more on theory than evidence.[15] At most, the theoretical models in question merely allude to historical facts as a way of providing motivation, rather than engaging seriously with the evidence. And even scholars who treat the evidence seriously are hampered by the limits of the available empirical base.

Consider the currency composition of foreign exchange reserves. We know something about this in 1899 and 1913, courtesy of the pioneering estimates of Peter Lindert.[16] We then know something about it starting in the 1970s, courtesy of the IMF and its Currency Composition of Official Foreign Exchange Reserves (COFER) database.[17] But we know little about the periods before or between.

These are thin empirical reeds on which to hang an encompassing narrative. Moreover, the traditional narrative is hard to square with even this limited evidentiary base. For the final decades of the twentieth century, the IMF's data confirm that the dollar accounts for the single largest share of identified foreign exchange reserves, but that this share is only on the order of 60 percent. Other currencies also played consequential international roles, in would appear.

Neither do Lindert's data support the assertion that international currency status is a natural monopoly. In fact they show other currencies in additional to sterling—the German mark and the French franc—also accounting for non-negligible shares of central bank reserves in 1899 and 1913.[18] (See Figures 1.1 and 1.2.)

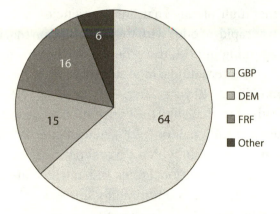

FIGURE 1.1. Shares of Currencies in Known Reserves, 1899 (percent).
Source: Lindert (1969).
Note: DEM, German mark; FRF, French franc; GBP, British pound.

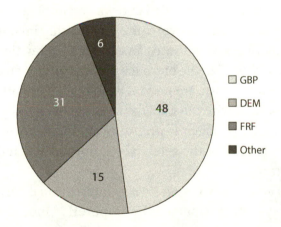

FIGURE 1.2. Shares of Currencies in Known Reserves, 1913 (percent).
Source: Lindert (1969).
Note: DEM, German mark; FRF, French franc; GBP, British pound.

New evidence on the period between 1913 (when Lindert's analysis ends) and the early 1970s (when the IMF's picks up) is equally hard to reconcile with the traditional view. Sterling, rather than remaining the preeminent international currency after World War I, in fact already shared that status with the dollar in the 1920s, suggesting that multiple international currencies can coexist. The dollar's rise was rapid, at odds with the presumption that persistence is strong. Beginning in 1913, the greenback went from being used hardly at all in the international monetary domain to being a coequal with the pound barely 10 years later.

All this leads us to challenge the conventional wisdom. We argue for replacing the traditional (or "old") view of international currencies with a "new" view, in which several national currencies can play consequential international roles and in which inertia and persistence are not as strong as traditionally supposed.[19]

This new view has a basis in theory as well. It builds on a literature on technology standards that emphasizes open systems, in which users of a particular technology or system can interact with those using other technologies or systems.[20] Network effects still exist, but the technical barriers between competing systems can be surmounted by so-called gateway technologies that enable suppliers or customers to overcome pre-existing incompatibilities and integrate rival systems into "an enlarged production system or extended network."[21] In the presence of these gateway technologies, interchangeability costs are no longer so high. Network increasing returns associated with the use of a particular technological system or standard are no longer as pronounced. First-mover advantage and the persistence of the established, dominant standard are no longer so strong.[22]

There is an analogy here between international currencies and operating systems for personal computers. Once upon a time, exchanging information across operating systems or platforms was costly and difficult. When buying a personal computer, it paid to buy one with the same operating system used by one's friends and colleagues. Network increasing returns were strongly increasing. Interchangeability costs (the costs of transferring data across platforms) were high. In the 1980s, Microsoft Word came in two versions. While one was compatible with the Apple Macintosh and the other was compatible with the IBM PC, the two were incompatible with each other. Switching costs (and hence the costs of experimenting with alternative platforms) were prohibitive, since one's existing files, generated for use with one system, were incompatible with the other. Everyone used Microsoft's disk-operating system (MS-DOS, which eventually morphed into Windows), because everyone else used it. Alternatives were for hobbyists, not for researchers or businesspeople.

With time, however, software engineers learned how to more easily move data across platforms. Interchangeability costs were cut. Software developers incorporated "translators" into updates of existing word-processing software and published new packages whose files were fully compatible across platforms. As a result, switching costs fell, and network increasing returns became less pronounced. Multiple operating systems, such as Microsoft Windows, Apple Mac OS X, and Linux, were now able to coexist in personal-computer space—making it possible for coauthors with personal computers running different operating systems to collaborate on this book.

For the modern-day foreign exchange market, this twenty-first-century picture of low costs of information, transactions, and coordination is clearly more plausible than the traditional assumption of high switching costs and costly information. In the age of high-speed communications, it is straightforward for potential customers to get real-time quotes on the price of foreign exchange and compare the prices of commodities denominated in different currencies. When more than half of all foreign exchange transactions occur on electronic platforms, it is possible to purchase and sell multiple currencies at microscopic bid-ask spreads in a matter of milliseconds. This is true not only for high-speed traders utilizing Thomson-Reuters servers and for large financial institutions with interbank electronic platforms, but also for retail investors with access to Internet-based foreign-exchange gateway technologies like Oanda and World First.

Likewise, it is now possible for a firm to obtain protection from future exchange rate changes that might otherwise distort its costs and revenues by purchasing and selling currency forwards, swaps, and other foreign exchange derivatives—transactions that can be undertaken at low cost on high-tech twenty-first-century financial markets. Hence the need for a firm to price its exports in the same currency in which its imported inputs are invoiced is no longer as pressing as before. And as more countries open the capital accounts of their balance of payments, more national markets acquire the depth and liquidity necessary to render assets traded there attractive to international investors.

For all these reasons, it is increasingly difficult to sustain the traditional argument that the currency of the leading economy, in which the majority of international transactions are concentrated, possesses such a pronounced advantage in terms of liquidity and transactions costs as to acquire natural monopoly status.[23]

More surprisingly, what is true for twenty-first-century foreign exchange market turns out to be true as well for nineteenth- and early twentieth-century currency markets, as new evidence and analysis suggest. In recent work, Marc Flandreau and Clemens Jobst develop a theoretical model of the international monetary system along the lines of the open-systems literature described above.[24] They apply it to the pre-1914 era to investigate whether the conditions were present for natural monopoly and lock-in or whether, instead, several widely traded international currencies could coexist and the identity or identities of the leading currencies could change. Their analysis highlights the need to distinguish network effects giving rise to a degree of persistence from very strong externalities giving rise to lock-in and natural-monopoly effects.[25] In the absence of those very strong externalities, of the network variety or other, international currency status will still display inertia. But several international currencies can coexist, and they can come and go.

Flandreau and Jobst's empirical estimates of network effects in pre-1914 international money markets support the view that these externalities mattered but reject the hypothesis that they were so strong as to produce lock-in and winner-takes-all effects. This helps us understand the coexistence of several international financial centers and the use of several key currencies in nineteenth-century foreign exchange and money markets. Flandreau and Jobst's analysis of the foreign exchange and money markets before World War I shows there were in fact three main international currencies against which other currencies were traded. Evidently, the financial-engineering expertise needed to create a reasonably open financial system, in which multiple international currencies or standards could coexist, was not beyond the capacity of nineteenth-century financiers.

Thus, where the old view suggested that network increasing returns are so strong that only one true global currency can exist at any point in time, the new view suggests that increasing returns are not so strong as to rule out a role for several currencies. Where the old view found support in the dollar's dominance in the second half of the twentieth century, the new view finds support in other periods during which several currencies simultaneously played consequential international roles. The old view implied that the dollar's dominance might persist for an extended period, whereas the new view predicts that the dollar will have rivals sooner rather than later.

Why It Matters

The idea that a particular national currency can continue to dominate international transactions even after the issuer has lost its economic, fiscal, and political might has uncomfortable implications. Marcello de Cecco has emphasized the relative economic decline of Britain before 1913 together with the continued dependence of the world economy on a sterling-centered system as factors in the financial tensions and imbalances leading up to World War I.[26] With other countries now growing more rapidly than the more mature British economy, the British market was no longer large enough to accommodate the distress goods of other countries. British lending, countercyclical or otherwise, no longer sufficed to stabilize monetary and financial conditions worldwide. The Bank of England no longer possessed the financial leverage needed to conduct the international orchestra.[27]

Similarly, in his account of the 1930s, Charles Kindleberger blamed the onset of the Great Depression on the continued dependence of the world economy on sterling and London after the conditions leading to their preeminence had passed and Britain had lost its capacity to stabilize the international system. Still others link the global imbalances of the early twenty-first century and the financial crisis that followed to the world's reliance for international liquidity on a United States that accounted for a declining share of an expanding global economy. The United States therefore possessed a diminished capacity to provide safe and liquid assets on the requisite scale, leading it to substitute subprime-mortgage-linked securities, whose stability and liquidity turned out to be less than met the eye.[28] This is one way of understanding the chronic fragility of the international monetary system and the instability of global finance, phenomena that have long troubled historians and policy makers.

In contrast, the idea that there can be several consequential international currencies and several sources of international liquidity at a point in time suggests the possibility of a better match between the structure of the global economy and its international monetary and financial system. If international currency status is not a natural monopoly in which strongly increasing returns produce lock-in, then other countries need not depend exclusively for their liquidity needs on a relatively mature, slowly growing economy in relative decline. The twenty-first-century version of the Triffin Dilemma—in which that relatively mature, slowly growing country by itself cannot continue indefinitely to meet the global economy's liquidity needs—can be resolved through the development of other national sources of international liquidity.[29] For countercyclical and emergency lending, the world need not rely on the judgment and goodwill of one central bank and one national government alone. If the central bank that is traditionally the source of emergency liquidity assistance to other countries refuses for domestic political reasons to again come to their aid, then others with the wherewithal can step in.

Contrary to this view of the stability of a global system with several consequential international currencies is the fear that the exchange rates among the currencies in question will become dangerously volatile and unstable. The existence of several liquid markets will enable central banks and other investors to rapidly rebalance their portfolios. They will be able to dump one of the currencies comprising their stock of foreign assets at the first sign of trouble, since they will have alternatives into which to shift. Small shocks or even minor bits of news may then cause sharp changes in the exchange rates between the currencies of the major countries, creating problems for their economies and for the smaller countries with which they have economic ties. Whether this is a real and pressing danger, and under what circumstances, are presumably questions on which history can shed light.

Finally, which of the two views is more accurate has implications for the benefits (sometimes known as the "exorbitant privilege") accruing to the issuer of the international currency or currencies. When a national currency is used widely in cross-border transactions, demand for it is apt to be stronger than otherwise. The issuer will be able to place debt securities denominated in that currency at a lower cost; as a result, the cost to it of financing budget and current account deficits will be less. The issuer also enjoys a kind of automatic insurance: when a serious negative shock hits the world economy, investors will rush into its financial markets, since there is nothing that they value more than liquidity in a crisis. This tendency was evident in 2007–2008, when investors rushed into the dollar, which strengthened against other currencies, even though the United States itself was the source of the subprime crisis and then the Lehman Brothers shock.

But if multiple international currencies can exist simultaneously, any such benefits will be more widely shared. These will not accrue to just one country, the United States, the situation that led French officials responsible for the phrase to characterize that privilege as "exorbitant."[30]

What We Do

We start in Chapter 2 by sketching the background to our story, describing the origins of the practice of holding foreign balances (bank deposits and securities denominated in a foreign currency and held in a foreign financial center) by firms, banks, and governments. This enables us to describe the contours of the international monetary and financial system from the late nineteenth century to the eve of World War I. Chapter 3 then tells the next installment of the story, which extends from the outbreak of the war to the early 1920s (and from the Jekyll Island meeting in 1910 that paved the way for founding the Federal Reserve and the subsequent process of dollar internationalization) to the Genoa Conference in 1922, at which it was agreed to move to a foreign-exchange-based monetary and financial system.

Chapters 4 through 6 then present new evidence for reserve currencies in the 1920s and 1930s, for the use of currencies in trade finance in this same period, and for the use of currencies as vehicles of long-term international investment. This is where we present our central evidence for the "new view."

Chapters 7 through 11 bring the tale up to date. Chapter 7 describes changes in the relative importance of different national currencies as international reserves from the end of World War II through the beginning of the twenty-first century. It also provides evidence on the changing importance of network increasing returns, other sources of persistence (such as custom and tradition), and the policies of the reserve-currency-issuing countries. Chapters 8 and 9 then turn to a pair of cases with the capacity to shed light on the future. Chapter 8 focuses on sterling balances in the aftermath of World War II and the efforts of the British authorities to manage an international currency in decline. Chapter 9 considers the abortive rise of the yen as an international currency. It looks at the attempts of the Japanese authorities to internationalize their currency and discusses why these efforts proved unsuccessful.

These two case studies speak to the question of whether the euro area and China will succeed in internationalizing their currencies and whether the euro and renminbi are likely to emerge as consequential rivals to the dollar. They raise the question of what history can tell us about the prerequisites for currency internationalization, and how the United States should respond to the emergence of a rival and how it should conceivably manage the loss of dollar dominance. We consider these issues in Chapters 10 and 11, which look respectively at the euro and renminbi's prospects as international currencies.

Chapter 12, in concluding, considers the broader implications for the dollar and the world economy.

In what follows, we use a combination of historical and statistical—some would say narrative and econometric—evidence. Economic theory structures and informs our analysis, as will be evident from this chapter. But we present that theory verbally rather than laying it out in gory detail in order to make the analysis accessible to the widest possible audience.[31] We are also aware of the limits of the evidence, which prevent us from drawing some conclusions as firmly as others. For example, in seeking to show that multiple international currencies can coexist, we can invoke evidence from a variety of different periods and international monetary regimes: the gold standard, the interwar gold-exchange standard, the Bretton Woods period, and the post–Bretton Woods period. In contrast, in seeking to establish that the persistence of international monetary and financial dominance is not always what it is cracked up to be, we are inevitably limited by the fact that there has been only one consequential change in that dominance in the modern period, from sterling to the dollar, and that the circumstances surrounding that shift were special in important respects. But consequential historical events are always special. Whether our arguments are convincing and general is for the reader to judge.

2

The Origins of Foreign Balances

The practice by central banks of holding foreign exchange reserves developed in the nineteenth century. Previously, national banks of issue (where they existed) had held their reserve assets, which they maintained as backing for their liabilities, in gold and silver bullion.[1] The case of the Bank of England is illustrative. The Bank Charter Act of 1844, which gave the Bank of England a monopoly over note issuance, required it to hold gold equal to 100 percent of its notes after allowing for £14 million backed by other securities.

Yet just a few years later, in 1850, a newly created bank of issue, the National Bank of Belgium, began accumulating foreign-currency-denominated assets that it used in foreign exchange market intervention and other operations. Its practices were ad hoc and opportunistic. But when its charter was renewed in 1872, new provisions allowed the Bank to treat those assets as part of its official reserve.[2]

Where the National Bank of Belgium led, other central banks followed. Foreign exchange reserves rose rapidly in the final years of the nineteenth century and early years of the twentieth. According to Bloomfield (1963) and Lindert (1969), the foreign assets of 18 leading banks of issue and national treasuries rose eightfold from $102 million at the end of 1880 to $814 million at the end of 1913.

Their gold reserves, in contrast, rose from $1 billion at the end of 1880 to $4.9 billion at the end of 1913, a relatively modest fivefold increase. Whereas foreign exchange had accounted for less than 10 percent of total reserves in 1880, it accounted for nearly 15 percent in 1913.

Development of Foreign Exchange Markets

In fact, this practice of holding securities and deposits abroad was neither new nor novel. Raymond De Roover, the foremost historian of early modern European money markets, emphasizes the role of bills of exchange in the development of the practice.[3] The bill of exchange arose out of the needs of international commerce. A banker, approached by a merchant wishing to make a payment in a foreign city, would issue a *lettera di cambio* or *lettre de change*. This bill or letter would then be conveyed to the foreign city where it would be paid. The originating banker, holding money on deposit with a correspondent in that foreign city, would instruct the latter to pay the foreign merchant and debit the banker's account.

A secondary market then developed in these bills of exchange. They were purchased by third parties wishing to acquire balances abroad and use them in their own international payments. Because these bills of exchange were for payment in a foreign market, they were denominated in a foreign currency. But when traded on the local market, they were purchased using local currency. The market price of these promises to pay in foreign currency was thus the exchange rate of one currency against the other. The market for bills of exchange was, in modern parlance, the foreign exchange market.

For this system to work, prior arrangements had to be made for a banker in the first city to use the facilities provided by the banker in the second when the deposits of the first banker did not suffice. But the banker in the second city would only be willing to let his correspondent overdraw his account if that correspondent was creditworthy.[4] Hence the quality of the signature on the bill—the reputation of the banker originating it, in other words—was paramount.

Hence the rise of financial centers where these kinds of transactions were concentrated and reputation could be cultivated: Florence, Venice, Genoa, Augsburg, Antwerp, and the towns of the Hanseatic League in the Middle Ages and Renaissance; Amsterdam in the seventeenth and eighteenth centuries; and London and Paris in the eighteenth and nineteenth. Their most reputable banking houses—long lived, well endowed with capital, and possessing extensive international connections—attracted deposits from merchants, landowners, princes, and other banks while in turn extending them credit. The cities with which they were associated became international financial centers. In the phrase of the financial historian Youssef Cassis, they became "capitals of capital."[5]

Some centers were more central than others. First-tier financial centers populated by reputable houses offered higher returns to foreign depositors and lower costs to foreign borrowers. Lesser-known banks in second-tier centers held balances in first-tier centers. First-tier centers, meanwhile, forged direct links with one another. The branches of the Rothschild family, present in first-tier centers like London, Paris, Vienna, Frankfurt, and Naples, illustrate the point.

The growth of these first-tier centers was fostered by positive feedbacks—network externalities in the terminology of Chapter 1. The larger a first-tier center grew and the more second-tier centers linked up with it, the richer and more diverse became the resulting ecology of banks and merchants. Information about market conditions, signatures, and reputations accumulated in such centers. With different market participants borrowing and lending at different times, the market acquired liquidity, enabling such centers to offer more attractive lending and deposit rates.

As more resources, both financial and informational, were concentrated in the leading financial centers, banks there were able to offer a greater range of services, including long-term foreign loans to governments and companies. The liquidity and information services of banks in the leading financial centers shaped the decisions of borrowers about where to issue bonds and in what currency to issue them.[6] When floating a bond, a government or private borrower arranged for the services and sponsorship of an underwriter. After raising the money, the underwriter retained the principal amount, transferring funds according to the needs of the borrower while retaining a balance for interest payments, amortization and other costs.[7]

In this way long-term foreign loans were transformed into short-term deposit balances. The practice of holding these deposits expanded from bankers holding foreign balances (to service the needs of the merchants who were their customers) to governments and other borrowers, who held such deposits to meet their current expenditures. The nineteenth and early twentieth centuries offer many examples of this behavior. The Brazilian government maintained balances with Rothschild in London. The Chilean government held balances with Rothschild and three German banks that underwrote its bonds. After 1890, the Russian government maintained deposits, also referred to as reserves, with its Paris underwriters.[8]

These practices rested on the informational advantages of the underwriter, the reputability of the banking house in convincing investors of the creditworthiness of the borrower, and the liquidity of the market, which together enabled the banker to put otherwise idle balances to work. They rested, in other words, on the positive feedbacks and network effects that characterized the leading financial centers.

Importantly, however, those positive feedbacks were not so strong as to produce the winner-take-all or natural-monopoly outcome predicted by the traditional or "old" view of international finance, as this school is referred to in Chapter 1. Flandreau et al. (2009) provide evidence on this for the mid-eighteenth century, documenting the presence of bills of exchange in European cities in which there was an active foreign exchange market. No one financial center and currency, they show, possessed anything resembling a natural monopoly, although Amsterdam and the guilder were clear leaders. Bills on Amsterdam could be found in about 60 percent of all foreign exchange markets. However, bills on London and Paris could be found in about 40 percent of all markets, while bills on Hamburg circulated in 30 percent of all markets. Although the guilder possessed a lead, it had not crowded out other international currencies.

In addition there were subsidiary international currencies with non-negligible reach, each of which was traded in roughly 20 percent of all foreign exchange markets: those of Livorno, Lyon, Genoa, Venice, and Vienna. Active trading in the currencies of these once-great money centers attests to the persistence of international financial arrangements. At the same time, the continuing prominence of these Renaissance centers, notwithstanding the rise of Amsterdam, gives further grounds for questioning the winner-takes-all or natural-monopoly view.

Central Banking and the Gold Standard

Over the course of the nineteenth century, this city-centered, merchant-bank-led system of bills of exchange was supplemented by central bank credit. Banks of issue emitted notes convertible into bullion. These notes were utilized for settling financial transactions once the issuing central banks developed regional branch networks. This de facto situation was ultimately acknowledged de jure as these notes acquired legal-tender status. Their de jure status was of course purely domestic, that being the domain of national law. But these developments also set the stage for national currencies to supplant city-based units as the basis for international transactions.

Another key development was the emergence of the international gold standard. The 1860s saw agitation for a common international standard to facilitate the expansion of trade. Gold was the basis for the currency of Great Britain, the world's leading trading and financial power. Recent gold discoveries in California and Australia promised adequate supplies. Germany initiated the transition, using the proceeds of the indemnity received at the end of the Franco-Prussian War, followed quickly by France. Because France had previously helped stabilize the relative price of gold and silver through the operation of its bimetallic system, its move away from bimetallism dented the credibility of silver in international markets. Massive discoveries led to a fourfold increase in world silver production in the final quarter of the twentieth century, launching the silver standard onto what turned out to be an inexorable decline.[9]

In this environment, where bimetallism was problematic and silver-based currencies tended to depreciate, a gold-backed currency was an attractive alternative. But it was costly to acquire the gold needed for internal circulation or for backing that circulation in countries operating a gold bullion standard.[10] Real resources were needed to mine or import the yellow metal. Doing so was especially challenging for poor countries.[11] In rich but small open economies like Belgium, gold was more rapidly lost than gained, given that its market was used as an arbitrage and clearing center by international financiers.

Here the Belgian example showed the way forward. Gold reserves could be supplemented with interest-bearing assets denominated in a unit convertible into gold, such as the bills of exchange on foreign financial centers held by the National Bank of Belgium. These assets threw off interest income: Conant (1909) describes how the government of the Philippines obtained a return of 4 percent on deposits held with foreign money-center banks. Governments could use the international market to borrow the funds needed to acquire interest-earning foreign assets, especially if they were ready to keep the resulting funds as sight or time deposits with the foreign banks underwriting the loan. In this way the cost of operating a gold standard could be reduced.

And so the gold-exchange standard developed in the second half of the nineteenth century. With it came the practice of holding foreign exchange reserves as a de facto and, sometimes, de jure feature of the monetary system. By the end of the century, the gold-exchange standard prevailed in India, the Philippines, Mexico, Panama, Japan, and other relatively poor economies where the resource costs of a purely gold-based system were prohibitive. But the arrangement was also attractive to a variety of richer economies, both small ones like the Netherlands, Denmark, Sweden, and Norway, and large ones like Austria-Hungary and Russia, which similarly sought to economize on the costs of operating a commodity-backed currency system.

The Role of Sterling

This growing demand for convertible foreign balances—or equivalently, for safe and liquid assets denominated in a currency readily convertible into gold—was accommodated by a growing supply. Great Britain was the foremost supplier beginning around 1870, when the practice of holding foreign balances became widespread, reflecting its well-developed banking system, long record of gold convertibility, and liquid financial markets backed by a central bank conscious of its lender-of-last-resort responsibilities.

That Britain possessed a well-developed banking system, especially in its international aspect, had obvious appeal to foreign investors. The years prior to 1870 had seen the formerly fragmented British banking system undergo consolidation. Cottrell (2009) describes the 1850s through the 1870s as London's "First Big Bang," owing to the growth of overseas lending and the liberalization of company legislation. This more widely branched and diversified banking system was perceived, according to contemporaries like Keynes, as increasingly mature and stable, inspiring greater confidence on the part of investors, both foreign and domestic.

Confidence—specifically, confidence in the convertibility of the currency into gold at a fixed price—was critical for attracting and retaining those foreign investors. It helped that Britain had been on the gold standard for longer than any other country. By the 1870s it had maintained gold convertibility for a century and a half, notwithstanding an interruption during the Napoleonic Wars. To be sure, the Bank Charter Act was suspended in 1847, 1857, and 1866. But on each occasion the key provisions were restored subsequently, and the sterling price of gold remained the same. Britain in the nineteenth century practiced what economists refer to as "the resumption rule," a fact that the British authorities advertised via their consular representatives abroad.[12] As a result, investors came to expect this behavior. Confidence in sterling's convertibility, if not absolute, was considerable.

Sterling's attractions included also the fact that London was the world's leading gold market, more so from the 1870s when Paris, its rival, was struggling to pay an indemnity to Germany following the conclusion of the Franco-Prussian War.[13] The majority of Alaska's, Australia's, and South Africa's newly mined gold passed through London. Gold could always be obtained in London, where, reflecting the depth of the gold market, its price was relatively stable. The Bank of England, which had more experience with the gold standard than other central banks and also had the powerful lever of the London money market, smoothed the operation of the gold standard and stabilized the level of prices, accumulating gold when supplies were abundant and disgorging it when they were scarce.

The period starting in 1870 also saw the growing circulation of Treasury bills and bonds.[14] These securities provided the banking system with a liquid asset in which to invest and the Bank of England with instruments to conduct open market operations. Increasingly, the Bank bought and sold Treasury securities as a way of stabilizing interest rates at desired levels.[15] With interest rates and security prices stable, Treasury bills and bonds became an attractive alternative to bank deposits for governments and central banks seeking safe and liquid foreign assets. With the discount market languishing, it is unlikely that London would have been as attractive a destination for foreign balances in their absence.

Finally, sterling was attractive because the Bank of England could act as an emergency provider of liquidity to the market. Deposits in British banks were secure because when liquidity grew scarce, banks could turn to the Bank of England to rediscount their bills. Exactly when the Bank first acknowledged this responsibility—and, more importantly, acted on it—is disputed. Already at the beginning of the nineteenth century, Henry Thornton (1802) pointed to the Bank's unique position as a source of liquidity to the financial system. In 1873 Walter Bagehot described how the Bank *should* act in this context, although he also raised questions about whether the Bank fully understood its role.[16] Lovell (1957) suggested that the Bank already operated as a lender of last resort in the eighteenth century, increasing its discounts in times of crisis. Collins (1989) pointed to the failure of the City of Glasgow Bank in 1878 as the critical turning point. Others argue that the transition occurred between the Overend, Gurney Crisis in 1866, when the Bank purchased a wide variety of assets from an unusually broad range of counterparties, and the Baring Crisis in 1890, when the Bank supplied emergency liquidity in the context of a lifeboat operation.[17]

Whatever the dating, Britain unquestionably possessed one of the longest lived and most experienced central banks. Investors had more reason to anticipate the provision of emergency liquidity than did participants in the financial markets of countries like, inter alia, the United States, which still lacked modern central banking institutions.

London's Rivals

Observations like these are invoked in support of the view that London and sterling dominated the international monetary and financial landscape toward the end of the nineteenth century. But even though it is true that some potential rivals, like the United States and the dollar, lacked essential prerequisites for an international role—the United States lacked both a lender and liquidity provider of last resort and commercial banks with international reach—the same was not true of other countries, such as Germany and France.

Figure 2.1, reproducing evidence from Flandreau and Jobst, describes the state of the system circa 1900, enumerating the number of markets in which different currencies were traded.[18] Again there is evidence of persistence insofar as the previous hierarchy of cities (Amsterdam, London, Paris, and Hamburg) is reflected in the ranking of countries and their respective currencies: the guilder, sterling, the franc, and the mark.

But Figure 2.1 is at odds with the natural-monopoly interpretation of international currency competition as a winner-takes-all game. While the pound sterling, widely acknowledged as the leading international currency, was traded on all markets worldwide for which there is information, the French franc was also traded on 80 percent of those markets and the German mark on 60 percent. This evidence from the foreign-exchange market in 1900—that several national currencies played significant international roles, if somewhat unevenly—matches Lindert's evidence on the currency composition of foreign exchange reserves (see Figure 1.1). It is easier to reconcile that evidence with the new view, which, while not

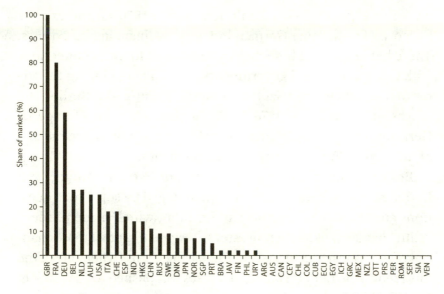

FIGURE 2.1. Diffusion of Monetary Denominations circa 1900 (percentage of all markets).
Source: Flandreau and Jobst (2005).
Note: GBR, United Kingdom; FRA, France; DEU, Germany; BEL, Belgium; NLD,
Netherlands; AUH, Austria-Hungary; USA, United States; ITA, Italy; CHE, Switzerland;
ESP, Spain; IND, British India; HKG, Hong-Kong; CHN, China; RUS, Russia; SWE, Sweden;
DNK, Denmark; JPN, Japan; NOR, Norway; SGP, Strait settlements (Singapore); PRT,
Portugal; BRA, Brazil; JAV, Dutch East Indies (Java); FIN, Finland; PHL, Philippines; URY,
Uruguay; ARG, Argentina; AUS, Australia; CAN, Canada; CEY, Ceylon; CHL, Chile; COL,
Colombia; CUB, Cuba; ECU, Ecuador; EGY, Egypt; ICH, French Indochina; GRC, Greece;
MEX, Mexico; NZL, New Zealand; OTT, Ottoman Empire; PRS, Persia; PER, Peru; ROM,
Rumania; SER, Serbia; SIA, Siam; VEN, Venezuela.

denying the existence of network increasing returns, questions that
they are so strong as to leave room for only one true international
currency.

French and German financial institutions competed for these
international roles. In France, important new deposit banks were
founded starting in the 1860s. The foreign deposits of the three largest banks, in particular, grew rapidly as Paris became a major source
of foreign loans. The Bank of France amassed enormous gold reserves, potentially to be made available to holders of franc balances.[19]

The German banking system similarly grew rapidly. The Great
Banks with their universal structure were the most prominent
German institutions, but they were only one component of a highly
articulated financial system (Guinnane 2002). Among the new banks

were some like Deutsche Bank, founded in 1870 for the express purpose of promoting German industry by financing its exports. These banks opened branches overseas and forged connections with foreign firms and governments, in turn encouraging the latter to bring their financial business to Hamburg and Berlin. The Reichsbank, founded in 1876, 5 years after the creation of Imperial Germany, amassed a considerable gold reserve, not as large as that of the Bank of France but extensive nonetheless.

Besides being facilitated by the rise of Paris, Hamburg, and Berlin, reserve diversification was encouraged by sotto voce questions about financial practices in London, which made prudent central bankers, like other investors, hesitate to put all their financial eggs in one national basket. The Baring Crisis (when one of the most reputable London financial houses was pushed to the brink in 1890) highlighted those questions.

In addition, preceding decades had seen the rapid growth of joint-stock banks (modern-style banks with multiple shareholders, as distinct from the earlier six-partner model), which now competed with the Bank of England in the discount market.[20] It thus became more difficult for the Bank of England to make its policy interest rate ("Bank rate") effective, in the sense of having an effect on flows of capital and gold.[21] To enhance its leverage, the Bank sought to enlist the cooperation of the joint-stock banks, an effort that met with mixed success. The Bank next resorted to the so-called gold devices, changing the terms on which it paid out gold.[22] Although this helped regulate gold flows and defend the Bank's reserve, it raised questions about whether sterling was "as good as gold."

Empires and Alliances

Since rivalry between London, Paris, and Berlin involved not just their financial markets but also their overseas empires and alliance politics, these political dimensions also affected the practice of holding foreign balances. Colonies regularly held reserves in the metropole, whether with a central bank or a commercial banking establishment. De facto dependencies like the Philippines and

Panama did likewise. Marcello de Cecco describes British possessions as having little choice: "Should they have a surplus, they were
denied the right to choose between gold and sterling; they had to
deposit any surplus in London."[23]

India is a case in point.[24] The India Office controlled the financial (as well as other) affairs of the provinces of British India. The
Presidency Banks were owned by British subjects; other banks were
dominated by British directors.[25] India had to pay the British government for debt service and pay the War Office for maintenance
of the Indian Army, transfers that were known as "Home Charges."

The result was close connections with London and sterling.
These links took three forms. First were the Raj's cash balances.
Cash balances were held in rupees in India and sterling in London.[26]
The share of cash balances in sterling fluctuated between one- and
two-thirds. The sterling portion was held partly in an account at
the Bank of England, but mainly was lent for short periods to other
financial institutions.

Second was the Paper Currency Reserve held as backing for
notes. These were gold and foreign exchange reserves held as part
of the gold-exchange standard provided for by the Gold Note Act
of 1898. That act and subsequent statutes set a relatively low ceiling
on the portion that could be invested in securities, and in sterling
securities specifically; the remainder was held mainly in the form
of gold in London and India. Circa 1912, roughly 6 percent of the
Currency Reserve was held in sterling securities, 15 percent in rupee
securities, and 56 percent in gold.[27]

Finally, starting in 1900, the Indian authorities accumulated a distinct Gold Standard Reserve using seigniorage earned from injecting
subsidiary silver coin into circulation. Initially, two-thirds was held
in the form of gold in India, while the remaining third was invested
in British government securities. With the British government under
pressure to place the debt issued to finance the Boer War, a larger
and larger share, eventually approaching 100 percent, was invested
in British Exchequer bonds, treasury bills, and consols. Starting in
1908, the Government of India also invested modest amounts of the
Gold Standard Reserve on the London money market.[28]

India thus provides an example of a dependency encouraged to operate a gold-exchange standard by holding its reserves in the form of securities and short-term money on call in the metropolitan financial center. Sterling reserves were held not just by India but also by the governments of Ceylon, Australia, and Canada. Other examples can be found in the formal and informal empires of the other leading financial powers: France; Germany; and, in the second tier, the Netherlands and United States. Paris introduced a similar system in French Indochina. The Netherlands operated one in the Dutch East Indies, Germany in West Africa. The United States imposed such a system as part of its currency reforms in the Philippines and Panama.[29]

And where empire strictly speaking was not involved, empire broadly defined—alliance politics, to put it another way—generally was. Japan held sterling in London to solidify its ties with Britain, an alliance designed to counter the Russian-led, French-supported military threat in the Far East. Russia held deposits in Berlin to mollify a potentially bellicose Germany and then, when this effort failed, in Paris to solidify its alliance with France. The Bank of Greece, the Italian Treasury, and the Austro-Hungarian authorities held balances in Paris for analogous reasons, while the Greeks hedged their bets by also holding balances in London. These alliance-related foreign balances were, if anything, more important than those of empire; revealingly, Japan's sterling reserves were larger than India's.

The Japanese case is an especially good example of the links between alliance politics and the accumulation of foreign exchange reserves.[30] Japan went on the gold standard in the 1890s using an indemnity received from China. China was required to pay its indemnity in gold. It did so in London, that being the principal world gold market and a logical place to borrow to fund the indemnity. The Japanese then maintained those balances in London, with the Bank of England opening an account for the Yokohama Specie Bank. British officials worried (not without reason) about the impact on confidence, and perhaps on the Bank of England's reserves, of Japan shipping large amounts of gold out of London. They therefore encouraged the Japanese to stretch out the associated transactions.

In the meantime, the Bank of Japan issued yen notes backed by money on deposit in London. Herein lay the origins of the de facto gold-exchange standard that developed in Japan in the 1890s.[31]

For British and Japanese policy makers, monetary cooperation was a way of signaling their commitment to the Anglo-Japanese Alliance of 1902, in which each government was obliged to provide military aid to the other if either went to war with two or more powers. These monetary arrangements and political entanglements were then elaborated as a result of the Russo-Japanese War. Starting in 1904, Takahashi Korekiyo, a Bank of Japan official and the country's future finance minister, arranged for the flotation of sterling bonds to finance Japanese government imports of armaments. The proceeds were initially maintained on deposit in London.[32] The Japanese government then continued borrowing in London, through government agencies and state companies, while holding its excess funds there as a reserve. Those funds were in the form of demand deposits, partly at the Bank of England, and in short-term sterling bills (both Treasury bills and sterling bills of exchange that originated in overseas trade).

As this account of diplomatic and military alliances makes clear, the political outlook grew more worrisome in the run-up to World War I. De Cecco (1984) points to the Boer War as a watershed; by bringing down the curtain on this period of peace, it undermined confidence in the security and convertibility of foreign balances in London, Paris, and Berlin, inaugurating a movement back toward holding gold. The imperial conflict between the French and German governments in Morocco, culminating in the Agadir Crisis in 1911, worked in the same direction. Although the overall stock of foreign exchange reserves continued to grow until 1914, gold itself was the fastest-growing component in the years leading up to the Great War.[33] In a sense, these events presaged the liquidation of foreign exchange reserves in the run-up to World War II. They illustrated the fragility of the gold-exchange standard and the extent to which its operation hinged on that delicate quality of confidence.

3

From Jekyll Island to Genoa

The international monetary arrangements of the 1920s differed from those before 1913. Foreign exchange constituted a larger fraction of the international reserves of central banks and governments (especially for European central banks and governments)—as much as 42 percent of the total in 1928, up from 15 to 20 percent in 1913, depending on whether one includes for the earlier year total monetary gold stocks or only official gold reserves.[1] In many cases, arrangements governing those reserves were formalized by new central bank statutes and, where necessary, by the creation of new central banks. The monetary landscape was transformed by the rise of New York, the decline of Paris and Berlin, and London's struggles to reassert its dominance (although with what implications exactly for the currency composition of foreign exchange reserves is not, on the basis of prior scholarship, entirely clear).

The two most important events from the point of view of subsequent developments were passage of the Federal Reserve Act in 1913 followed the next year by the outbreak of World War I. Both worked to enhance the international role of the American dollar. The fact that, to this point, the U.S. currency played little role in international monetary and financial affairs—aside from its use as reserves in exceptional cases like the Philippines, Panama, and Mexico as discussed in Chapter 2—was in some sense deeply anomalous. The United States had long since overtaken Britain as the world's largest economy. It was now poised to overtake Britain as the largest trading nation.

But America's restrictive banking legislation and underdeveloped financial infrastructure, reinforced by the head start of sterling and other European currencies, prevented the dollar from playing a larger role. Here restrictive banking legislation refers to the provisions of the National Banking Act and associated state statutes preventing U.S. banks from branching abroad. Deep-seated American suspicion of concentrated financial power resulted in the adoption of statutes limiting the ability of U.S. banks to branch in general and across state lines in particular. Allowing banks to branch abroad would have enabled them to subvert the intention of those restrictions on the scope of their activities.

Not being able to branch abroad hindered the ability of U.S. banks to originate foreign business and provide international financial services to their customers. To be sure, trust companies (which managed money and undertook transactions on behalf of estates, trusts, and the like) were sometimes able to circumvent these restrictions. While a handful of trust companies opened foreign branches prior to 1913, they engaged in only a limited range of transactions, enabling them to provide only some services to their clients.[2] In addition, private banks like J.P. Morgan & Co. had close relations with fraternal financial institutions abroad, often overseen by members of the same extended family, favorably positioning them to engage in international business.

Most U.S. banks provided international financial services to their customers through correspondent banking relationships. When a U.S. importer needed to pay a foreign supplier, the importer's local bank transferred funds (or made a commitment to do so) to a corresponding institution, generally located in London. The foreign correspondent would then make payment in pounds sterling to the supplier, irrespective of whether the latter resided in Britain or a third country. These arrangements reinforced London's position at the center of the monetary and financial system. They limited the incentive for foreigners trading with and investing in the United States to hold balances in dollars in New York in order to facilitate their transactions. They disadvantaged American importers and exporters by requiring them to pay two commissions—one to their local bank and another to its correspondent—to make or receive international transfers.

It Came from Jekyll Island

The dearth of international bonds, international bank transactions, and foreign trade credits denominated in dollars would have been paradoxical, given the size and international connections of the U.S. economy, were it not for this absence of supporting infrastructure. In particular, prior to 1914 there was no central bank to provide liquidity to the markets and backstop them in times of crisis. Contemporaries like Edwin Kemmerer—Princeton University professor, advisor of central banks and governments, and prominent advocate of the gold-exchange standard—pointed to the seasonal and cyclical instability of U.S. interest rates. They attributed this situation to the absence of a central bank to accommodate the market's fluctuating liquidity needs (to the absence, in contemporary parlance, of "an elastic currency"). They cited this cyclical and seasonal instability as a deterrent to doing business in dollars—international transactions being where market participants had a choice.[3] Observations like these contributed to the groundswell of support, from financiers and merchants alike, to do something about the problem.

That something, it turned out, was the creation in 1913 of the Federal Reserve System. Admittedly, the decision to establish a central bank after a hiatus of more than three-quarters of a century (since Andrew Jackson vetoed the bill renewing the charter of the Second Bank of the United States in 1832) reflected a confluence of factors. The secret 1910 meeting on Jekyll Island, off the coast of Georgia, produced a blueprint for what became the Federal Reserve System. The meeting brought together politicians and experts concerned with the volatility of U.S. financial markets (something

that had been highlighted by the 1907 financial crisis), seasonal fluctuations in interest rates (which created problems for commodity
producers and traders), and the absence of a proper fiscal agent for
the federal government.[4] But another important consideration, as
Lawrence Broz (1997) has emphasized, was the desire to foster wider
international use of the dollar and limit the dependence of American
merchants and investors on London and the pound sterling.

Efforts to foster currency internationalization started, logically,
with measures to develop a market in trade credits ("trade acceptances") denominated in dollars, provided by U.S. banks now permitted to branch abroad and originate international business, and
supported by a central bank that stood ready to act as market maker
and liquidity provider.[5] The new central bank would act as purchaser
of last resort of such acceptances, ensuring that dollar-denominated
credits would be available to finance trade in the requisite quantities
at predictable prices, which would in turn draw other participants
into the market. And once the dollar was widely utilized to finance
merchandise imports and exports, it would assume the other functions of an international currency: as an invoicing currency in which
prices were quoted, as a currency of denomination for international
bonds, and as a currency in which foreign central banks and governments held their international reserves.

This had been the experience of Great Britain, where the wider
international use of sterling developed out of the early provision of
sterling-denominated bills by specialized discount houses and merchant banks for the purposes of financing overseas trade. It had been
the experience of Germany, where the establishment of Deutsche
Bank to arrange export finance and of the Reichsbank to backstop
the market led to the growth of a market in mark-denominated credits. The latter was an experience on which the German-American
financier Paul Warburg drew when formulating plans for the institution that became the Federal Reserve System and when sharing them
with his colleagues at Jekyll Island.[6] It was similarly the experience of
the United States following the founding of the Federal Reserve and
with the support provided by the new central bank to the fledgling
market in trade acceptances.

Consequences of World War I

This process was then helped along by World War I. The British authorities sought to husband credit available in London for the war effort. In addition, the war limited the flow of credit to the London market from Continental European financial centers.

U.S. importers and exporters, when doing business in Latin America and Asia, therefore out of necessity turned to domestic sources of trade credit, which a growing number of American banks sought to provide. The dollar acceptance market already showed signs of life in 1915, although the amount of credit provided was still modest. The supply of dollar acceptances then rose to higher levels starting in 1916–1917, when the Federal Reserve banks began purchasing them in growing numbers for their own accounts.

Other wartime changes worked in the same direction. World War I was more financially damaging to the United Kingdom than to the United States. Britain was directly engaged in hostilities for more than 4 years, the United States for just 2. The public-debt-to-GDP ratio of Britain, at 122 percent in 1920, was more than four times that of the United States.[7] Although Britain raised output between 1914 and 1919 as successfully as the United States, it did so by eating its seed corn: the net capital stock was lower in 1919 than in 1914 by approximately 4 percent.[8] Estimates for the United States are not directly comparable but point to a significant increase in the net capital stock over the period.[9]

The United States was also transformed from a net international debtor to a net creditor, as foreigners liquidated more than half of their prior investments in the United States to fund purchases of arms and matériel, and U.S. investments abroad nearly doubled.[10] The United Kingdom, for its part, incurred substantial debts to the United States, first to private creditors (as institutions like J.P. Morgan & Co. provided the British government with credits, which Morgan then securitized, selling the bonds to private investors) and then directly to the U.S. government once America entered the war in 1917. As a result, Britain's war debt to the United States came to nearly $5 billion at conclusion of hostilities.

Finally, there were wartime and immediate postwar movements in prices and exchange rates. In the United Kingdom, where money finance of wartime expenditure was extensive, wholesale prices rose by more than 150 percent between 1914 and 1919; in the United States they rose by a more modest 100 percent.[11] Prices were then pushed down in the 1920–1921 recession but, since they fell in both countries, the immediate postwar deflation did little to erase the earlier divergence. Combined with the different paths of the two countries' capital stocks during wartime, these trends explain the problems of international competitiveness that bedeviled the United Kingdom in the 1920s.

In principle, the discrepancy could have been neutralized by changes in exchange rates. The depreciation of sterling during the war had been limited by the maintenance of exchange and capital controls. With the end of hostilities in early 1919, many of these controls lost their force, or at least their support, and the convertibility of sterling into gold was temporarily suspended, allowing the currency to depreciate further. The United States, in contrast, remained on the gold standard at an unchanged parity throughout.[12]

The pound might have been stabilized at a gold price 10 percent higher than in 1914 and at a dollar exchange rate 10 percent lower, consistent with the analysis and arguments of Keynes.[13] The case against doing so was that abandoning the customary parity would diminish London's stature as an international financial center and sterling's prospects as an international currency. So the decision was taken in 1925 to return to gold at the traditional parity and dollar exchange rate of $4.86. As to whether restoration of the prewar parity would in fact have the desired effect on sterling's postwar position in the international monetary and financial system, only time would tell.

Efforts to Promote the Use of Foreign Exchange Reserves

The rise in price levels in Britain, Europe, and the United States during and after World War I had the further effect of raising doubts about whether global stocks of monetary gold were still adequate for supporting the customary volume of transactions. While price levels had risen substantially, the production of new gold declined as the relative price of the metal fell—wholesale prices rising worldwide, as noted, but the nominal price of gold remaining fixed in sterling and dollar terms.

Given the reluctance of governments like Britain's to contemplate raising the price of gold, and the equally strong reluctance of workers and producers to acquiesce to further cuts in wages and prices, financial experts devised schemes for supplementing those limited stocks of monetary gold. Their discussions culminated in the resolutions of the Financial Convention at the Genoa Conference in 1922 to formalize and encourage the holding of foreign exchange reserves.

Before Genoa, however, there was Brussels. The Brussels International Financial Conference in 1920 was the first attempt to grapple in a comprehensive way with postwar economic and financial problems. Awkwardly, the conference was convened while the issue of German reparations was still outstanding. It was convened, moreover, by the Council of the League of Nations, explaining why the United States sent only an unofficial representative rather than an official delegation.[14]

Discussions focused on the pressing problems of containing inflation, balancing budgets, and jumpstarting trade and capital flows. But, in addition, discussions at Brussels set the stage for the Genoa Conference 2 years later by forging a broad international consensus on the desirability of delegating the conduct of monetary policy to "autonomous" central banks free of political control. Agreement extended to the desirability of restoring the gold standard, so long as this objective could be achieved without unleashing destructive deflationary repercussions.[15] Background material was provided by five eminent economists, including Gustav Cassel of Sweden, whose scholarly writings had highlighted the potential for conflict between the objectives of exchange rate stability and price stability.[16]

It fell to the delegates to the Genoa Conference in 1922 to flesh out these ideas. Genoa came after the reparations question had been settled (for the time being) by the London Schedule of Payments laid down by the Reparations Commission in May 1921. While the

conference was called at European behest, this time the League of
Nations was circumvented in order to encourage U.S. participation,
the Europeans realizing that no comprehensive solution to postwar
financial problems was possible without the active participation of
one of the world's leading economic and financial powers. But to the
disappointment of its European partners, the Harding Administration, fearful that the issue of war debts would be reopened, again
agreed to send only an "unofficial observer," Richard Washburn
Child, who as American ambassador to Italy was close at hand.

The work of the Conference was divided into four commissions;
the commission on financial questions took up the issue of monetary
stabilization. The monetary experts assembled first for a preparatory
meeting in London, where Ralph Hawtrey, director of Financial
Enquires at the Treasury, presented a preliminary set of draft
resolutions.[17] The Genoa Resolutions on finance, agreed on by the
full conference, closely followed Hawtrey's draft. They endorsed a
return to the gold standard at suitable parities, without specifying
what constituted suitable.[18] But, importantly, they acknowledged
the prospect of a shortage of monetary gold. They warned against
the "simultaneous and competitive efforts of countries to secure
metallic reserves" (*Report of the Financial Commission of the Genoa
Conference,* reprinted in Federal Reserve Board 1922, 678) and of
the deflationary consequences that would flow from such efforts.
As a solution, they advocated a system of reserve centers situated
in countries whose central banks would hold their reserves entirely
in gold. Other countries would then hold their reserves
in a combination of gold and foreign bills and balances in the reserve
centers in question.

Effectively, this plan was a formalization and extension of the
gold-exchange standard of prewar years. But the justification was
now different. The rationale then had been to limit the real resource
cost of gold, enhance diplomatic leverage, and secure capital market
access. Now instead it was to reconcile limited global gold supplies
with a higher price level.

The identity of the reserve centers, like the appropriate level of
parities, was left carefully unspecified. But it was clear that the United

States, which had amassed more than 40 percent of the world's monetary gold stock, would be one. Hawtrey and his colleagues evidently anticipated, extrapolating prewar practice, that the United Kingdom would be the other. Tradition militated in London's favor, as did the reputation of British financial institutions—including the Bank of England—and the liquidity and efficiency of British financial markets. The benefits of reserve center status might be substantial. Foreign purchases of British Treasury bills and bonds, and capital inflows into Britain generally, would relax the balance-of-payments constraint. Making London a reserve center would help attract other international financial business, insofar as the accumulation of official reserves and other transactions went together. As Hawtrey and his Treasury colleagues saw it, sterling and the dollar would share the role of reserve currency in the 1920s, in proportions to be determined.

To foster the practice of holding foreign reserves, the Genoa Resolutions foresaw a number of further reforms. Reserve-holding decisions, following the Brussels recipe, would be delegated to "autonomous" central banks free of political interference. To this end, such central banks, with modern statutes specifying the share of reserves that could be held in the form of foreign exchange, would be established where they did not already exist. Finally, where statutes specifying that the legal reserve should be held exclusively in the form of gold for reasons of custom or tradition, and could not be changed, central banks might still be encouraged to hold any excess reserves above the legal minimum in the form of foreign exchange.

With the reserve base now augmented by foreign exchange, and with central banks holding reserves above the legal minimum, these banks might be able to take active steps to stabilize the price level, in contrast to the situation before 1913. Cassel emphasized the need to supplement restoration of the gold standard with "endeavours to keep the value of gold as constant as possible" (where the reference was to the value of gold in terms of a basket of commodities, meaning the price level).[19] The Genoa Resolutions called for negotiating a convention based on the gold-exchange standard "with a view to preventing undue fluctuations in the purchasing power of gold." The idea was to create an environment in which "credit will be regulated, not only with a view to maintaining the currencies at par with one another, but also with a view to preventing undue fluctuations in the purchasing power of gold." (*Report of the Financial Commission of the Genoa Conference,* reprinted in Federal Reserve Board 1922, 678). Hawtrey, in his commentary on the resolutions, translated this into clear English: "In other words we want to stabilize prices."[20] This could be done by adjusting the interest rate at which the central bank provided credit to the private sector (Hawtrey being the leading analyst and proponent of "Bank rate policy" in this period).

The constraint was that no one central bank could unilaterally reduce its discount rate and expand credit to head off an incipient deflation without seeing its currency weaken and losing reserves. Hence the Genoa Resolutions spoke of the need for "continuous" central bank cooperation for the acceptable operation of the gold-exchange standard. Otherwise, central banks would be caught between the Scylla of deflation and the Charybdis of exchange rate instability—as they were in the 1930s, when cooperation collapsed. In this case, confidence in the foreign-exchange component of reserves would be an early casualty.[21] This constraint was also a departure from the prewar gold-exchange standard; where central bank cooperation then had been episodic, it was now to be systematic and ongoing.[22]

Furthermore, it was important, in the language of Genoa, that the new gold-exchange standard and cooperation supporting it be "encompassing." If a central bank holding a substantial fraction of global reserves failed to cooperate, it might be impossible for the others to take steps to stabilize prices without threatening their parities and hence the stability of the system. Implicitly, this was a reference to the Federal Reserve System, the central bank of a country not officially represented at Genoa.

The Bank of England was tasked with hosting an international conference of central banks, separate from direct government (read "political") involvement; this separation, it was thought, might encourage American participation. In the event, its efforts to organize such a conference came to naught. European leaders were preoccupied by reparations, disarmament, and monetary stabilization. U.S. leaders feared being asked to make concessions on war debts. On both sides of the Atlantic, politicians were reluctant to see their central banks convene a joint meeting. (So much, then, for the fiction of "autonomous" central banks.) Federal Reserve officials, for their part, worried that they might be pressured into policy adjustments that were undesirable from a strictly domestic point of view.[23]

In the end, the London meeting of central banks was not convened. Central bank cooperation in the subsequent period was again episodic rather than continuous, haphazard rather than systematic. Ultimately it failed to head off global deflation and the collapse of the gold-exchange-standard system after 1929.

Implementing Genoa

None of this prevented governments, with support from the League of Nations, from attempting to implement Genoa's plans. Austria, Bulgaria, Danzig, Estonia, Greece, and Hungary stabilized their currencies with help from the Financial Committee of the League, the proto-International Monetary Fund of the 1920s.[24] These countries' newly established central banks, endowed with statutes drafted with guidance from the League, were authorized to hold the entirety of their reserves in convertible foreign exchange. Other countries establishing or reforming central banks were authorized to hold a specified proportion of their reserves in this form. Still other central banks, such as those of Japan and Norway, were limited to holding the legally required reserve backing in gold but maintained excess reserves in the form of foreign bills and balances.[25]

London and New York competed as gold centers for the business of these countries. British officials played a prominent role in the League of Nations' monetary stabilization efforts, leading the French to complain that the Financial Committee was so influenced by the Bank of England's Montagu Norman as to be effectively his "personal agent."[26] European countries taking the advice of the League were encouraged to adopt the gold-exchange standard and, implicitly, to hold the resulting foreign exchange reserves in London. In countries in Britain's postwar sphere of influence, such as Greece and Bulgaria, the Bank of England drafted central bank statutes and organized central bank operations.[27] Similarly, the proceeds of stabilization loans raised in Britain, with help from the Bank of England, were logically maintained in London.

The alternative source of advice was the Federal Reserve Bank of New York, which delegated the task of money doctoring to Professor Kemmerer.[28] U.S. involvement and receipt of the Kemmerer–New York Fed seal of approval heightened the prospects for placing a stabilization loan in the United States. In turn, the proceeds of a stabilization loan placed in the United States were logically held on deposit in New York until they could be put to further use.

This narrative points to several tensions in the historical literature. The close-fought rivalry between the Bank of England and Federal Reserve Bank of New York and between the financial centers of London and New York sits uneasily with accounts in which it is asserted that the pound sterling remained the dominant international and reserve currency until after World War II. The effort to construct a gold-exchange standard that was more durable than its pre–World War I predecessor and that did a better job of reconciling exchange rate and price stability is hard to square with the subsequent instability of prices, exchange rates, and indeed the system as a whole. Was the new reserve system badly designed or just badly managed? Answering questions like these requires a closer look at the evidence.

4

Reserve Currencies in the 1920s and 1930s

Until recently, the currency composition of foreign exchange reserves in the 1920s and 1930s was something of a statistical black hole. In the interwar years, central banks published figures for total gold and foreign exchange reserves but not for the currency composition of those reserves. Estimates of that composition are sparse, undocumented, and conflicting. In 1928, Federal Reserve Board staff conjectured that "perhaps as much as $1,000,000,000 of the operating reserves of foreign central banks was held in the form of dollar balances, bills and bonds."[1] If so, this accounted for roughly half of the foreign exchange reserves of leading central banks as tabulated by Ragnar Nurkse in his analysis of international currency experience.[2] Other scholars of international monetary relations, such as Robert Triffin, offered sharply contrasting estimates; according to Triffin (1964), sterling's share of global foreign exchange reserves remained on the order of 80 percent circa 1928. Others, like Aliber (1966) and Chinn and Frankel (2008), generalized from the assertions of Triffin and others, suggesting that the dollar first rivaled and surpassed the pound sterling as a reserve currency only after World War II. This long lag between U.S. economic and financial supremacy and the dollar overtaking sterling as a reserve currency is seen as testifying to the advantages of incumbency and the power of network effects, which bestow inertia on the currency composition of foreign exchange holdings and leave room in the market for only one true international currency.

In fact, these earlier estimates for the 1920s and 1930s are based on only fragmentary evidence and conjecture. Triffin's widely cited estimates, for example, are undocumented and unexplained.

In this chapter, we take a first step toward filling this gap, providing evidence on the currency composition of foreign exchange reserves in the 1920s and 1930s. We use evidence from contemporary ledgers and accounts housed in the archives of central banks. Inevitably there are gaps, but our estimates at their most complete cover more than 75 percent of foreign exchange reserves worldwide.

Our new estimates are at variance with previous pictures. We find that the dollar first overtook sterling as the leading reserve currency not in 1928, 1938, or 1948 but already in the mid-1920s, and it then widened its lead in the second half of the decade. Evidently incumbency and inertia did not delay the transfer of leadership for as long as suggested by earlier scholars.

With the U.S. economic and financial crisis of the early 1930s, culminating in devaluation of the dollar in 1933, the greenback then lost its supremacy. This loss was part of the broader liquidation of foreign exchange reserves resulting from the instability of exchange rates, including the exchange rates of the major reserve currencies. The principal exception was the continued maintenance of pound sterling reserves by members of the eponymously named Sterling Area—economies with close commercial, financial, and political ties to the United Kingdom. These trends in the 1930s may explain why scholars like Triffin misconstrued developments in the 1920s and international currency experience in the interwar period more generally.

Our evidence for the 1920s and 1930s is inconsistent with the notion that there is room in the international system for only one dominant reserve currency, conceivably complemented by a competitive fringe of minor players, owing to strong network increasing returns. A plausible reading is that sterling and the dollar shared reserve currency status more or less equally, depending on the year, for much of the interwar period. The prewar oligopoly described by Lindert (1969), where market share was split among sterling, the French franc, and the German mark, was effectively replaced by a sterling-U.S. dollar duopoly.

Data and Methods

Several compilations document the evolution of aggregate gold and foreign exchange reserves in the interwar years. Bank for International Settlements (1932) covers 1924–1932. The statistics it provides are annual, except for 1931–1932, for which it provides quarterly data. Twenty-six European countries and the United States are included, and all data are in Swiss francs.[3] Another widely cited source is Nurkse (1944), published under the auspices of the League of Nations. Nurkse's statistics are annual. They cover 24 European countries during 1924–1932 and are in U.S. dollars.[4]

Nurkse's series appear to have been compiled from contemporary periodical sources. The League of Nations published information on gold and foreign exchange reserves in its annual *Statistical Yearbooks* and occasional *Memoranda*.[5] Economists and statisticians at the League worked with official central bank returns and communicated with statisticians at the central banks, thus explaining a number of adjustments. These sources report data in local currency units. Another reference is the *Monetary Statistics* of the Federal Reserve Board (1943), which seems to have been the source for or at least used a methodology similar to Nurkse's.[6] It is also possible that the League of Nations is the source for Nurkse's tabulations, since Nurkse worked for the League from 1933 through 1945.[7]

As mentioned, although these sources provide information on the total volume of foreign exchange reserves, none provides information on their currency composition. Central banks were reluctant, then as now, to publish such information, fearing that they would be front-run by other investors and realizing that purchases or sales of the assets of other countries could be politically controversial. Even now, nearly a century after the fact, many continue to regard these data as sensitive. We know only one case, Italy, where a central bank has published the currency decomposition of its foreign exchange reserves.[8] Another partial exception is monthly material published by Brazil's currency board for 1927–1929.

We have therefore attempted to retrieve data on the currency composition of foreign exchange reserves from the archives of central banks. Generally these are contained in handwritten or type-written ledgers. They vary in whether the amounts they report are in domestic or foreign currency.

Material from the archives does not always match the totals published by the Bank for International Settlements (BIS) and the League of Nations. This may reflect valuation effects: it is not always clear what exchange rates were used when the BIS and League reported the value of foreign exchange reserves in Swiss francs or U.S. dollars.[9] It is possible that central banks, when publishing information on their foreign exchange reserves and reporting to the League of Nations, included only a subset of their reserves, for example, "foreign exchange held for cover purposes" (the reserves required as statutory backing for domestic liabilities) and not also "other foreign exchange." It is possible that they reported not only their own reserves but also those held on behalf of other agencies of government.[10]

Where national and League of Nations sources differ, we have taken the national sources as definitive. We have sought to value gold and foreign exchange reserves at market prices, something that was not always the practice of contemporary central banks.[11] Our efforts have produced data for 18 countries, albeit with gaps. In practice, for any given year we are able to include about 15 countries, encompassing Western Europe, Eastern Europe, Asia, and Latin America. The central banks in question account for roughly three-quarters of global foreign exchange reserves. Table 4.1 provides a summary of the information we have assembled.[12]

TABLE 4.1. Coverage of Data on Reserve Currency Composition

Country	Source	Period	Valuation
	Gold Bloc Countries		
France	Bank of France	1928–1939	Market exchange rates
Italy	Collana Storica	1920–1939	Market exchange rates
Switzerland	Swiss National Bank	1920–1939	
Netherlands	Bank of the Netherlands	1920–1931	Market exchange rates
	Central Europe		
Austria	Bank of Austria	1923–1929, 1932–1937	Market exchange rates
Czechoslovakia	Bank of Czechoslovakia	1921–1938	Market exchange rates
Romania	Bank of Romania	1929–1934, 1937	Market exchange rates
	Sterling Area		
Denmark	Bank of Denmark	1919–1939	Book exchange rates
Finland	Bank of Finland	1921–1938	Book echange rates
Norway	Bank of Norway	1920–1939	Book exchange rates
Portugal	Bank of Portugal	1931–1939	Book exchange rates
Sweden	Riksbank	1926–1939	Market exchange rates
	Other Europe		
Spain	Bank of Spain	1920–1936	Market exchange rates
	Latin America		
Brazil	Reports of the *Caixa de Estabilização*	1927–1929	Book values coincide with fixed exchange rate prevailing during available dates
Colombia	Bank of Chile	1926–1929, 1932–1933, 1936–1939	Market exchange rates
Chile	Bank of the Republic	1923–1939	Market exchange rates
	Asia		
Japan	Bank of Japan	1920–1939	Market exchange rates

Note: Italy is counted as a member of the Gold Bloc.

One Reserve Currency or Several?

Figure 4.1 is a snapshot of the composition of foreign exchange reserves in 1929, at the apex, if you will, of the interwar gold-exchange standard. The 16 countries included in the figure (Austria, Brazil, Chile,

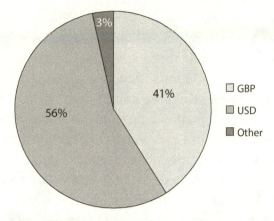

FIGURE 4.1. Aggregate Foreign Currency Holdings
(16 countries), 1929.
Source: Constructed on the basis of data drawn from the
archives of the central banks reported in Table 4.1.
Note: GBP, British pound; USD, U.S. dollar.

Colombia, Czechoslovakia, Denmark, Finland, France, Italy, Japan,
Netherlands, Norway, Romania, Spain, Sweden, and Switzerland)
held a total of $1.9 billion in exchange reserves. This is 82 percent of
Nurkse's global total for the end of 1929 and approximately 75 percent
of the global total, given Nurkse's incomplete country coverage.

The picture leaves little room for doubt. In 1929 there were
essentially two true reserve currencies, the dollar and sterling, which
together accounted for some 97 percent of global foreign exchange
reserves. So much, then, for the idea that there is room in the market
for only a single reserve currency at any point in time. This is strong
support for the so-called new view of international currency competition, according to which several international currencies can coexist.

Note also that our new estimates support the Federal Reserve
Board's conjecture for 1927 of approximately $1 billion of dollar-
denominated global exchange reserves (out of a roughly $2.1 billion
total) while contradicting the suggestion by Triffin that sterling still
accounted for 80 percent of global foreign exchange reserves. Thus,
dollar supremacy so measured did not have to wait until after World
War II, as has been repeatedly conjectured.

It seems unlikely that adding more countries would significantly
change the picture. The most important omission is Germany, which

held less than 1 percent of global foreign exchange reserves as of 1929. We suspect that it split them fairly equally between New York and London—or even held the bulk of those reserves in New York, given that the majority of German foreign borrowing in the 1920s was sourced there. Austria held more dollars than sterling (see below), and it is unlikely that Germany's behavior was significantly different.[13]

But the possibility of room in the market for more than one consequential reserve currency does not mean that an infinite number of such currencies existed. Aside from sterling and the dollar, other currencies pale in comparison. The Swiss franc and Dutch guilder, the two next most important currencies in central banks' portfolios, accounted for only about 2 percent of the global total. What was true in 1929 was true more broadly. Reserves held in currencies other than sterling and the dollar generally hovered around 5 percent of the global total; their share was significantly greater only in 1932 and 1933, when doubts about the stability of the U.S. and British currencies were at their peak. See Figure 4.2.

Also interesting is the negligible share of French francs in foreign exchange reserves. The franc had a troubled history, having experienced rapid inflation and currency depreciation in the 5 years ending in 1926.

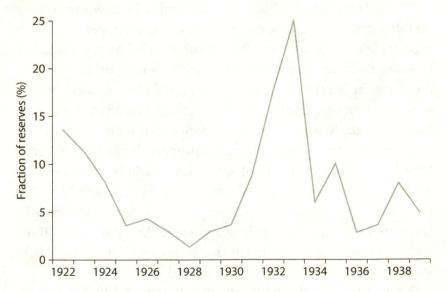

FIGURE 4.2. Fraction of Reserves in Third Currencies, 1919–1939 (percent).
Source: Constructed on the basis of data drawn from the archives of the central banks reported in Table 4.1.

The summer of the latter year saw the famous Poincaré stabilization, which brought 5 years of chronic currency depreciation to a close.[14] The franc then appreciated sharply over the subsequent 6 months before de facto stabilization at the end of 1926 and de jure stabilization, which cemented the currency's gold-standard status, in June 1928.

Confidence having been restored, French investors repatriated large amounts of flight capital. To prevent the currency from appreciating excessively and the country's hard-earned competitive advantage from being lost, the Bank of France intervened with purchases of foreign exchange; its foreign currency reserves rose rapidly, from a mere $50 million at the end of November 1926 to more than $770 million at the end of the subsequent May. The majority of the inflow reportedly came from London in the form of sterling. It followed that more than half of the Bank of France's foreign exchange portfolio was initially made up of sterling, with the remainder in dollars. The French central bank then made controversial efforts in 1927 and 1928 to convert a portion of its sterling into gold and dollars—to the extent that by 1929, the majority of its foreign exchange reserves was in dollars.[15] See Figure 4.3.

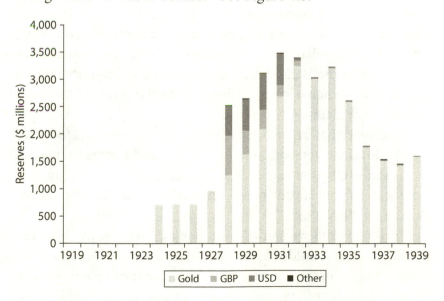

FIGURE 4.3. French Foreign Exchange and Gold Reserves, 1928–1939 ($ millions).
Source: Data drawn from the archives of Bank of France.
Note: No data available on foreign exchange reserves for 1924–1927. GBP, British Pound; USD, U.S. dollar.

At this point the French financial community, official as well as private, launched a campaign to restore the stature of Paris as an international financial center and the franc as an international currency of the first rank.[16] Figure 4.1 suggests that they made little progress. Evidently, the effects of years of inflation and currency instability were difficult to surmount. Then at the beginning of the 1930s, when France was finally in a position to surmount them, general disenchantment with the practice of holding foreign exchange reserves set in. Soon thereafter the French economy descended into the Great Depression, creating fears, not unfounded, that the franc might suffer the fate of sterling and the dollar—namely, that it might ultimately be devalued against gold.

The Rise and Fall of the Dollar

Pinpointing the date at which the dollar overtook sterling is more difficult, since information on the currency composition of foreign exchange reserves in the first half of the 1920s is fragmentary.[17] For four countries (Italy, Norway, Spain, and Switzerland), we have a continuous run of currency-composition figures for the 1920s: as shown in Figure 4.4, these suggest that the dollar overtook sterling circa 1924. The dollar then maintained its leadership through the second half of the 1920s, when sterling was continuously "under the harrow"—when doubts persisted about the ability of the Bank of England to maintain convertibility.[18]

For a somewhat larger group of countries (the previous four plus Czechoslovakia, Denmark, Finland, Japan, and Portugal), we can do the same thing starting in 1923. The result (Figure 4.5) suggests that the dollar had already overtaken sterling as the leading reserve currency in 1924–1926.

Finally, in 1928 we can add the Bank of France, by this time the single-largest holder of foreign exchange reserves. The sheer size of France's exchange reserves means that sterling temporarily regained its reserve-currency leadership as a result of the Bank of France's accumulation of London bills and balances. ("Regained," because France accumulated the vast majority of these balances

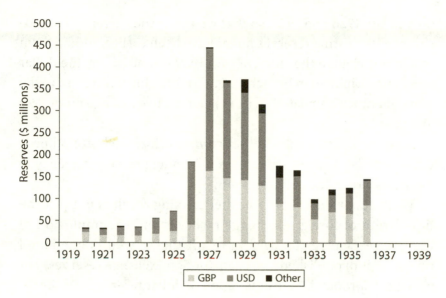

FIGURE 4.4. Currency Composition of Reserves for Four Countries, 1920–1936 ($ millions).
Source: Constructed on the basis of data drawn from the archives of the central banks reported in Table 4.1.
Note: GBP, British Pound; USD, U.S. dollar.

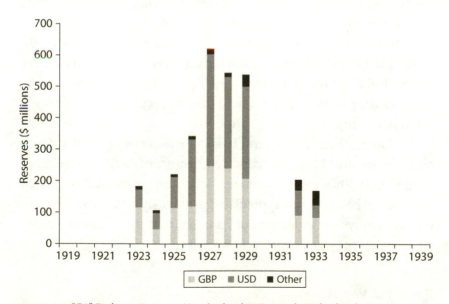

FIGURE 4.5. "G9" Exchange Reserves (Czechoslovakia, Denmark, Finland, Italy, Japan, Norway, Portugal, Spain, and Switzerland), 1923–1933 ($ millions).
Source: Constructed on the basis of data drawn from the archives of the central banks reported in Table 4.1.
Note: GBP, British Pound; USD, U.S. dollar.

only in late 1926 and 1927, so that whatever the currency composition of its existing reserves might have been earlier, adding them would not change the story.) From 1929 on, however, the dollar was again dominant in French and therefore global reserves, as the Bank of France liquidated sterling balances in exchange for dollars and gold.

As always, historical reality is complex. But the bottom line is that the dollar overtook sterling as the leading reserve currency in the 1920s, not in the 1940s or 1950s.

What about the 1930s? Another striking result is not just the liquidation of foreign exchange reserves and the implosion of the gold-exchange standard (a result that is well documented on the basis of published aggregate foreign exchange reserves) but also the disproportionate liquidation of dollar reserves and the renewed dominance of sterling. At this point the Bank of France no longer figures in the story; by 1932 it had liquidated most of its dollar and sterling claims, and by 1933 it had liquidated these entirely but for a small dollar balance. In other countries, however, sterling regained its predominance relative to the dollar, a predominance that appears to have been sustained for the remainder of the 1930s. Adding still other countries for which we have information for the 1930s (Ireland, Australia, and New Zealand) only reinforces the picture, since these countries held the entirety of their reserves in pounds sterling.

Strikingly, then, the Federal Reserve's estimates of dollar dominance in the late 1920s and Triffin's conjecture of sterling dominance in the late 1930s were both correct. Why the compatibility of their conjectures has not been appreciated previously is also now evident: it is not always the case, it would appear, that the status as leading reserve currency, once lost, is lost forever.

Regional Variations

Was sterling's recovery as the leading reserve currency in the 1930s purely a matter of the Sterling Area? Figure 4.6 provides circumstantial evidence that the Sterling Area was a large part of the story.

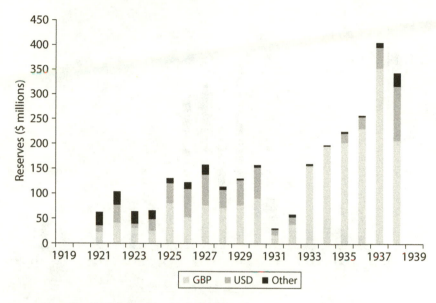

FIGURE 4.6. Non-English-Speaking Sterling Area Exchange Reserves, 1917–1934 ($ millions).
Source: Constructed on the basis of data drawn from the archives of the central banks reported in Table 4.1.
Note: GBP, British Pound; USD, U.S. dollar.

The non-English-speaking members of the Sterling Area—here, the Scandinavian countries and Portugal—liquidated both sterling and dollar reserves in 1931–1932. Then starting in 1933, with the recovery of their economies and exports, they sought to rebuild those reserves. But reflecting U.S. President Roosevelt's embargo of gold exports, their accumulation of reserves was entirely in the form of sterling. The Scandinavians and Portuguese added small amounts of dollars to their portfolios in 1935–1936 and then larger amounts in 1937 and 1938, with the approach of World War II. But the pound remained far and away the dominant reserve currency in the Sterling Area. The same was true, as noted above, in Australia and New Zealand.[19]

The story elsewhere was different. The Bank of France, one of the principal holders of foreign exchange reserves, liquidated its sterling in 1931–1932 and held small dollar balances thereafter. The other members of the gold bloc—Belgium, Italy, the Netherlands, Poland, and Switzerland—similarly sought to dispose of their unstable sterling and dollars after 1930. The years 1931–1932 found them holding much smaller foreign exchange reserves in a portfolio divided

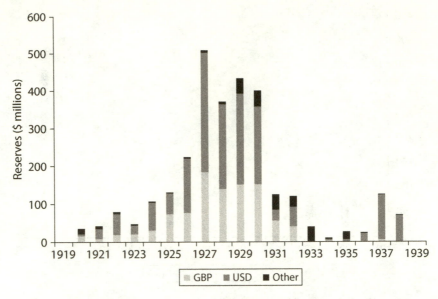

FIGURE 4.7. Gold Bloc Exchange Reserves (excluding France), 1920–1938 ($ millions).
Source: Constructed on the basis of data drawn from the archives of the central banks reported in Table 4.1.
Note: GBP, British Pound; USD, U.S. dollar.

evenly between sterling, dollars, and now, interestingly, French francs. By 1933 the franc had given way at least temporarily to the Dutch guilder. Then after 1936, with the collapse of the gold bloc and approach of World War II, these countries shifted into dollars even more markedly than did the members of the Sterling Area. See Figure 4.7.

Our data for Latin America paint a similar picture. The liquidation of foreign exchange reserves after 1930 was rapid, and sterling balances were liquidated even faster than dollars were (Figure 4.8). Spain is an exceptional case: the country was not on the gold standard in this period. The Spanish peseta depreciated significantly against the gold currencies between 1928 and 1932, insulating Spanish exports from the Depression (Choudhri and Kochin 1980) and allowing the central bank to accumulate additional foreign exchange reserves.[20]

Figure 4.9 shows a sample of Central European countries. Despite the role of the Bank of England in inflation stabilization in Central Europe, the dollar dominated sterling in the exchange reserves of

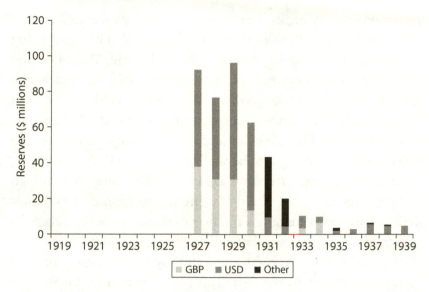

FIGURE 4.8. Latin American Exchange Reserves (Chile and Colombia), 1926–1938 ($ millions).
Source: Constructed on the basis of data drawn from the archives of the central banks reported in Table 4.1.
Note: GBP, British Pound; USD, U.S. dollar.

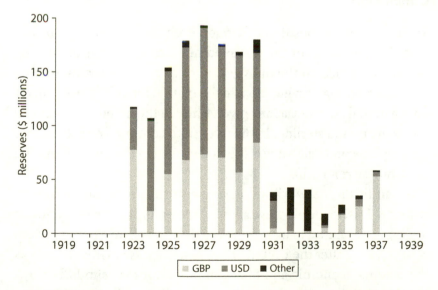

FIGURE 4.9. Central European Exchange Reserves (Romania, Austria, and Czechoslovakia), 1923–1937 ($ millions).
Source: Constructed on the basis of data drawn from the archives of the central banks reported in Table 4.1.
Note: Authors' computations from database. Undocumented amounts were allotted according to the distribution of documented amounts. Breakdowns for 1930 and 1931, as a result, are estimates. GBP, British Pound; USD, U.S. dollar.

the region's central banks after 1924. A temporary exception is 1930, when the National Bank of Czechoslovakia took a bet on sterling at what turned out to be the worst possible time. Thereafter the region participated aggressively in the process of foreign exchange liquidation. With the pound's departure from the gold standard, not just sterling but also dollar reserves were liquidated.[21] We also see a rise in the role of the French franc, which strongly dominates the region's reduced foreign exchange reserves in 1933. Interestingly, when Central European central banks partially rebuilt their foreign exchange reserves, they held sterling rather than dollars. Their sterling balances were only a fraction of those of the Sterling Area countries in terms of value but were substantial nonetheless.

Thus, while the resurrection of sterling as the leading reserve currency in the 1930s was heavily a phenomenon of the Sterling Area, other countries and regions were involved.

Conclusion

The currency composition of foreign exchange reserves is a prominent battleground for the so-called new and old views of international currencies. In the old view, network effects and increasing returns are strong, leaving room in the market for only one dominant international currency at any given time. In the nineteenth century it was the pound sterling. In the twentieth century—or at least that century's second half—it was the dollar. And in the future it may be the Chinese renminbi.

In addition, network increasing returns are a source of persistence. This, in the old view, allowed the pound sterling to continue to dominate central bank reserve portfolios well into the twentieth century, long after the United States had surpassed Great Britain as the leading economic and financial power. It may similarly allow the dollar to dominate those portfolios well into the twenty-first.

The new view, in contrast, questions whether reserve currency status is a natural monopoly. It challenges the presumption that persistence is overwhelmingly strong. It suggests that several national units have regularly shared the reserve currency function over the course of the past century.

A principal field of combat on this battleground is the interwar period, when sterling, it is said, continued to dominate reserve portfolios, illustrating the power of network increasing returns and the strength of persistence. The evidence presented here is inconsistent with this interpretation. It shows that reserve currency status was evenly shared in the 1920s, challenging the natural monopoly view. It shows that the dollar had already overtaken sterling as the leading reserve currency by the middle of the decade, in a manner inconsistent with the image of strong persistence. The picture is complicated by the collapse of the gold-exchange standard in the 1930s and the growing instability of the leading reserve currencies in the 1930s. These events led to the liquidation of both sterling and dollars, then to some rebuilding of reserve balances in London by the members of the Sterling Area, and finally to the accumulation of official dollar balances in New York by countries anticipating the outbreak of World War II. But the evidence overall strongly favors the so-called new view.

Reserve currency status is only one aspect of a national unit's international means of payment, unit of account, and store of value function. Subsequent chapters will therefore investigate whether what is true of reserve currency status is also true of the other dimensions.

5

The Role of Currencies in Financing International Trade

This chapter provides evidence on the role of national currencies in financing international trade. Specifically, we consider the role of sterling and the dollar in the provision of trade credit in the 1920s, the years of transition between British and U.S. monetary and financial leadership. Both currencies, we find, accounted for significant fractions of finance for international trade.

Serving as a unit of account, means of payment, and source of credit for imports and exports are among the key functions of an international currency. Upward of 60 percent of world trade, according to one widely cited estimate, was invoiced, financed, and settled in pounds sterling before World War I.[1] Not only Britain's own imports and exports but also the majority of the imports and exports of other countries—including large countries like the United States and France—were financed and settled using trade credit sourced in London and denominated in sterling.

Today the dollar's role as an invoicing and settlement currency for merchandise imports and exports similarly exceeds the weight of America in global trade. Data on these practices are incomplete, but

Ito and Chinn (2014) conclude on the basis of the available evidence that some 60 percent of the imports of countries other than the United States is invoiced in U.S. dollars.[2] What is true of imports is similarly true of exports.[3] For countries as diverse as Australia, Indonesia and Thailand, the dollar is the invoicing currency for more than 80 percent of exports, even though the United States is the destination of less than 15 percent of their trade.

Thus, the preponderance of first sterling and now the dollar in global import and export trade is seen as lending strong support to the traditional view that the leading national unit will heavily dominate international financial transactions. Contrast this with the behavior of central banks: when deciding in what currencies to hold their reserves, central banks will not pay close attention to pecuniary costs and returns. Other considerations, including the political, may figure more importantly and create a simultaneous demand for several different currencies as reserve units.[4] By comparison, when importers and exporters decide where to source trade credit and in what unit to invoice and settle transactions, cost considerations will be central to their calculus.

Moreover, the cost and convenience of using a specific national unit, whether sterling in the nineteenth century or the dollar in the twentieth, may depend heavily on which unit is used by other importers and exporters. Denominating one's exports in the same currency as other exporters enables potential purchasers to compare prices and facilitates the efforts of entrants to break into international markets. The cost of trade credit is likely to be lowest in the deepest and most liquid financial market, which possesses that depth and liquidity because it is the market to which established importers and exporters turn when sourcing trade finance. Hence network increasing returns are likely to be more evident in the market for trade credit than in the choice of international reserves. It follows that if network increasing returns are significant, then the dominance of a particular national currency at any given point in time should be more evident in trade finance than in the currency composition of reserves. And if network increasing returns discourage agents, in the absence of a mechanism for coordinating their decisions, from moving to alternatives, the persistence of the incumbent's dominance should similarly be more evident in trade finance.

It is therefore striking that we find the dollar able to complete the transition from being a negligible source of trade credit in 1914 to achieving essentially coequal status with sterling a handful of years later. The shift to the dollar as a source of trade credit had already begun during and immediately after World War I, not in the late 1920s or even, as sometimes asserted, after World War II. These facts are inconsistent with the presumption that inertia is powerful in the international financial realm and that there is room in the market for only one dominant international currency. Rather, the experience of this period is more supportive of the "new view" that several international currencies can coexist.

The full story is complex. The rapid rise of the dollar as a source of trade credit reflected not just market forces but also government action. And not all the achievements of the 1920s were sustained in the 1930s. But history is rarely straightforward.

Background

Exporters need credit to purchase materials and pay their bills while their merchandise is in transit. Standard practice before 1913 was for an American exporter to go to his bank with documents showing that he had shipped his goods and indicating what he would be paid. If his credit was good, he could get his money immediately rather than having to wait for the goods to arrive in the foreign market and for the buyer's payment to arrive in the United States.

The exporter's bank arranged this advance by drawing on a correspondent with whom it had made prior arrangements. On receipt of the bill, which specified the commodities shipped and the name of the U.S. bank drawing the bill, the correspondent whose name was mentioned in the document accepted the security, providing payment in return. The resulting instruments were thus known as "acceptances." Triply guaranteed by the merchandise, by the drawer, and by the acceptor, the claim could then be sold to other investors.

A simple bank-to-customer credit was thereby transformed into a liquid, tradable instrument.

By 1912 the United States was the leading trading nation. It is thus striking that virtually no acceptance credit was provided by U.S. banks or denominated in dollars. Instead, American banks offering such services did so through correspondent banks in London. It followed that their acceptances were denominated in sterling, since that was the currency with which the London banks, the secondary-market investors to whom they sold the paper, and the Bank of England were all accustomed.

These arrangements and their implications did not sit well with American exporters and financiers, and their shortcomings were prominent in the debates surrounding the creation of the Federal Reserve System, an institutional innovation designed in part to correct them. In a pamphlet written for the National Monetary Commission in 1910, Lawrence Jacobs deplored that U.S. bankers were forced to transact via London, observing how this "adds to the importance of London and militates against the development of New York as a financial center."[5] John J. Arnold, first vice president of the First National Bank of Chicago, argued that the "three-cornered arrangement" by which London banks financed American foreign trade was costly and cumbersome. He urged its elimination by creating a "direct dollar exchange market" between the United States on the one hand and South America and the Far East on the other. Doing so would deny London "the undue advantage which this center has had in the past."[6] The German-American banker Paul Warburg referred to the amount paid annually to British banks in acceptance fees as "tribute," in language designed to build support for efforts to internationalize the dollar and transform New York into a global financial center.[7]

In seeking to explain sterling's dominance, contemporaries like Jacobs pointed to the unparalleled strengths of the London market. The City, as the British financial capital was known, had a large and diverse population of banks, including so-called merchant banks with origins, tellingly, in helping merchants with the finance of trade, but also private banks, joint stock banks, and colonial banks, all with international reach. Having acquired networks of overseas correspondents, these banks were able to originate a large volume of trade acceptances. Having originated them, they could distribute them to a secondary market of individual and institutional investors familiar with the instrument. With the help of specialized bill brokers, the banks could sell their acceptances either individually or in packages known as parcels.[8] In the unusual event that there was no ready purchaser but the bank in question did not wish to hold the paper on its own balance sheet, the market maker of last resort, the Bank of England, stood ready to buy it at a discount.[9]

These three factors—the merchant banks' first-mover advantage, a large and active secondary market, and a market maker of last resort—made for low costs, high liquidity, and increasing returns. They explain why sterling was the leading international currency and why London dominated the provision of trade credit.

In seeking to explain why London succeeded in attracting so much of this business at New York's expense, other contemporaries emphasized instead the role of regulatory prohibitions and institutional limitations that made it hard for American banks to penetrate this market. Under the National Banking Act, American banks were prohibited from branching abroad, for much the same reason that they were prohibited from branching across state lines and, in some cases, from branching at all. Americans had a deep-seated aversion to concentrated financial power. Farmers feared that widely branched banks would divert their savings into industrial and commercial uses in other regions at the expense of finance for planting and crop-transport activities; allowing U.S. banks to branch abroad might be even worse from this point of view. In addition, federal legislation prevented banks from dealing in trade acceptances, or so it was argued in legal circles.[10] Last but not least, the United States lacked a central bank to act as market maker of last resort.

It is worth emphasizing that these two interpretations of the situation before World War I had quite different implications for how the market might develop. That emphasizing Britain's first-mover advantage—as a result of which the country possessed experienced intermediaries with extensive international contacts, a deep and liquid secondary market, and an experienced central bank—suggested that the future would resemble the past. The provision of trade credit was subject to increasing returns, placing London at the center of the trade credit network. Even a sharp shock like World War I was unlikely to erode sterling's dominance.

In contrast, the interpretation emphasizing U.S. regulatory and institutional limitations implied that legislative initiatives relaxing those constraints might enable U.S. banks to rapidly penetrate the market. This was what the framers of the Federal Reserve Act had in mind when advancing legislation that authorized U.S. banks to branch abroad, removed ambiguity about the permissibility of banks dealing in trade acceptances, and created a central bank with the capacity to act as market maker and liquidity provider of last resort. If what mattered was not so much Britain's first-mover advantage as the absence of these prerequisites, then New York might quickly come to rival London.

The Rise of New York

Figure 5.1 uses money market rates of interest to gauge the competitive positions of London and New York from 1900 to the late 1930s. While the cost of acceptance credit also had other components (taxes, the bank's commission, and insurance against exchange risk), the interest rate constituted the largest part (Vigreux 1932). In Figure 5.1 the rate shown for London is the open market rate—the rate at which acceptances were bought on the market by investors. We compare this to the open market rate on U.S. acceptances when possible—that is, starting in January 1917. Because U.S. rates for acceptances only become available at that time, we also show prime U.S. commercial paper rates (i.e., the rate on prime short-term credit instruments issued by corporate borrowers of high standing), which begin earlier. This is a reasonable comparison insofar as commercial paper benefited in similar fashion from the new institutional arrangements. The Federal Reserve Act was designed to promote the commercial paper market. Federal Reserve rediscount rates on commercial paper were close to, if slightly higher than, the rate on acceptances after 1916.[11]

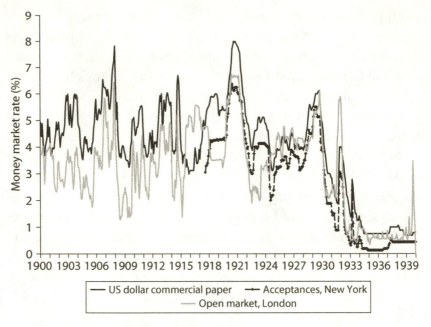

FIGURE 5.1. London and New York Money Market Rates, 1900–1939 (percent). *Source*: Federal Reserve statistics and *Acceptance Bulletin*.

The period around 1915 saw a sharp shift in the relative position of London and New York. This is when the interest differential in Figure 5.1 reversed and significant numbers of dollar acceptances began to appear on the books of the banks. The Guaranty Trust Company claimed to have been the first American intermediary to originate acceptances and to allow foreign correspondents to draw on it.[12] Guaranty Trust listed some $18.2 million of acceptances on its December 1914 balance sheet, when the market as a whole was probably not much bigger (Guaranty Trust 1919).[13]

In subsequent years, more banks entered the market. Figure 5.2 shows the impact on the supply of dollar acceptances and compares it with the comparable stock of acceptances denominated in sterling. The comparison is based on sterling acceptances drawn both abroad and domestically, along with the corresponding U.S. totals.[14] The value of dollar and sterling acceptances was quite close in the 1920s. These figures for private international claims thus resemble the findings in Chapter 4 for official international reserves.[15] Again, this supports the so-called new view of international currency competition.

FIGURE 5.2. Dollar and Sterling Acceptances, 1927–1937 (£ millions).
Source: Calculations based on data drawn from the *Acceptance Bulletin* and archival documents described in Eichengreen and Flandreau (2010).

Reinforcing the point, Figure 5.3 compares the market spreads for London and New York. After 1922, spreads in the two markets are quite similar.

Figure 5.4 indicates that the American market in acceptances experienced two boom-and-bust cycles. A sharp increase occurred in the last years of World War I, coincident with the hike in U.S. trade associated with direct American military involvement. The peak was then reached in 1919–1920. This was the eve of the post–World War I recession. The Fed had started tightening in November 1919, raising the discount rate in response to a gold cover ratio that had fallen close to the 40 percent minimum specified in the Federal Reserve Act. Gold stopped flowing out in April 1920, but the higher cost of credit created difficulties for commodity producers and manufacturers. Industrial production peaked in early 1920 before heading sharply lower in late 1920 and early 1921. Merchandise exports and imports fell moderately in 1920 and then rapidly in 1921, reflecting the impact of the recession, the end of the postwar restocking boom, and the increased cost of trade credit.

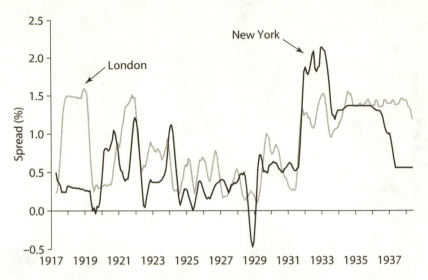

FIGURE 5.3. Spreads between Official and Market Rates in London and New York, 1917–1939 (percent).
Source: NBER Historical Macroeconomic Database.

FIGURE 5.4. Total Outstanding Acceptances and Amounts Held by the Federal Reserve Board, Own Account or for Account of Foreign Correspondents, 1917–1939 ($ billions).
Source: Federal Reserve statistics and *Acceptance Bulletin*.

The second upswing started in 1922–1923 with recovery from the postwar recession. It peaked shortly after the stock market and industrial production in 1929. There was only a modest decline in the volume of outstanding trade acceptances in 1929–1930, coincident with the onset of the Great Depression, but an accelerating decline starting in 1931.[16]

As with official reserves, the dollar's share fell relative to that of sterling in the crisis of the 1930s. Where the value of sterling acceptances fell by half between the peak in 1929 and the mid-1930s, dollar acceptances in 1935 were barely a seventh what they had been in 1929. Again this parallels what we found for changes in the composition of international reserves between the 1920s and 1930s. For acceptances as for reserves, part of the explanation is that the U.S. depression was more severe, and U.S. trade contracted more rapidly than did British trade. But a complete account of the decline in the market for U.S. trade acceptances has other elements as well.

The Fed as Market Maker

The Federal Reserve Board's second *Annual Report* for 1915 is the first publication commenting on this new market.[17] It points to official intervention as playing an important role. The Federal Reserve Bank of Boston is described as having made "every effort to further and develop that business" by purchasing acceptances from Massachusetts banking institutions engaged in financing "hides and wool from South America and cotton and jute from the orient and other sections of the world" in the early months of 1915, trade that had previously been financed "through credits drawn on European centers."[18]

The motivations for the Fed's involvement can be inferred from the minutes of the Open Market Investment Committee, created in 1923 to monitor the System's investment policies and security market operations. A statement adopted during the April 1923 meeting contrasted the relatively hands-off stance of the Bank of England, appropriately for a central bank overseeing a relatively well-developed market. That stance permitted the maintenance of a consistent spread between the open market rate and the rediscount rate of the central bank. In contrast, the committee recommended a more interventionist policy for the Federal Reserve.

> A policy as drastic as that of the Bank of England, for instance, which always aims to make the market pay a penalty rate upon recourse to the bank, is not always suited to the American bill market, and if applied might have an adverse effect upon the establishment of dollar credit and dollar bills in overseas trade and world markets, and it seems reasonably certain that the sterling credit would quickly drive the dollar credit from those markets. It is probable therefore that we must continue for some time a somewhat paternalistic attitude towards the market for dollar bills in this country.[19]

It would appear that American officials were skeptical that simply removing statutory and institutional constraints was enough to jump-start the market in dollar acceptances, given London's first-mover advantage. In addition it was necessary for the Federal Reserve to subsidize the secondary market by offering ready-to-purchase trade acceptances at a concessionary rate. Once a more liquid market developed, that subsidy could be withdrawn and the involvement of the Federal Reserve System could be curtailed.

But, for the moment, that involvement was considerable, as can be seen in Figure 5.4. In these early years, Federal Reserve Banks typically held, either for their own account or on behalf of foreign correspondents (principally foreign central banks), about half of all trade acceptances. When uncertainty spiked and private demand evaporated (notably in April 1917 when the United States entered the war), the Reserve Banks stepped in, purchasing essentially all outstanding acceptances. In contrast, when private demand was strong, as in 1924, the Reserve Banks were able to step out of the market. On average the Federal Reserve System held about half of all outstanding acceptances on the market.

Figure 5.5 juxtaposes two indicators of official support for the market. The dashed line is Federal Reserve holdings as a share of outstanding acceptances. The solid line is the spread between the

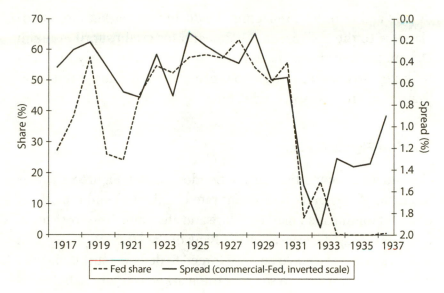

FIGURE 5.5. Share of the Fed in the Acceptance Market (left axis) and Relative Interest Rates (right axis), 1917–1937 (percent).
Source: Authors' calculations based on Federal Reserve statistics.
Note: Data are annualized.

Federal Reserve discount rate and market rate for acceptances. (The scale for this variable, on the right-hand side of the figure, is inverted.) The narrower is the spread, the stronger is the support. Except in 1921 and 1931, the Fed kept its rate close to the market rate and purchased a substantial fraction of acceptances outstanding. Again, this is consistent with the view that the U.S. central bank played an active role in fostering the market in trade credit.

The differential in the discount rate market was on the order of 20–60 basis points, and the Fed's share of outstanding trade acceptances, as noted, was on the order of a half. Two exceptions occurred: in 1920–1921 and in October 1931. In the earlier episode (noted above), the Fed raised its discount rate in response to gold losses, causing a sharp decline in both economic activity and its share of outstanding acceptances. In the October 1931 episode, the central bank once more raised the discount rate in response to gold losses (this time precipitated by sterling's departure from the gold standard), causing its share of acceptances to fall sharply. The spread of the discount rate over the market rate continued to widen

in 1932 and into 1933, reflecting the decline in market rates associated with the collapse in the demand for credit, until Franklin
Delano Roosevelt was inaugurated as president in early 1933 and
took steps to counter expectations of deflation, leading to the stabilization and recovery of market rates.

London Fights Back

We turn next to conditions on the London market. Figure 5.6 shows
the Bank of England's rediscount rate (Bank rate) and the rate of
discount on the open market before and after 1914. The correlation
declines during the war, when the Bank of England, grappling with
a weak sterling exchange rate and forced to defend a shrinking gold
reserve, was not able to support the market as freely as before.[20]
Sterling depreciated against the dollar, and statutory restrictions
were placed on the ability of London banks to provide finance not
just to enemies but also to neutrals and allies. All this presumably
helped American entrants solidify their position at the expense of
the British incumbents.

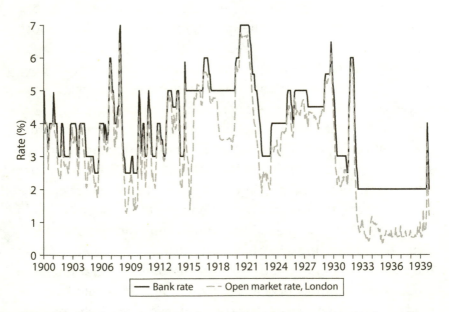

FIGURE 5.6. Bank of England Rediscount Rate and Open Market Rate, 1900–1939 (percent).
Source: NBER Historical Macroeconomic Database.

But the war also created opportunities for London. German banks, often operating through their London branches, had been active in the provision of trade credit to Latin America, Central Europe and the East in the years leading up to 1914. In Latin America, for example, the role of the German mark in financing the region's trade had expanded on the basis of rising German industrial exports. Integral to this process were German overseas banks: the Banco Alemán Transatlántico, the Deutsch-Südamerikanische Bank, Brazilianische Bank für Deutschland, and the Bank für Chile und Deutschland, which were active in providing trade credit to the importers and exporters in question.[21]

With the outbreak of the war, the London branches of German overseas banks were shuttered or expropriated.[22] British merchant and overseas banks sought to capitalize on the information obtained through these expropriations. The British government seized the London branch of the Anglo-Austrian Bank, a leading Vienna-based institution with links to Germany that was active in Central Europe and the Near East. Once the government and private sector accessed its records and correspondence, they could see how its affiliated institutions operated in Central Europe. This knowledge "eased the way for private British interests to seize control of the Anglo-Austrian network."[23]

After the war, these expropriations were recognized by Article 248 of the Versailles Treaty. Legal status facilitated the organization of a new Anglo-Austrian Bank in 1922 under the aegis of the Bank of England. The reconstituted Anglo-Austrian bank, now under British control, in turn controlled the new Anglo-Czech Bank that was formed to take over the branches of the former Anglo-Austrian bank in Czechoslovakia. Similar policies were pursued in Turkey, where German banks had played a prominent role before World War I.

Table 5.1 shows data for 1913 and 1921, from the *Bankers' Almanac*, comparing Germany's four Latin American banks with three British rivals. It shows how the German overseas banks lost their connections in London and were replaced by British merchant banks. The merchant houses in question, the likes of Kleinworts, Schroeders, and Seligmans, were London institutions of German origin with a strong German information base. Whereas the capital and balance sheets of British and German banks operating in Latin America had

TABLE 5.1. German and British Overseas Banks in Latin America: 1913 vs. 1921

Bank	Main London Agent		Total Assets (1913 £ million)		Capital (1913 £ million)	
	1913	1921	1913	1921	1913	1921
German Foreign Banks in Latin America						
Banco Aleman Transatlantico	Deutsche Bank	Kleinwort	14.0	7.0	2.0	0.1
Deutsch-Sudam. Bank	Dresdner Bank	Kleinwort, Shröder, Japhet	7.0	1.9	1.0	0.1
Bank für Chile und Deutschland	Disconto	None[1]	3.0	0.2	0.2	0.0
Brasilianische Bank für Deutschland	Disconto	None[1]	7.0	0.8	0.5	0.1
Total			30.9	10.0	3.5	0.4
Main British Overseas Banks in Latin America						
Anglo-South American	Own	Own	14.0	57.6	1.3	3.5
London and River Plate	Own	Own	35.0	41.7	1.2	1.4
London and Brazilian Bank	Own	Own	20.0	25.7	1.0	1.0
Total			69.0	125.0	3.5	5.9

Sources: Authors' estimates from Banker's Almanac (see Eichengreen and Flandreau (2010) for further details). Conversions into sterling made using price indices from Mitchell (1998a) (1921 prices converted to 1913 prices) and the 1913 sterling parity of £1 = 20.4 German marks.

Note: Disconto, Discontogesellschaft Bank.

[1]According to the Banker's Almanac.

been comparable in 1913, by 1921 British banks were much larger. Evidently, accounts suggesting that the shock of the war was responsible for the shift of a significant share of the acceptance market from London to New York are misleading. Arguments that the war was good for the United States but bad for Britain are at best incomplete. The use of political means to eliminate German competition could and, in some cases did, reinforce London's competitive position.[24]

Regression Analysis

We now look more closely at the supply of dollar acceptances in the 1920s. Recall that a first interpretation of this phenomenon is that it was market led. U.S. banks were capable of entering the market if they were freed from regulatory restrictions. Once so freed, in 1914, they could open foreign branches and build on existing U.S. trade. The second, competing interpretation is that the transition was government led. Sterling still benefited from incumbency, and a significant rise in the dollar's share would not have occurred had the Fed not provided a subsidy by substituting for the missing secondary market. In this view, the Fed's purchases of acceptances—and not the establishment of foreign branches or extent of U.S. trade flows—was the key determinant of the dollar market's growth.

We test these hypotheses using data for individual banks in different years. The dependent variable, the value of bank acceptances on the balance sheet of bank i in year t, is assembled for 20 banks between 1915 and 1939.[25] The panel is unbalanced (we lack observations for some banks in some years, since certain banks were merged, while others were closed). While we provide estimates in Table 5.2 with and without clustered standard errors, the latter may be appropriate, since we are combining bank-level and macroeconomic variables.

Balance sheets were used to gather figures for other bank attributes (capital, reserves, total assets, etc.). We assume that value of acceptances originated by a bank depended on the number of its foreign branches but also on its capital, reserves, and the size of the overall market as captured by the total value of acceptances or, alternatively, total U.S. imports plus exports.[26]

While some banks branched more heavily than others, it is hard to know how to weigh, say, a single branch in Paris against several branches in Cuba. We therefore use a zero/one dummy variable for the existence of branches (the results are not noticeably affected by alternative specifications).[27]

In Table 5.2, bank size, whether measured by total assets or capital, tends to be positive and significant.[28] The economy-wide variables—acceptances and total trade—are similarly significant and positive more often than not.[29]

Branching is also significant: the existence of branches is associated with a roughly 60 percent increase in outstanding acceptances.

TABLE 5.2. Determinants of Banks' Acceptances

	Without Clustering						
	(1)	(2)	(3)	(4)	(5)	(6)	(7)
Total assets/ Liabilities	0.90 (12.19)	0.72 (13.53)	0.73 (13.21)	—	—	—	0.59 (3.91)
Capital, surplus, and undivided profits	—	—	—	0.94 (13.45)	0.67 (12.43)	0.72 (12.36)	0.15 (0.99)
U.S. total trade (exports + imports)	0.68 (4.70)	—	0.08 (0.68)	0.83 (5.86)	—	0.25 (2.10)	0.12 (1.01)
Total U.S. acceptances outstanding	—	1.05 (12.72)	1.03 (11.61)	—	0.96 (11.10)	0.88 (9.37)	0.99 (10.34)
Branching	0.30 (2.41)	0.57 (6.09)	0.55 (5.71)	0.32 (2.66)	0.64 (6.79)	0.58 (5.79)	0.54 (5.53)
Intercept	−8.92 (−6.25)	−8.77 (−14.27)	−9.36 (−8.77)	−8.35 (−6.23)	−6.37 (−11.01)	−8.25 (−7.74)	−9.27 (−8.65)
N	262	249	249	263	250	250	249
Adjusted R^2	0.51	0.72	0.72	0.55	0.70	0.71	0.72
	With Clustering						
	(1)	(2)	(3)	(4)	(5)	(6)	(7)
Total assets/ Liabilities	0.90 (11.64)	0.72 (8.46)	0.73 (8.49)	—	—	—	0.59 (2.48)
Capital, surplus, and undivided profits	—	—	—	0.94 (13.15)	0.67 (8.43)	0.72 (8.70)	0.15 (0.73)
U.S. total trade (exports + imports)	0.68 (4.66)	—	0.08 (0.42)	0.83 (5.68)	—	0.25 (1.32)	0.12 (0.65)
Total U.S. acceptances outstanding	—	1.05 (10.88)	1.03 (9.44)	—	0.96 (8.42)	0.88 (7.08)	0.99 (9.91)
Branching	0.30 (1.47)	0.57 (3.55)	0.55 (3.26)	0.32 (1.55)	0.64 (3.58)	0.58 (2.94)	0.54 (3.15)
Intercept	−8.92 (−6.96)	−8.77 (−16.28)	−9.36 (−6.39)	−8.35 (−6.20)	−6.37 (−9.36)	−8.25 (−4.98)	−9.27 (−6.35)
N	262	249	249	263	250	250	249
R^2	0.52	0.73	0.73	0.56	0.71	0.71	0.73

Notes: Dependent variable: Ln (acceptances outstanding, bank i, t). Estimates obtained by ordinary least squares. All variables in logs, except Branching. —, variable excluded from the specification.

The top four banks controlled about 30 percent of the market for dollar acceptances in 1928. Our estimates imply that, had it not been for their branches, they would have had 20 percent of the market. Evidently, while branches helped, they were not indispensible to the growth of the acceptance market. Banks that did not branch overseas were still able to compete, making use of their connections with U.S. importers and exporters and other financial institutions.

The next two tables assess the contribution of the Federal Reserve System to the growth of acceptances. Table 5.3 considers a narrow definition of Fed's support: total acceptances held on the Fed's own account. This variable tends to be statistically significant at conventional confidence levels even when it is lumped together with total acceptances outstanding and U.S. trade, with which it is correlated.[30]

TABLE 5.3. Determinants of Banks' Acceptances, Including Federal Reserve's Own Market-Making Activities

	With Clustering						
	(1)	(2)	(3)	(4)	(5)	(6)	(7)
Total assets/ Liabilities	1.00 (10.36)	0.94 (9.26)	0.94 (9.30)	—	—	—	0.72 (2.71)
Capital, surplus, and undivided profits	—	—	—	0.97 (15.72)	0.92 (11.60)	0.93 (11.83)	0.72 (2.77)
U.S. total trade (exports + imports)	−0.09 (−0.69)	—	−0.10 (−0.68)	0.10 (0.70)	—	0.08 (0.56)	−0.04 (−0.25)
Total U.S. acceptances outstanding	—	0.42 (2.65)	0.42 (2.65)	—	0.21 (1.27)	0.21 (1.22)	0.34 (2.26)
Fed acceptances/ "Own" account	0.27 (3.17)	0.15 (1.64)	0.18 (2.12)	0.27 (3.03)	0.27 (2.86)	0.24 (2.67)	0.20 (2.18)
Branching	0.22 (1.44)	0.30 (1.96)	0.31 (2.09)	0.32 (2.07)	0.39 (2.38)	0.37 (2.27)	0.30 (2.02)
Intercept	−3.80 (−3.31)	−6.48 (−8.99)	−5.80 (−5.64)	−3.28 (−2.83)	−3.59 (−3.72)	−4.18 (−3.63)	−5.52 (−5.37)
N	205	205	205	205	205	205	205
R^2	0.72	0.74	0.74	0.71	0.72	0.72	0.74

Notes: Dependent variable: Ln (Acceptances Outstanding, bank i, t). Clustered standard errors. All variables in logs, except Branching. —, variable excluded from the specification.

The point estimates suggest that Fed purchases were as important as the aggregate growth of the market. Knowing that it might be possible to lay off acceptances on the Fed caused banks to respond twice as fast to market growth as otherwise (since the banks could generate revenue by originating acceptances but would not have to hold them on their own balance sheets and tie up capital). Banks were more willing to originate acceptances because they knew that there was a secondary market maker.

In practice, the Fed also received deposits from foreign central banks (notably from the Bank of France), many of which it invested in the acceptance market. In Table 5.4 we add these acceptances held by the Fed for the account of others to acceptances purchased for its own account. The official-purchases variable is now even more

TABLE 5.4. Determinants of Banks' Acceptances, Including Federal Reserve's Own Market-Making Activities and Holdings on Foreign Account

| | With Clustering | | | | | | |
	(1)	(2)	(3)	(4)	(5)	(6)	(7)
Total assets/ Liabilities	0.90 (10.00)	0.83 (8.84)	0.83 (8.76)	—	—	—	0.66 (2.80)
Capital, surplus, and undivided profits	—	—	—	0.88 (13.92)	0.80 (11.43)	0.81 (11.01)	0.19 (0.94)
U.S. total trade (exports + imports)	-0.12 (-0.77)	—	-0.13 (-0.83)	0.12 (0.72)	—	0.08 (0.50)	-0.07 (-0.45)
Total U.S. acceptances outstanding	—	0.53 (3.66)	0.54 (3.66)	—	0.41 (2.71)	0.40 (2.59)	0.49 (3.67)
Fed acceptances/ "Own" account	0.22 (12.71)	0.14 (4.35)	0.14 (5.14)	0.19 (9.00)	0.14 (4.33)	0.14 (4.59)	0.15 (5.19)
Branching	0.31 (1.95)	0.40 (2.51)	0.42 (2.57)	0.36 (2.15)	0.47 (2.76)	0.45 (2.49)	0.40 (2.48)
Intercept	-2.76 (-1.96)	-6.59 (-9.13)	-5.45 (-4.14)	-2.62 (-1.79)	-3.77 (-4.54)	-4.48 (-2.91)	-5.31 (-3.98)
N	249	249	249	250	250	250	249
R^2	0.74	0.76	0.76	0.73	0.74	0.74	0.76

Notes: Dependent variable: Ln (Acceptances Outstanding, bank i, t). Clustered standard errors. All variables in logs, except Branching. —, variable excluded from the specification.

TABLE 5.5. Robustness: With Fed-Commercial Spread Replacing Fed Holdings

	With clustering						
	(1)	(2)	(3)	(4)	(5)	(6)	(7)
Total assets/	0.82	0.75	0.74	—	—	—	0.64
Liabilities	(9.66)	(8.79)	(8.60)				(2.67)
Capital, surplus, and	—	—	—	0.84	0.73	0.73	0.12
undivided profits				(12.08)	(9.44)	(8.65)	(0.57)
U.S. total trade	−0.71	—	−0.35	−0.27	—	−0.04	−0.30
(exports + imports)	(−2.57)		(−1.62)	(−1.05)		(−0.18)	(−1.34)
Total U.S. acceptances	—	0.92	0.89	—	0.75	0.75	0.86
outstanding		(7.47)	(8.20)		(6.00)	(6.41)	(8.54)
Spread	−0.92	−0.15	−0.36	−0.71	−0.24	−0.26	−0.35
(Fed-commercial)	(−5.52)	(−1.26)	(−2.75)	(−4.22)	(−1.89)	(−1.93)	(−2.69)
Branching	0.42	0.52	0.54	0.42	0.56	0.57	0.53
	(2.63)	(3.14)	(3.22)	(2.47)	(2.95)	(2.90)	(3.13)
Intercept	4.72	−7.97	−4.46	2.44	−5.02	−4.61	−4.56
	(1.70)	(−10.26)	(−2.44)	(0.97)	(−6.25)	(−2.38)	(−2.51)
N	245	245	245	246	246	246	245
R^2	0.63	0.72	0.72	0.64	0.70	0.70	0.72

Notes: Dependent variable: Ln (Acceptances Outstanding, bank i, t). Estimates obtained by ordinary least squares. All variables in logs except Branching and Spread (Fed-Commercial). —, variable excluded from the specification.

significant, reinforcing the conclusion that the central bank played an important market-making role.

Table 5.5 substitutes an alternative measure of Fed support, namely, the spread between the official and commercial discount rates on acceptances. The results are as before: they strongly support the hypothesis that official intervention mattered.

Table 5.6 addresses the concern that Fed investments in acceptances and total investments in acceptances are simultaneously determined by redefining the dependent variable as the market share of an individual bank in an individual year. The results are consistent with what we found before, except that the effect of branching is now larger. The second panel of the table, where we include the Fed's share as an explanatory variable, suggests that official support for the market favored the big players disproportionately (big banks dominate our sample).

TABLE 5.6. Robustness: Using Log Market Share as Dependent Variable

	With Clustering		
	(1)	(2)	(3)
Total assets/Liabilities	0.72	—	0.62
	(8.67)		(2.58)
Capital, surplus, and undivided profits	—	0.67	0.11
		(8.80)	(0.53)
Branching	0.57	0.65	0.57
	(3.52)	(3.60)	(3.50)
Intercept	−8.45	−6.64	−8.24
	(−8.21)	(−24.37)	(−11.39)
N	249	250	249
R^2	0.66	0.63	0.66
	Controlling for Federal Reserve Share		
	(1)	(2)	(3)
Total assets/Liabilities	0.77	—	0.73
	(9.47)		(3.03)
Capital, surplus, and undivided profits	—	0.69	0.04
		(10.20)	(0.20)
Branching	0.50	0.61	0.50
	(3.20)	(3.41)	(3.19)
Federal Reserve share	0.07	0.06	0.07
	(3.23)	(2.19)	(3.15)
Intercept	−8.58	−6.62	−8.50
	(−18.35)	(−25.41)	(−11.77)
N	249	250	249
R^2	0.68	0.65	0.88

Notes: Dependent variable: Ln (Market Share, bank i, t). Estimates obtained by ordinary least squares. All variables in logs, except Branching. —, variable excluded from the specification.

The Retreat of the Market

The markets in sterling and dollar acceptances moved in parallel between 1927 and 1931. As can be seen in Figure 5.2, the value of dollar acceptances peaked later, toward the end of 1929. But the parallelism is clear both in the late stages of the 1920s expansion and then with the onset of the Great Depression.

After 1933, in contrast, the two series diverge. While the value of sterling acceptances stabilizes, the value of dollar acceptances continues to fall until it is only half its sterling equivalent. Put another way, it falls to levels not seen since the early 1920s.

Why the gains of the 1920s did not survive the 1930s is difficult to say. The United States experienced a deeper depression: U.S. merchandise exports fell to 47 percent of 1929 levels in 1936 (valued at current prices), whereas U.K. exports fell to "just" 60 percent of their 1929 level. Less trade meant less acceptance business. That said, in the period when the volume of acceptances on the two markets diverged (between 1933 and 1936), U.S. exports were actually growing faster than British exports, reflecting the American economy's relatively strong expansion.

In addition, U.S. financial markets experienced more difficulty between 1930 and 1933. Thousands of banks failed in America; few if any in the United Kingdom. That said, most U.S. failures were of small banks not involved in originating acceptances. And after mid-1933, when the series for the two countries diverged, the United States had put this problem of bank failures behind it.

The other change in this period, evident in Figure 5.4, is that the Federal Reserve Banks essentially withdrew from the market. The 1932 Glass-Steagall Act expanded the range of assets that the Federal Reserve was permitted to purchase. Monetary activism in 1932–1933 was dominated by the Reconstruction Finance Corporation and not the Fed. Then in 1934 the Fed's Board of Governors grew increasingly concerned about the excess reserves of the banks and the specter of inflation and financial speculation. To combat these perceived dangers, the discount rate and the Fed's buying rate for acceptances were kept significantly above the open market rate for acceptance paper. As a result, the Fed's acceptance portfolio fell from $10 million in the spring of 1934 to negligible levels thereafter.

This last observation is not inconsistent with our finding that Federal Reserve support was important for nurturing the growth of the market in the 1920s. But the central bank's heavy intervention was supposed to be temporary. The hope was that it could be curtailed once a proper secondary market in trade acceptances developed. Yet

20 years after that intervention commenced, the secondary market was still underdeveloped by the standards of the United Kingdom. A contemporary argument, recounted by Mehrling (2010), is that by driving up the price of and driving down the return on acceptances in the 1920s, the Fed rendered them less attractive to private investors. Banks were encouraged to invest instead in more remunerative over-the-counter security-repurchase agreements and loans to stock brokers and dealers. One wonders whether the Federal Reserve, by so dominating the market, discouraged the participation of other investors.

Conclusion

In the provision of credit for international trade, even more than in the holding of assets by central banks as international reserves, it is argued that a single currency will dominate the market at any point in time. Network increasing returns are strong; it therefore pays to use the same currency used by other importers and exporters when invoicing, financing, and settling trade-related transactions. Persistence is therefore strong; the secondary market in credit instruments denominated in that currency is deep and liquid, because this is the market in which everyone is accustomed to transact. Thus the pound sterling and City of London dominated this market when Britain emerged as the leading trading nation in the nineteenth century, and they retained that dominance well into the twentieth. Only after a long lag and the shock of World War II were they supplanted by New York and the dollar.

The evidence in this chapter, covering the period from the founding of the Federal Reserve to the end of the 1930s, confirms the importance of liquid markets and commercial contacts. But it shows that these conditions do not entirely explain why sterling dominated the market in acceptance credit as late as 1913. Sterling's potential competitor, the dollar, was held in check by legal barriers to U.S. banks originating acceptances and branching abroad and by the absence of a central bank to backstop the market. Once those obstacles were removed and the Federal Reserve moved to provide a secondary market for trade acceptances, trade credit denominated in dollars quickly grew to match and, for a period, surpass trade credit denominated in sterling. Sterling had the advantage of a head start, but that head start was not insurmountable. Persistence was not as strong as sometimes supposed. Increasing returns did not prevent sterling and the dollar from sharing this, like other, international currency functions.

The most difficult challenge for the aspiring issuer of the new international currency was the creation of a deep, liquid, and stable secondary market in the relevant financial assets. Federal Reserve efforts to finesse this constraint produced mixed results. Indeed, the presence of the Fed as purchaser of last resort may have discouraged the participation of other investors and slowed the development of this segment of the market. This is a cautionary tale for Chinese officials seeking to deepen markets in renminbi-denominated assets as part of the campaign to internationalize their currency.

Data for Regression Analysis

BANK BALANCE SHEET DATA

Balance sheet data used in this chapter are extracted from balance sheets as of December 31 or the closest available date for the banks listed here. Balance sheets were collected from Baker Library (Harvard University, Cambridge, MA), Columbia University Library (New York), British Library (London), and the Graduate Institute Library (Geneva). The banks in the sample are as follows (periods for which we have data are indicated).

American Exchange Irving Trust, 1927–1928
Bank of New York and Trust Company, 1922–1938
Bank of the Manhattan Company, 1924–1935 (some years missing)
Bankers Trust Company, 1915–1935
Central Hanover Bank and Trust Company, 1930–1935
Chase Bank, 1915–1938 (some years missing)
Chemical Bank and Trust Company, 1929–1935
Commercial National Bank and Trust Company of New York, 1929–1939
Continental Illinois National Bank and Trust Company, 1932–1935
First National Bank of Boston, 1915–1935
First National Bank of Chicago, 1915–1935
Guaranty Trust, 1914–1937
International Acceptance Bank, 1929
Irving Bank-Columbia Trust Company, 1920–1926

Manufacturers Trust Company, 1924–1935
Marine Midland, 1929–1935
National Bank of Commerce in New York, 1923–1928
National City Bank of New York, 1915–1935
New York Trust Company, 1920–1935
Old Colony Trust Company 1919–1929 (some years missing)
Philadelphia National Bank, 1926–1935 (some years missing)
Wells Fargo, 1921–1935

Branching Variable

Dummy variable equals 1 for Chase Bank, First National Bank of Boston, Guaranty Trust, National City Bank, 0 otherwise.

Total Acceptances Outstanding

December totals from Acceptance Bulletin and *Federal Reserve Bulletin* and *Federal Reserve Annual Reports*, as described in the text.

Federal Reserve Holdings of Acceptances

December observations of holdings for own and foreign accounts are from Federal Reserve publications.

6

Evidence from International Bond Markets

This chapter presents evidence from the 1920s and 1930s on the use of sterling and dollars in international financial transactions. It addresses a further dimension of international currency status, namely, the use of currencies as vehicles for cross-border investment. We focus on the bond market, bonds being the principal instrument for cross-border lending and borrowing. Considering this additional aspect of international currency competition is useful for establishing the generality of the new view of international currency status, according to which multiple international currencies can coexist.

We employ data on the currency denomination of international public debt for 33 countries between 1914 and 1946. We focus on bonds issued in foreign markets, so-called international bonds, because these were denominated in international currencies to appeal to international investors.[1]

Our analysis supports the new view in that both sterling and the dollar were used as currencies of denomination in international debt markets in the 1920s and 1930s. This finding is again at odds with the presumption that the market has room for only one dominant international currency.

In addition, our empirical results suggest that the effects of inertia on international currency use are not insurmountable. When we exclude Commonwealth countries, which were heavily inclined toward sterling issuance for political reasons, we show that the dollar overtook sterling as early as 1929. We find that financial development was an important determinant of the ability of the dollar to overcome sterling's initial advantage. This points to the importance of structural factors, such as market liquidity, in the acquisition and retention of international currency status.

Data

For data on the currency composition of foreign debt, we draw on United Nations (1948). This compendium was assembled by statisticians employed by the United Nations and its predecessor, the League of Nations, drawing on official sources that include accounts prepared by ministries of finance, annual and special reports of central banks and national statistical institutes, and national statistical yearbooks.[2]

As with all debt data, there is always the possibility that the UN data are not strictly comparable across countries. Some debt floated in foreign financial centers may be purchased by domestic residents. Some national statistical agencies may include, along with foreign debt, domestically issued securities purchased by foreign investors. The authors of the UN compendium describe their attempts to adjust for these problems insofar as possible.

What is key for our purpose—which is to gauge the importance of sterling, the dollar, and other currencies as vehicles for international financial transactions— is that the public debt categorized as foreign is distinguished by currency of denomination.[3] The United Nations applied consistent criteria when categorizing countries' foreign debts by their currency of denomination. Each foreign debt issue was classified according to "the original currencies in which it was raised." The authors distinguished the currency of issuance from the currency of the country in which the bonds were issued. They accounted for the fact that not every bond issued in London was denominated in sterling, that the currency in which the bond was issued was not always the same as the currency in which it was redeemed, and that both the currency of issuance and currency of redemption could differ from the currency of the country where it was issued.[4]

We use data on foreign public debt for 33 countries (including five Commonwealth countries) around the world: Argentina, Australia, Austria, Belgium, Bolivia, Brazil, Canada, Chile, Colombia, Costa Rica, Cuba, Denmark, Dominican Republic, Finland, France, Guatemala, Haiti, Honduras, India, Japan, New Zealand, Nicaragua, Norway, Panama, Peru, Poland, Portugal, Romania, Siam, South Africa, Switzerland, Turkey, and Uruguay. Countries that provide data on their overall stock of foreign debt but not on its currency composition (e.g., Italy) were necessarily excluded.

Annual observations are available from 1914 to 1944. Between 14 and 24 countries report data from 1914 to 1927 (see Figure 6.1), while about 30 countries report data from 1928 to 1939, and between 19 and 27 countries do so from 1940 to 1944.

Foreign public debt is recorded in 19 currencies: sterling, U.S. dollar, French franc, Swiss franc, German mark, Austrian schilling, Belgian franc, Canadian dollar, Czechoslovak crown, Danish crown, Dutch florin, Dutch guilder, Italian lira, Norwegian crown, Scandinavian crown, Spanish peseta, Swedish crown, Argentinean peso, and Romanian leu.[5] While roughly a third of the countries in our sample (e.g., Cuba, Dominican Republic, Haiti, India, New Zealand, Panama, Portugal, South Africa, Switzerland, and Siam) had foreign debt in only one currency (either sterling or dollars), others had foreign debt denominated in 10 or more currencies. Romania had foreign debt in a total of 14.

Debt in minor currencies was occasionally denominated in units of constant gold content: Argentine gold pesos, Austrian gold crowns, Austrian gold florins, French gold francs, Italian gold lire, and Romanian gold lei. Argentina, Austria, France, and Romania had all been off the gold standard for extended periods or suffered high inflation, leading investors to insist on this practice.[6] However, the value of foreign bonds denominated in currencies of constant gold content was relatively small, on the order of 3 percent of the

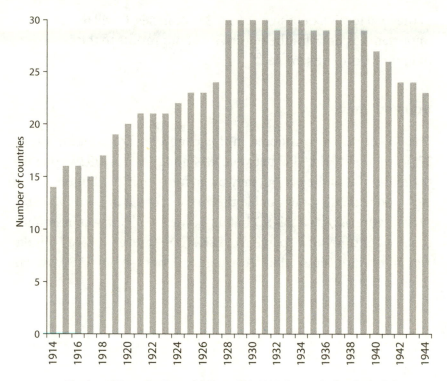

FIGURE 6.1. Number of Countries Reporting Data, 1914–1944. Source: Authors' calculations based on data from United Nations (1948).

Note: The figure shows for each year between 1914 and 1944 the number of countries reporting data on the currency composition of their foreign public debt.

global total. There were almost no dollar or sterling loans of constant gold content.[7] Turkey issued such bonds between 1933–1934 and 1938–1939 but in negligible amounts (some $6–9 million).

We take the book value of outstanding amounts and convert them into dollars by using end-of-year market exchange rates.[8] Debt in gold currency is converted to dollars using the exchange rate under the gold standard that is nearest to the year when such debt was issued.[9]

Another issue is treatment of war-related debts. France is the most notable case: 80–90 percent of its foreign public debt was owed to allied governments and incurred during World War I. Moreover, France's foreign public debt, at some $6–7 billion, was by far the largest outstanding at this time, the equivalent of more than a third of the total foreign debt stock of our 33 countries. It will therefore be important to check for the sensitivity of our results to the exclusion of France from the sample.[10]

Stylized Facts

The 33 countries considered in this chapter accounted for about 37 percent of world GDP between 1914 and 1946.[11] By 1929, roughly the mid-point of the period, they owed more than $17 billion of foreign public debt, about double the amount owed in both 1920 and 1939 (Figure 6.2).[12] Of this $17 billion, some $10 billion was in sterling (equivalent to about 50 percent of U.K. GDP) and another $7 billion was in dollars (equivalent to roughly 7 percent of U.S. GDP).

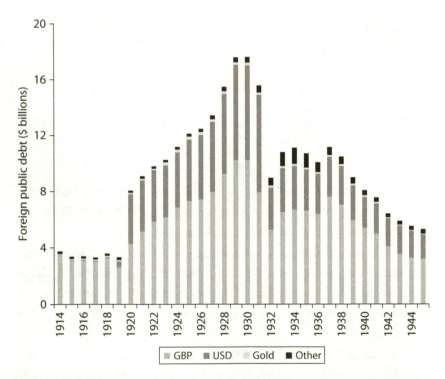

FIGURE 6.2. Global Foreign Public Debt, 1914–1945 (U.S. $ billions at current exchange rates). Source: Authors' estimates based on United Nations (1948), "Global Financial Data" and "Measuring Worth" databases.
Note: Calculated using the full set of 33 countries and broken down into selected currencies. GBP, British Pound; USD, U.S. dollar.

Clearly, the shares of both currencies were substantial. This is consistent with the new view: it suggests the possibility of having more than one international financing currency at a time.

But the possibility of room in the market for more than one consequential international currency does not mean that there existed a large number of them at any given time. Sterling and the dollar between them accounted for about 97 percent of global foreign public debt in this period. Much as we saw for foreign reserves in Chapter 4, currencies other than sterling and the dollar paled in comparison. In particular, the comparatively minor role of the French franc is again notable, consistent with what we found for reserves.

The distribution of foreign public debt denominated in different currencies was markedly different across regions (Figures 6.3 and 6.4). Almost 80 percent of dollar-denominated debt was owed by European countries. Of that amount, the main debtor was France, which alone accounted for almost 60 percent of global foreign public debt denominated in dollars. This reflected France's heavy involvement in World War I. U.S. loans to the French government, first

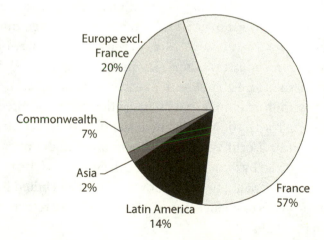

FIGURE 6.3. Global Foreign Public Debt in U.S. Dollars—Main Debtors, 1929 (percentage of total at current exchange rates). Source: Authors' estimates based on United Nations (1948) and on "Global Financial Data" and "Measuring Worth" databases. Note: Shown is the global stock of U.S. dollar-denominated foreign public debt (amounting to $6,828 million) broken down by main debtor regions for 1929 (roughly the mid-point of our sample).

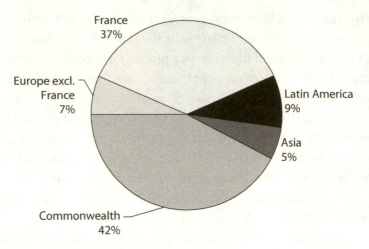

FIGURE 6.4. Global Foreign Public Debt in Sterling—Main Debtors, 1929 (percentage of total at current exchange rates). Source: Authors' estimates based on United Nations (1948) and on "Global Financial Data" and "Measuring Worth" databases.
Note: Shown is the global stock of sterling-denominated foreign public debt (amounting to $10,232 million) broken down by main debtor regions for 1929 (roughly the mid-point of our sample).

through the agency of U.S. banks and then by the U.S. government itself, amounted to just over $4 billion when converted into long-term bonds in the early 1920s.[13] Most of the remainder was owed by Latin American countries (Cuba, Dominican Republic, Haiti, and Panama all issued foreign public debt exclusively in dollars). This reflected the strong economic and financial ties that the United States had developed with the region since the turn of the century and during and after World War I (Mitchener and Weidenmier 2005). The rest was owed by two Commonwealth countries (Australia and Canada) and by Japan. Japan had borrowed in the United States as early as 1904–1905 to finance its war with Russia and returned to the market in the 1920s.[14]

About 40 percent of sterling-denominated debt was owed by Commonwealth countries, reflecting their strong ties to the United Kingdom. A further 40 percent was owed by European issuers. France was again the main European originator, accounting for a third of foreign public debt denominated in sterling. Asia (that is,

Japan and Siam) accounted for around 5 percent of foreign public debt in sterling, while Latin America (Argentina, Bolivia, Brazil, Chile, Costa Rica, Guatemala, Honduras, Nicaragua, Peru, and Uruguay) accounted for a further 9 percent.[15]

When Did the Dollar Surpass Sterling?

As Figure 6.5a shows, the share of the dollar was almost equal to that of sterling by 1931. But including the five Commonwealth countries may skew the results, due to their strong political links with the United Kingdom.[16] When one excludes them, the crossover date becomes 1929, earlier than before (Figure 6.5b). Sterling's postwar lead was largest in 1924, although the dollar's share of the market was already substantial. The second half of the 1920s then saw the dollar close the gap; this was the period, in the words of Cleona Lewis, marked by "the scramble for 'investment opportunities.'"[17] It was also an era when the British authorities, concerned by the weakness of the balance of payments, used moral suasion and controls to restrain long-term foreign lending (Moggridge 1971).

Sterling regained market share after 1933 and again ran neck and neck with the dollar at the end of the decade. U.S. experience with foreign public debt in this period was unhappy; some two-thirds of outstanding issues lapsed into default, roughly double the share of sterling-denominated debt (Winkler 1933). Bonds issued in dollars were more marginal credits. U.S. underwriters were less experienced, and sterling-denominated bonds issued by members of the British Commonwealth and Empire were faithfully serviced all through the 1930s (Mintz 1951; Eichengreen and Portes 1990). Widespread defaults on dollar-denominated debts demoralized the New York market and limited foreign issuance there. The Johnson Act of 1934 then prohibited governments in default on their sovereign debts from marketing new loans in the United States.[18]

History is messy, and this certainly was true of the 1930s. But the fact that a variety of special factors caused the dollar's lead to narrow does not change the fact that the greenback already had emerged as a major vehicle for long-term foreign lending in the 1920s. Indeed, it reinforces the point that fortunes can change quickly and that the advantages of incumbency can be exaggerated.

Moreover, that the share of the dollar rose sharply after 1914 was not simply a reflection of World War I. It also reflected the Federal Reserve Act's lifting of the ban on foreign branching by U.S. banks. This set the stage for the first wave of expansion of U.S. banks abroad (Phelps 1927). U.S. banks opened foreign branches, underwrote foreign bonds, and sold them to domestic customers for the first time. All this points to the role of financial

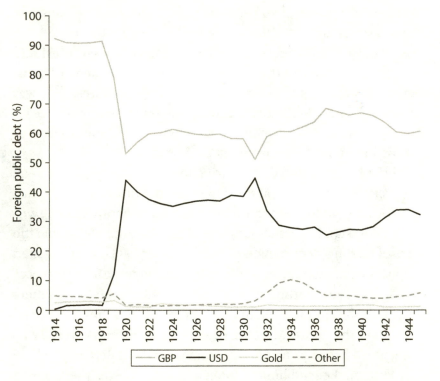

FIGURE 6.5A. Global Foreign Public Debt—Full Sample, 1914–1944 (percentage of total at current exchange rates).

Source: Authors' estimates based on United Nations (1948) and on "Global Financial Data" and "Measuring Worth" databases.

Note: Shown is the global stock of foreign public debt (in percentages and at current exchange rates) based on our full sample of 33 countries. Data for Australia, Canada, New Zealand, and South Africa refer to the location (London or New York) where debt was "payable," "redeemable," or "due" and are not strictly comparable with those of the remaining 29 countries whose data refer to actual foreign currency debt denomination. GBP, British Pound; USD, U.S. dollar.

development—including financial development policies—as a determinant of the rise of the dollar as an international borrowing currency.

The dramatic rise in the share of the dollar in the early 1920s could conceivably reflect the fact that the currency shares reported in Figure 6.5b are calculated as weighted averages (with weights proportional to the value of debts). The largest debtors, including America's wartime allies, might therefore have a disproportionate influence on aggregate changes. But in fact, calculating shares as unweighted averages (as in Figure 6.5c) does not significantly alter the finding. Not only does the share of the dollar still rise swiftly, but the greenback already overtakes sterling in the mid-1920s and not only in 1929.

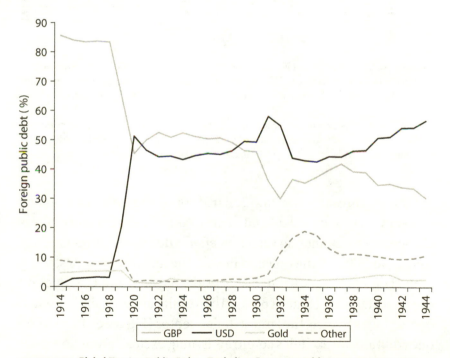

FIGURE 6.5B. Global Foreign Public Debt—Excluding Commonwealth Countries, 1914–1944 (percentage of total at current exchange rates). Source: Authors' estimates based on United Nations (1948) and on "Global Financial Data" and "Measuring Worth" databases.
Note: Shown is the global stock of foreign public debt (in percent at current exchange rates) based on a restricted sample of 28 countries (i.e., the full sample minus our five Commonwealth countries: Australia, Canada, India, New Zealand, and South Africa). GBP, British Pound; USD, U.S. dollar.

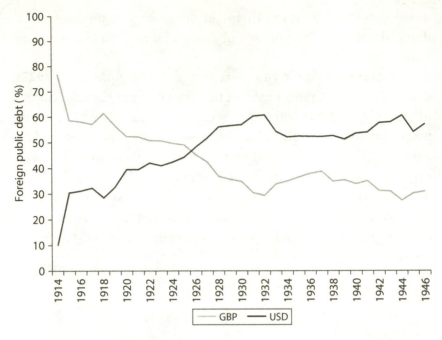

FIGURE 6.5C. Global Foreign Public Debt—Excluding Commonwealth Countries, Arithmetic Averages, 1914–1946 (percentage of total at current exchange rates). Source: Authors' estimates based on United Nations (1948) and on "Global Financial Data" and "Measuring Worth" databases.
Note: Shown are the shares of sterling and the U.S. dollar calculated as cross-country arithmetic averages and based on 28 countries (i.e., the full sample minus our five Commonwealth countries: Australia, Canada, India, New Zealand, and South Africa). GBP, British Pound; USD, U.S. dollar.

The picture of a sterling-dollar duopoly again obtains when currency shares are calculated at constant rather than current exchange rates, eliminating valuation effects due to the devaluation of sterling in 1931 and the dollar in 1933.[19] The dollar surpasses sterling in the late 1920s and maintains its lead even after the U.S. goes off the gold standard (Figure 6.6a). The results are also similar when one excludes France, the largest dollar debtor (Figure 6b) and when one additionally excludes countries issuing exclusively in dollars or sterling (Figure 6.6d).[20]

Finally, including the Commonwealth countries and using unweighted averages does not modify the conclusion (Figure 6.6c). By this metric, the dollar already had overtaken sterling in the mid-1920s.

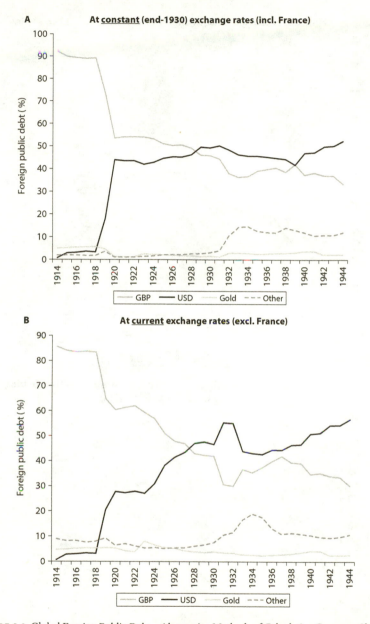

FIGURE 6.6. Global Foreign Public Debt—Alternative Methods of Calculating Currency Shares, 1914–1944 (percentage of total). Source: Authors' estimates based on United Nations (1948) and on "Global Financial Data" and "Measuring Worth" databases.

Note: Shown are the shares of sterling, U.S. dollar, gold, and other currencies in the global stock of foreign public debt using alternative methods to calculate currency shares and for panels A and B, based on the sample of 28 countries (i.e., the full sample minus our five Commonwealth countries: Australia, Canada, India, New Zealand, and South Africa). Panel C includes all 33 countries. Panel D excludes France and other countries issuing only in U.S. dollars or sterling.

C **At <u>current</u> exchange rates, arithmetic average across 33 countries**

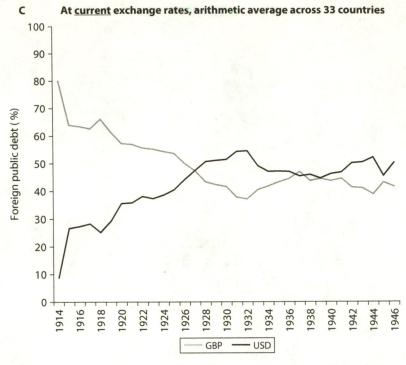

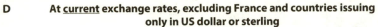

D **At <u>current</u> exchange rates, excluding France and countries issuing only in US dollar or sterling**

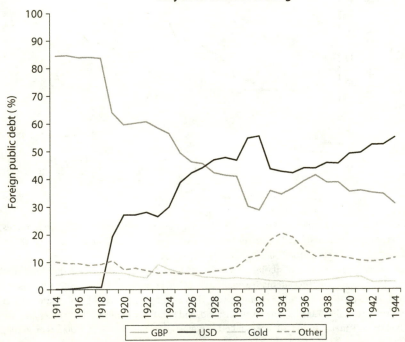

Figure 6.7 shows that during World War I, the dollar was the dominant currency of foreign debt denomination for Belgium, the Dominican Republic, Haiti, Panama, Poland, and Switzerland.[21] The efforts of New York underwriters to attract foreign borrowers were actively supported by the State Department, which saw foreign dependence on U.S. lending as a lever for opening foreign markets to American exports. Bolivia, Brazil, Chile, Guatemala, Norway, Peru, Romania, and Uruguay increased the share of their foreign currency debt in dollars in the course of the 1920s, this being when American promoters aggressively "search[ed] the world over for foreign borrowers."[22]

Only in Austria, Colombia, and Finland did the share of the dollar decline markedly in the interwar years. In Austria this reflected the growing dependence of the government on Paris, the one market that remained open in the early 1930s. Finland borrowed in Swedish kronor (for, inter alia, extension of its telephone system). After engaging in a borrowing binge in New York in 1927–1928, when it issued two mega-loans in dollars, Colombia borrowed modestly in both sterling and dollars, as well as in French francs in the case of a substantial 1931 loan floated in Paris. There was similarly some movement by central banks into subsidiary currencies like the French franc and Swedish kronor in the 1930s when problems affected the markets in dollars and sterling, but it was again limited in incidence and magnitude (Eichengreen 2011).

Econometric Specification

We now estimate the determinants of currency shares of foreign public debt. Since our panel has a three-dimensional structure with country, currency, and time dimensions, we allow for unobservable country, currency and time effects:

$$y_{i,j,t} = \alpha_{i,j} + \beta s_{j,t} + \gamma' X_{j,t} + \theta' D_t + \varepsilon_{i,j,t}$$

where i, j, and t are the country, currency, and time dimensions, respectively; y is the share of currency j in country i's foreign public debt in year t; s is a measure of financial depth; X is a vector of other key determinants of international currency status (including inertia, size, and credibility effects in the baseline specification); and D is a

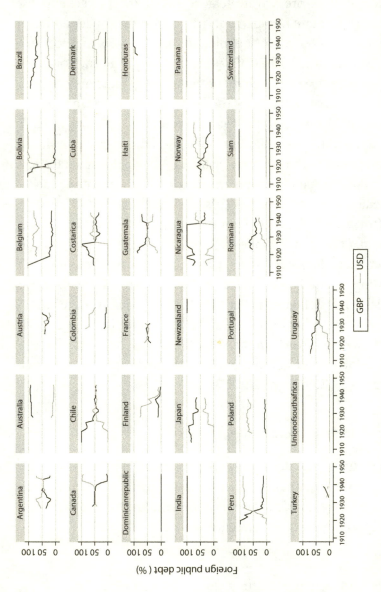

FIGURE 6.7. Share of U.S. Dollar/Sterling Debt in Foreign Public Debt—Breakdown by Country, 1914–1944 (percent at current exchange rates). Source: Authors' estimates based on United Nations (1948) and on "Global Financial Data" and "Measuring Worth" databases.

Note: Shown are the shares of the U.S. dollar and sterling in the foreign public debt of each of our 33 countries. Data for Australia, Canada, New Zealand, and South Africa refer to the location (London or New York) where debt was "payable," "redeemable," or "due" and are not strictly comparable with those of the remaining 29 countries, whose data refer to actual foreign currency debt denomination.

vector of time effects. We reduce the dimensions of our panel from three to two by distinguishing country-currency (subsequently referred to as "group") and time dimensions. With 28 countries and two currencies, we have 56 groups, and control for unobserved effects at the group level, denoted α. The estimable parameters are therefore α, β, and the vectors γ and θ. The specification is akin to that in Chinn and Frankel (2007, 2008) and Frankel (2011).

We estimate the equation above with fixed effects and report standard errors robust to heteroskedasticity and clustered heterogeneity. The dependent variable is the share of currency j in country i's foreign public debt in year t. Given that currency shares are, at any point in time and in any country, bounded between zero and one, a tobit estimator might be thought to be warranted, but since our data are censored neither from above nor from below, this is unnecessary. That said, we also report results using alternative estimators including tobit and the Arellano-Bond (1991) two-step generalized method of moments procedure.

The disturbances are split into unobserved group effects, with variance σ_α^2, and panel-level effects, with variance σ_ε^2, which are assumed to be independent. To gauge whether group fixed effects are required, we calculate the ρ-statistic, which measures the contribution of the variance of the disturbances due to group effects to the total variance of the disturbances:

$$\rho = \frac{\sigma_\alpha^2}{\sigma_\varepsilon^2 + \sigma_\alpha^2}$$

When ρ is close to zero, estimates with group-level effects are not significantly different from the standard ordinary least squares (OLS) estimate. Formal comparisons of the two models can be conducted with a likelihood-ratio test, where the null hypothesis is that a standard OLS model is better suited than a model with group-level effects.

Building on the literature on the macroeconomic determinants of currency shares, we focus on four categories of explanatory variables. The first of these is network externalities. An international currency, like a domestic currency, is more useful when others use it. That is to say, a currency used in international debt markets is more likely to be used in international trade transactions, in foreign exchange trading, as an anchor currency or as a reserve currency, which gives rise to economies of scope. This network effect creates inertia or incumbency effects. To capture them, we include the lagged value of y in $\mathbf{X}$, our vector of explanatory variables.

A second potential determinant is country size. The currency of an economy with a large share in global output, trade and finance has a natural advantage, to paraphrase Chinn and Frankel (2007). To capture this effect, we use the time-varying shares of the United States and the United Kingdom in global output.[23]

A third potential determinant is confidence in a currency's value. An international currency being a store of value, investors will want to know that its value is stable. As a proxy for confidence we use contemporaneous inflation, calculated using annual Consumer Price Index (CPI) data.[24]

Our fourth potential determinant of currency shares is financial depth s. Liquidity is widely recognized as an important determinant of the attractiveness of investing in a security, or for that matter in a security denominated in a particular currency. In turn, financial development is an important determinant of market liquidity. While financial depth has not been used in previous empirical studies of the determinants of choice of currency of denomination for, inter alia, central bank reserves, we showed in Chapter 5 that financial depth and development was a factor in the rise of dollar-denominated trade credits in the 1920s.[25] Moreover, the literature on the international role of the euro has stressed financial development and integration as determinants of the single currency's growing international profile (Portes and Rey 1998; Papaioannou and Portes 2008). As our measure of financial development we use bank assets relative to GDP, from Schularick and Taylor (2012).

In robustness checks in Appendix 6A at the end of this chapter, we consider several additional determinants of currency choice highlighted in the recent literature using firm-level data. An example of these is hedging. Firms issue debt in the currencies of countries in which they operate as a way of hedging their exposure to foreign exchange risk (Kedia and Mozumdar 2003). Specifically, the probability of issuing foreign currency debt is positively correlated with foreign-exchange exposure metrics, such as foreign sales as a fraction of total sales (Allayanis and Ofek 2001) and earnings and cash in foreign currency as a share of firm value (Allayannis, Brown, and Klapper 2003). To proxy for aggregate country exposure to foreign exchange risk in dollars and sterling, we use the share of the United States and the United Kingdom in a country's foreign trade.[26]

Another potential determinant is funding cost. McBrady and Schill (2007) suggest that deviations from interest parity may present opportunities for borrowers to reduce their costs by issuing in a foreign currency. Cohen (2005) and Habib and Joy (2010) find that interest rate differentials matter, suggesting that bond issuers choose their issuance currency to exploit arbitrage opportunities between funding currencies. As a proxy for this effect, we use the differential between the short-term interest rate in country i and that in the United States or the United Kingdom.

Finally, studies have shown that market liquidity matters for currency choice at the firm level. Firms facing domestic credit constraints have an incentive to broaden their investor base by issuing in foreign currency (Allayanis and Ofek 2001; Kedia and Mozumdar 2003). The larger the pool of national investors, the greater is the incentive to issue in their currency. Here we follow Flandreau and Jobst (2009), who argue that the short-term interest differential is a good measure of relative market liquidity and use the short-term dollar-sterling interest differential to capture this effect.[27] We define U.S. market liquidity as the differential between the U.S. short-term interest rate and the corresponding sterling rate (the lower the spread is, the higher the liquidity), and U.K. market liquidity as the same spread but with an opposite sign.

Results

To facilitate comparison with the determinants of the currency composition of foreign exchange reserves in Chapter 7, we initially exclude financial depth and focus on persistence (inertia), credibility, and scale effects (size). Table 6.1 presents the results. Sample size is constant throughout: estimation is carried out on our baseline sample of 28 countries, excluding members of the Commonwealth (whose strong political links with the United Kingdom constrained their ability to issue debt in currencies other than sterling) and covers the entire period of 1914–1946.[28]

A first finding in Table 6.1 concerns inertia effects. The point estimate on lagged currency shares of 0.90 corresponds to a half-life of about 7 years. This is similar to the estimates of Chinn and Frankel (2007, 303, their Table 8.4) of 0.90–0.96 using reserve data for 1973–1998.[29] But the estimate also indicates that the share of a

TABLE 6.1. Determinants of Currency Shares: Baseline Model Estimates

	(1)	(2)	(3)	(4)	(5)	(6)
Inertia	0.897***	0.896***	0.905***	0.904***	0.894***	0.903***
	(0.009)	(0.009)	(0.011)	(0.011)	(0.009)	(0.011)
Credibility		−0.109*		−0.151***		−0.082
		(0.058)		(0.054)		(0.060)
Size			0.349**	0.445***		0.992***
			(0.149)	(0.138)		(0.193)
Financial depth					0.088	0.338***
					(0.057)	(0.077)
Constant	4.390***	6.402***	−2.786	−2.772	−0.408	−34.285***
	(1.138)	(2.194)	(3.439)	(4.100)	(3.371)	(8.898)
Observations	1,061	1,061	1,061	1,061	1,061	1,061
No. of groups	56	56	56	56	56	56
R^2 (overall)	0.972	0.972	0.969	0.965	0.972	0.904
R^2 (within)	0.849	0.850	0.850	0.851	0.850	0.854
R^2 (between)	0.997	0.997	0.991	0.986	0.997	0.909
ρ	0.270	0.278	0.306	0.367	0.275	0.742
σ_α	3.698	3.761	4.022	4.598	3.735	10.18
σ_ε	6.075	6.066	6.060	6.041	6.071	5.995
log likelihood	−3377	−3375	−3374	−3370	−3376	−3361

Notes: Estimates of the baseline model based on our baseline set of 28 countries over 1914–1916 and including the main determinants of international currency status, group effects, and time effects. Standard errors reported in parentheses are robust to heteroskedasticity and clustered heterogeneity; ***, $p < 0.01$; **, $p < 0.05$; *, $p < 0.13$.

currency in global bond markets can be halved in a less than a decade, ceteris paribus, which is essentially what happened to sterling between 1914 and the mid-1920s.

Credibility also matters. Lower inflation significantly raises the share of a currency in a country's foreign public debt. The full model estimate (column 4 of Table 6.1) suggests that the short-run (1 year) effect of reducing the inflation rate by 10 percentage points is an increase in the share of the U.S. dollar (sterling) of about 1.5 percentage points. Again, our coefficient of -0.15 is fairly close to those of Chinn and Frankel (2007), who found estimates ranging between -0.07 and -0.14.

Scale effects are also important. The full model estimate suggests that the short-run (1 year) effect of an increase in the share of the U.S. (U.K.) economy in global output of 10 percentage points corresponds to an increase in the share of the dollar (sterling) of 4 percentage points. In this case the coefficient of 0.45 is larger than that of Chinn and Frankel (2007), whose estimates range from 0.09 to 0.12.

Columns 5 and 6 in Table 6.1 add financial depth. The point estimates for the persistence and credibility effects now change, with the size effect becoming larger than before and credibility losing statistical significance. Financial depth also exerts a significant effect on the share of the U.S. dollar (sterling) in global foreign public debt markets. The full model suggests that in the short run (1 year), an increase in the ratio of banking assets to GDP by 10 percentage points is associated with an increase in the share of the dollar (sterling) of about 3 percentage points.[30]

Figure 6.8 shows the contributions of size, credibility, and financial deepening to the change in the share of the dollar in foreign public debt between 1918 and 1932. The contributions are calculated using the estimated parameters of the benchmark model (Table 6.1, column 6), taking into account the effects of inertia arising from the persistence introduced by the lagged values of currency shares. For each year t between 1919 and 1932, we calculate the contribution of variable z (i.e., either size, credibility, or financial deepening) to the change in the average share of the U.S. dollar (sterling) in global foreign public debt y as $(\Sigma_{i=0,\ldots,\infty}\, \rho^i \theta dz_{t-i})/dy_t$, where θ is the estimated parameter for z, ρ is the estimated parameter for the lag of y, and $dy_t = y_t - y_{t-1}$. The overall contribution of z to the change in y is obtained by summing the 14 annual contributions between 1919 and 1932.

Figure 6.8 shows that financial deepening is the most important factor behind the increase in the share of the dollar as a currency of denomination for international bonds between 1918 and 1932, consistent with the findings in Chapter 5 for the market in trade acceptances. The rise in the ratio of U.S. banking assets to GDP from 70 percent to 100 percent of GDP over the period accounts for a 40 percentage point increase in the share of the dollar in global foreign public debt.[31] Next in importance is greater credibility due to lower U.S. inflation, although this impact is not statistically significant.[32]

Interestingly, country size contributed *negatively* to the rise of the dollar over this period, since the share of the United States in global

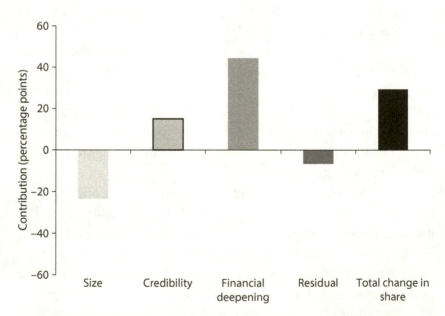

FIGURE 6.8. Estimated Contributions (Including Inertia Effects) to Change in the Share of the U.S. Dollar in Global Foreign Public Debt, between 1918 and 1932 (percent).
Note: Calculated using the estimated parameters of benchmark model (6) of Table 6.1. The estimates include inertia effects arising from the dynamic specification of the model. The estimated effect of credibility was found to be statistically insignificant.

output fell from 30 percent in 1918 to 22 percent in 1932, contributing to a decline in the share of the U.S. dollar of 20 percentage points.

Figure 6.9 shows the contributions for sterling. Here, too, financial deepening had a positive impact. But in this case country size is the most important factor explaining the fall in the average share of the currency between 1918 and 1932, with the share of the UK in global output falling from 13 percent in 1918 to 8 percent in 1932.[33] This result is consistent with the large literature emphasizing how slow growth and high unemployment handicapped Britain's efforts to maintain its financial preeminence and limited the role of sterling in the 1920s (Chandler 1958; Sayers 1976).

If one conducts a similar exercise for 1932–1939, during which the share of the U.S. dollar in foreign public debt declined by about 10 percentage points, it is again financial depth (in this period, *declining* financial depth) that contributes most (Figure 6.10); the ratio of bank assets to U.S. GDP fell by nearly 20 percent of GDP over this period as a result of the bank failures of the Great Depression.[34]

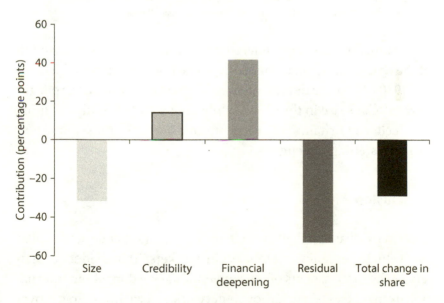

FIGURE 6.9. Estimated Contributions (Including Inertia Effects) to Change in the Share of Sterling in Global Foreign Public Debt, between 1918 and 1932 (percent).
Note: Calculated using the estimated parameters of benchmark model (6) of Table 6.1. The estimates include inertia effects arising from the dynamic specification of the model. The estimated effect of credibility was found to be statistically insignificant.

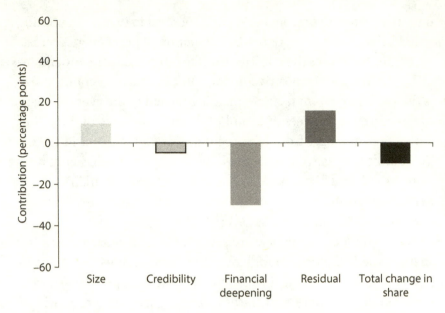

FIGURE 6.10. Estimated Contributions (Including Inertia Effects) to Change in the Share of the U.S. Dollar in Global Foreign Public Debt, between 1932 and 1939 (percent).
Note: Calculated using the estimated parameters of benchmark model (6) of Table 6.1. The estimates include inertia effects arising from the dynamic specification of the model. The estimated effect of credibility was found to be statistically insignificant.

In sum, the factors considered here explain a significant fraction of the change in currency shares in global bond markets in the 1920s and 1930s. Financial development is the most important determinant of the dollar's rise in the 1920s, while the extended slump resulting in a decline in Britain's relative economic size is the most important factor in sterling's decline.

Conclusion

This chapter has marshalled evidence on the emergence of the dollar as a vehicle currency in global debt markets. That evidence challenges the three aspects of the conventional wisdom about international currencies. First, although network externalities, first-mover advantage, and inertia matter, they do not dominate to the extent thought previously. Abstracting from Commonwealth countries, the dollar had already overtaken sterling in 1929, at least 15 years prior to the date cited in popular accounts. Even including the Commonwealth countries, which were wedded to sterling for political and institutional reasons, the dollar was within hailing distance of sterling as a currency of denomination for international bonds by the 1920s.

Second, our evidence challenges the presumption that once international monetary leadership is lost, it is gone forever. Although sterling lost its leadership as a vehicle for international investment in the 1920s, it recovered after 1933 and again ran neck and neck with the dollar toward the end of the decade.

Third, our findings challenge the presumption that there is room in the market for only one dominant international currency due to strong network externalities and economies of scope. International debt markets in the 1920s and the 1930s featured two important vehicle currencies, not just one.

Our regression results point to the development of U.S. financial markets as the main factor enabling the dollar to overcome sterling's head start. Financial deepening was the most important contributor to the increase in the share of the dollar in global bond markets between 1918 and 1932. In turn, the United Kingdom's falling share of global GDP was the most important factor accounting for sterling's decline.

These findings suggest that a shift from a unipolar dollar-based system to a multipolar system is not impossible, that it could occur sooner than often believed, and that financial deepening and market liquidity will be key determinants of the ability of other currencies to gain international currency status. Specifically, our results point to capital markets union (the European Commission's plan, announced in June 2015, to build deeper and more integrated capital markets) as important for the euro's acquisition of a greater international role. The results also indicate that the opening of the capital account of the balance of payments, along with exchange rate reform and development of liquid financial markets, are of key importance for wider international use of the Chinese renminbi.

Robustness

Table 6.A1 examines the robustness of the results to the use of a linear group-fixed effect estimator without time effects (column 1), a linear group-random effect estimator (column 2), and a panel

TABLE 6.A1. Determinants of Currency Shares: Estimates Using Alternative Estimation Methods

	(1) No Time Effects	(2) Random Effects	(3) Panel Tobit	(4) Griliches (1961) Liviatan (1963)	(5) Hatanaka (1974)
Inertia	0.901***	0.979***	0.975***		
	(0.010)	(0.004)	(0.007)		
Credibility	−0.026	−0.078	−0.078	−0.232**	−0.146*
	(0.028)	(0.060)	(0.059)	(0.101)	(0.080)
Size	0.425***	1.215***	1.198***	0.821**	0.887***
	(0.136)	(0.199)	(0.195)	(0.314)	(0.200)
Financial depth	0.090**	0.322***	0.325***	0.305**	0.338***
	(0.034)	(0.073)	(0.084)	(0.127)	(0.079)
Fitted inertia				0.879***	0.882***
				(0.028)	(0.016)
First stage residual					0.866***
					(0.030)
Constant	−9.340*	−29.980***	−33.420***	−24.847*	−29.835***
	(4.830)	(6.543)	(6.545)	(14.322)	(9.452)
Observations	1,061	1,061	1,061	1,003	1,003
No. of groups	56	56	56	54	54
R^2 (overall)	0.963	0.973	.	0.743	0.911
R^2 (within)	0.850	0.853	.	0.717	0.838
R^2 (between)	0.983	0.998	.	0.745	0.921
ρ	0.400	0	0.017	0.828	0.710
σ_α	4.888	0	0.788	17.600	9.467
σ_e	5.991	5.995	6.002	8.009	6.054
log likelihood	−3374	.	−3415	−3467	−3186

Notes: Estimates of the benchmark model (Table 6.1, column 6) based on baseline sample of 28 countries over 1914–1916 and using: (1) linear group-fixed effect estimator, but without time effects; (2) linear group-random effects estimator and (3) panel tobit estimator (also including currency effects); (4) Griliches (1961) and Liviatan (1963) estimator; and (5) Hatanaka (1974) estimator. Standard errors in parentheses are robust to heteroskedasticity and clustered heterogeneity; ***, $p < 0.01$; **, $p < 0.05$; *, $p < 0.1$.

tobit estimator (column 3). The results are close to our baseline estimates (note that the effect of credibility is again statistically insignificant and that of financial depth is smaller when time effects are excluded).

Some readers may worry that interpretation of the lagged dependent variable in terms of inertia is problematic, insofar as the latter is simply picking up persistent error terms. The combination of serially correlated errors and a lagged dependent variable also introduces the possibility of biased coefficient estimates due to possible correlation between the lagged variable and the error term. One way of dealing with this problem is to instrument the lagged dependent variable with its second lag and first lags of the independent variables (see, e.g., Griliches 1961; Liviatan 1963).[35] Intuitively, including only the predicted component of lagged currency shares enhances the plausibility that the lag is picking up inertia effects rather than persistent random errors. Another approach is that of Hatanaka (1974), which includes both the fitted value and the residual from the first-stage regression in the second stage and yields estimates that are both consistent and efficient.

Columns 4 and 5 of Table 6.A2 report results for the two approaches. The estimates are again close to those obtained with the baseline specification, in terms of sign, statistical significance and economic magnitude. In addition, the effect of credibility regains its previous statistical significance. Apparently we are picking up genuine inertia effects and not merely persistence in the error term.

In Table 6.A2, column 1, we exclude France, the single largest debtor in both dollars and sterling. In column 2 we control for the variation over time of the number of reporting countries, which could distort our baseline results if large outliers start (or discontinue) reporting data, thereby creating significant breaks in the series. We do this by including as an additional control the number of countries reporting foreign currency debt composition per year. The results again remain largely unaffected.

We can also use currency shares calculated at constant rather than current exchange rates (use of current rates being the established practice in the literature) to account for possible valuation effects arising from, for example, devaluations. The effect of persistence remains broadly unchanged, while that of size declines markedly in

TABLE 6.A2. Determinants of Currency Shares: Additional Sensitivity Tests

	(1) Excluding France	(2) Composite effects	(3) Constant shares	(4) Hedging and exposure	(5) U.S./U.K. market liquidity	(6) Cost of funding
Inertia	0.905***	0.903***	0.912***	0.920***	0.915***	0.894***
	(0.011)	(0.011)	(0.010)	(0.012)	(0.011)	(0.043)
Credibility	−0.105*	−0.082	0.011	0.064	0.151***	−0.107
	(0.058)	(0.060)	(0.051)	(0.047)	(0.049)	(0.085)
Size	0.999***	0.992***	0.517***	1.127***	0.951***	1.981***
	(0.201)	(0.193)	(0.148)	(0.285)	(0.250)	(0.528)
Financial depth	0.338***	0.338***	0.133**	0.424***	0.298***	0.810**
	(0.080)	(0.077)	(0.056)	(0.090)	(0.087)	(0.253)
Number of reporting countries		0.019				
		(0.087)				
Bilateral trade with U.S./U.K.				−0.004		
				(0.053)		
U.S.–U.K. spread					−1.102***	
					(0.311)	
Interest rate differential						−0.028
						(0.493)

TABLE 6.A2. (*continued*)

Constant	−34.062***	−35.384***	−14.734**	−45.473***	−36.443***	−87.689***
	(9.235)	(9.596)	(6.677)	(10.107)	(9.725)	(24.120)
Observations	1,024	1,061	1,061	729	729	125
No. of groups	54	56	56	39	39	8
R^2 (overall)	0.907	0.904	0.962	0.856	0.902	0.714
R^2 (within)	0.855	0.854	0.876	0.848	0.850	0.793
R^2 (between)	0.911	0.909	0.976	0.868	0.917	0.711
ρ	0.744	0.742	0.491	0.787	0.695	0.952
σ_a	10.220	10.180	5.465	11.610	9.040	22.310
σ_e	6.005	5.995	5.560	6.036	5.983	5.003
log likelihood	−3245	−3361	−3281	−2309	−2302	−356

Notes: Estimates of the benchmark model (Table 6.1, column 6) based on baseline sample of 28 countries over 1914–1916 and (1) excluding France (largest debtor) from the estimation; (2) controlling for the number of countries reporting data; (3) using currency shares calculated at constant exchange rates; (4) controlling for hedging and exposure considerations; (5) relative market liquidity; (6) cost of funding considerations. Standard errors in parentheses are robust to heteroskedasticity and clustered heterogeneity; ***, $p < 0.01$; **, $p < 0.05$; *, $p < 0.1$.

magnitude, and that of credibility is again insignificant (column 3). Importantly, the estimate for financial deepening remains significantly positive, although it is now smaller in magnitude.

Columns (4), (5), and (6) of Table 6.A2 provide evidence on firm-level determinants of currency choice in bond issuance, namely, hedging of foreign exchange exposures, market liquidity, and funding cost. We find empirical support only for market liquidity, although it is important to note that the size of our sample is now smaller for data-availability reasons. In line with expectations, the results in column 5 suggest that a higher U.S.-U.K. spread is associated with a significant decline in the respective international currency's share. Conversely, greater liquidity is associated with greater use of a particular unit in global debt markets. This result further supports our emphasis on financial development.

In this chapter, we provided evidence that financial development, as proxied by the ratio of bank assets to GDP, is an important determinant of the attractions of a currency as a unit of denomination for international bonds. Readers may be worried about reverse causality: the issuance of bonds in a market may be followed by the deposit, at least temporarily, of the receipts accruing to the issuer in the banks of that same market. Causality, in other words, may run from the value of bond flotations to the level of bank deposits as well as the other way around.

A counterargument is that our dependent variable is the share of bonds denominated in a particular currency and not the share floated in a particular national market.[36] Another counterargument is that even if issuers did temporarily deposit the receipts from bond issuance in banks of the country where the issue was floated, the money to buy the bonds would have come, in part, from the same place—that is, investors would have withdrawn money from those same banks to finance their purchases.

To get at this question, we instrumented bank deposits as a share of GDP using other dimensions of financial development less plausibly affected by bond issuance in the same country: broad money to GDP; private credit to GDP; and narrow money to GDP. In column 1 of Table 6.A3, only broad money to GDP is used as instrument, while in column 2, all three variables are used. The results confirm

TABLE 6.A3. Determinants of Currency Shares: Treatments for Endogeneity

	(1)	(2)	(3)	(4)
			Arellano and Bond (1991) estimates	
	Panel 2SLS Estimates			
Inertia	0.903***	0.871***	0.761***	0.755***
	(0.012)	(0.014)	(0.087)	(0.092)
Credibility	−0.085	−0.192***	−0.042	−0.122
	(0.060)	(0.067)	(0.048)	(0.088)
Size	0.967***	0.813***	0.976*	1.025
	(0.217)	(0.208)	(0.592)	(0.632)
Financial depth	0.322***	0.362***	0.292**	0.431**
	(0.099)	(0.090)	(0.132)	(0.195)
Constant	−38.491***	−36.392***	−25.204	−39.440*
	(10.930)	(9.908)	(16.066)	(20.571)
Observations	1,061	1,022	1,003	978
No. of groups	56	56	54	54
R^2 (overall)	0.908	0.918	—	—
R^2 (within)	0.854	0.834	—	—
R^2 (between)	0.914	0.927	—	—
ρ	0.731	0.696	—	—
σ_α	9.893	9.105	—	—
σ_ε	5.995	6.017	—	—
AR(1)	—	—	0.0006	0.0007
AR(2)	—	—	0.9937	0.9218
Sargan/Hansen χ^2-statistic	—	—	1.000	1.000

Notes: Estimates of the benchmark model (Table 6.1, column 6) based on baseline sample of 28 countries over 1914–1916 using (i) panel 2SLS estimator and (ii) 2-step GMM Arellano and Bond (1991) estimator. The instruments—together with lagged levels of currency shares and first-differenced errors for (ii)—include the ratio of broad money to GDP (in columns 1 and 3) as well as the latter, private credit to GDP and narrow money to GDP (in columns 2 and 4). Standard errors in parentheses; —, not available; 2SLS, two-stage least squares; GMM, Generalized methods of moments; ***, $p < 0.01$; **, $p < 0.05$; *, $p < 0.11$.

that the impact of financial development is not due to endogeneity, since the estimated coefficient is quite similar to that obtained before. The same is true of estimates obtained using the Arellano and Bond (1991) two-step generalized method of moments estimator.[37]

As a further robustness check, we added the five Commonwealth countries to the sample. The results are again similar (Table 6.A4)

The regression results on the importance of financial development will be spurious if this variable is nonstationary (i.e.,

TABLE 6.A4. Determinants of Currency Shares: Estimates Including Commonwealth Countries

	(1)	(2)	(3)	(4)	(5)	(6)
Inertia	0.897***	0.896***	0.903***	0.903***	0.894***	0.902***
	(0.009)	(0.009)	(0.011)	(0.011)	(0.009)	(0.011)
Credibility		−0.096*		−0.133***		−0.073
		(0.051)		(0.048)		(0.052)
Size			0.312**	0.396***		0.867***
			(0.133)	(0.124)		(0.174)
Financial depth					0.076	0.293***
					(0.050)	(0.069)
Constant	4.694***	6.278***	−1.833	−1.907	0.339	−29.147***
	(1.098)	(1.958)	(3.423)	(3.681)	(2.970)	(7.985)
Observations	1,214	1,214	1,214	1,214	1,214	1,214
No. of groups	66	66	66	66	66	66
R^2 (overall)	0.976	0.976	0.974	0.971	0.977	0.921
R^2 (within)	0.849	0.849	0.849	0.850	0.849	0.852
R^2 (between)	0.998	0.998	0.993	0.989	0.998	0.926
ρ	0.316	0.325	0.378	0.433	0.330	0.747
σ_α	3.871	3.945	4.425	4.951	3.994	9.657
σ_ε	5.689	5.682	5.676	5.661	5.686	5.624
log likelihood	−3785	−3783	−3782	−3778	−3784	−3770

Notes: Estimates of the benchmark model based on full sample of 33 countries over 1914–1916 (i.e., including the five Commonwealth countries in the sample: Australia, Canada, India, New Zealand, and South Africa) and the main determinants of international currency status, group effects, and time effects. Standard errors in parentheses are robust to heteroskedasticity and clustered heterogeneity; ***, $p < 0.01$; **, $p < 0.05$; *, $p < 0.13$.

trending). This is not the case, however. Although financial depth rose significantly in the United States in the 1920s, it collapsed in the Great Depression of the 1930s.[38] Estimates using first differences rather than levels (unlike the conventional specification used in the literature) confirm that financial development matters.[39] The effect of inertia almost vanishes, while that of size turns negative in two specifications, albeit becoming insignificant in the full model of column 6. But the results for credibility and—importantly—financial depth remain unchanged, which again supports our emphasis on financial development.

Finally, Table 6.A5 presents estimates for which the dependent variable is the share of debt denominated in dollars relative to that denominated in sterling (and the independent variables are U.S. relative to U.K. variables). This specification addresses possible ambiguities in the interpretation of developments on the two sides of the Atlantic. For instance, U.K. financial depth might well have increased on the whole but decreased relative to that in the United States. The results in Table 6.A5 are again qualitatively close to those in the baseline specification, however. In the full model (column 6), the estimated inertia coefficient remains unaltered; the credibility measure is insignificant; and the effect of size and financial depth are positive, significant, and even larger than before.

TABLE 6.A5. Determinants of Currency Shares: Estimates in Relative Terms

	(1)	(2)	(3)	(4)	(5)	(6)
Inertia	0.867***	0.867***	0.867***	0.867***	0.867***	0.867***
	(0.014)	(0.014)	(0.014)	(0.014)	(0.014)	(0.014)
Credibility		0.952		−0.258		1.228
		(0.617)		(0.783)		(0.767)
Size			0.489*	0.569		2.032***
			(0.250)	(0.349)		(0.572)
Financial depth					0.365***	0.813***
					(0.114)	(0.200)
Constant	−6.603	−9.909*	−10.607**	−9.549*	1.393	−53.468***
	(3.995)	(5.804)	(4.172)	(4.843)	(1.721)	(12.724)
Observations	517	517	517	517	517	517
Number of countries	28	28	28	28	28	28
R^2 (overall)	0.974	0.974	0.974	0.974	0.974	0.974
R^2 (within)	0.866	0.866	0.866	0.866	0.866	0.866
R^2 (between)	0.997	0.997	0.997	0.997	0.997	0.997
ρ	0.376	0.376	0.376	0.376	0.376	0.376
σ_α	8.745	8.745	8.745	8.745	8.745	8.745
σ_ε	11.27	11.27	11.27	11.27	11.27	11.27
log likelihood	−1958	−1958	−1958	−1958	−1958	−1958

Notes: Estimates of the benchmark model in relative terms (i.e., dollar share minus sterling share) based on baseline sample of 28 countries over 1914–1916 and including the main determinants of international currency status, group effects, and time effects. Standard errors in parentheses are robust to heteroskedasticity and clustered heterogeneity; ***, $p < 0.01$; **, $p < 0.05$; *, $p < 0.1$.

7

Reserve Currency Competition in the Second Half of the Twentieth Century

Widespread international use of the U.S. dollar in the second half of the twentieth century is regularly cited in support of the view that the currency of the country that is the leading economic and financial power tends to dominate cross-border transactions at any point in time. In this chapter, we examine this era more closely. We focus on the currency composition of foreign reserves from the late 1940s to the turn of the twenty-first century.

The use of national currencies as foreign reserves is only one aspect of international currency status. The advantage of focusing on this aspect is that it is possible to assemble a continuous series on the composition of international reserves for a substantial fraction of the world's central banks spanning this period. Data on currencies used for invoicing international trade, in contrast, are available only for scattered countries and years, while surveys of foreign exchange trading in different currencies, courtesy of the BIS, are available only from 1989. In Chapter 4 we saw how interwar evidence on the currency composition of foreign reserves could be used to shed light on (and more precisely, to challenge) the traditional view emphasizing network increasing returns, first-mover advantage, and the overwhelming dominance of a particular national currency in international transactions at any given time. In this chapter, we extend that analysis to the post–World War II period.

This era is important not only because it is strongly associated with dollar dominance but also because it is marked by sharp changes in financial technology, regulation, and policy. A dramatic decline in the cost of financial transactions made it easier for central banks, like other investors, to shift between currencies and reap the advantages of diversified reserve portfolios. Some governments took steps to actively encourage the use of their currencies as foreign reserves, while others sought to discourage the practice. Still other countries like Japan moved from one stance to the other. With the collapse of the Bretton Woods System in the 1970s, a growing list of countries moved from pegged to flexible exchange rates, something that was widely expected to affect their reliance on dollar reserves.

The picture in this chapter adds nuance to the traditional view of dollar dominance. We find that network effects appear to have weakened in recent decades, consistent with the idea that advances in financial technology have reduced the costs of currency transactions and encouraged portfolio diversification. But there remains evidence of persistence in currency choice, as if tradition and custom continue to matter in international financial markets. The stability and credibility of the policies of the reserve-issuing countries, as captured by such variables as the volatility of their exchange rates, have become increasingly important. Finally, we find that negative policy interventions designed to discourage international use of a currency have been more effective than positive interventions intended to encourage it.

Data

Our data on the currency composition of foreign exchange reserves are drawn from a volume published by the International Monetary Fund (IMF) to take stock of its first 20 years (Horsefield 1969), from which we extracted data for the 1940s and the 1950s; from the Fund's annual reports, which we used to gather data for the 1960s through 1990s; and from the Composition of Official Foreign Exchange Reserves (COFER) data base, which provides data for 1999–2013. These data are for "allocated" foreign exchange reserves; in other words, there is also a residual nondisclosed and unallocated component attributable to central banks that do not report the currency composition of their reserves.

The currency composition of disclosed reserves may not match that of nondisclosed reserves. But the importance of nondisclosed reserves is a recent phenomenon. It largely reflects the increase in China's reserve holdings after the turn of the century. Nondisclosed reserves accounted for about 47 percent of total foreign exchange reserves in 2014, compared to only about 20 percent in the late 1990s. Our results remain the same when we focus on a subset of advanced economies for which country-level data are available, as we describe below.

These sources report reserves held in U.S. dollars (including eurodollars) and British pounds from 1947, in French francs and Deutschemarks from 1970, and in Dutch guilders, Swiss francs, and Japanese yen from 1973. Reserves held in European Currency Units (ECU) are reported from 1987.[1] Australian and Canadian dollar reserves are reported starting in 2012.[2] In all, 11 currencies were reported as reserve currency units at one time or another.

Valuation effects due to exchange rate changes can produce changes in foreign reserves held in different currencies without any action by central banks. While the early literature ignored this complication, recent studies have computed currency shares at constant exchange rates and shown that such valuation effects can be important.[3] We report results both with and without valuation adjustments.

Figure 7.1 shows the currency composition of foreign reserves since 1947. The dominance of the British pound is evident in the aftermath of World War II, when it accounted for more than 80 percent of foreign exchange reserves. This is a striking exception to the picture of dollar dominance, although, as we show in Chapter 8, it was due to the unusual circumstances of the immediate postwar years. This is then followed by a sharp reversal, with the dollar quickly overtaking sterling and accounting for more than 50 percent of identified foreign exchange reserves by the early 1950s. The dollar's rise then continues through the mid-1970s.[4] Sterling's share similarly continues to fall, reaching the low single digits at around the same time.

Some fluctuations around these trends reflect exchange rate changes. For example, the dollar's declining share of global reserves after 1976 reflects its depreciation in the course of the subsequent decade, interrupted by its recovery in the first half of the 1980s. Sterling's accelerating fall in the late 1960s and early 1970s similarly reflects the impact of devaluation of the pound around the time of

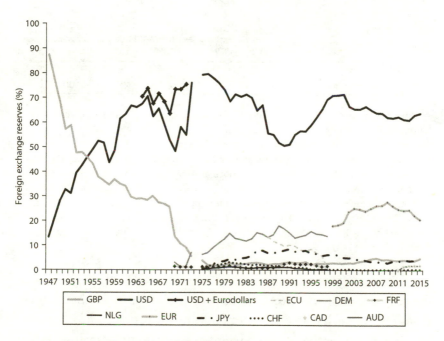

FIGURE 7.1. Currency Composition of Globally Disclosed Foreign Exchange Reserves, 1947–2015 (percent).

Source: Authors' calculations based on IMF data and sources.

Note: The currency shares are derived from U.S. dollar-denominated amounts for 1947–1969 and 1999–2015 as well as from Special Drawing Rights (SDR)-denominated amounts for 1970–1972. The currency shares for the period 1973–1999 are directly provided by the IMF in its annual reports (based on SDR valuation). Starting in 1979 the Fund added the SDR value of ECUs issued against the U.S. dollar to the SDR value of US dollar reserves; after 1987 the ECU was treated as a separate unit. The currency shares reported here exclude unallocated foreign exchange reserves post-1994 (i.e., about 40 percent of total foreign exchange reserves at the end of the sample). AUD, Australian dollar; CAD, Canadian dollar; CHF, Swiss franc; DEM, Deutschemark; ECU, European Currency Unit; EUR, euro; FRF, French franc; GBP, British pound; JPY, Japanese yen; NLG, Dutch guilder; USD, U.S. dollar.

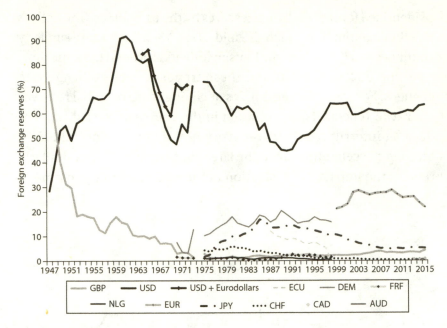

FIGURE 7.2. Currency Composition of Globally Disclosed Foreign Exchange Reserves at Constant Exchange Rates, 1947–2015 (percent).
Source: Authors' calculations based on IMF data and sources.
Note: See Figure 7.1. The currency shares at constant exchange rates calculated using the BIS methodology (and 2012 as base year), as described in Wong (2007). The currency shares reported here exclude unallocated foreign exchange reserves post-1994 (i.e., about 40 percent of total foreign exchange reserves at the end of the sample), as in Figure 7.1. AUD, Australian dollar; CAD, Canadian dollar; CHF, Swiss franc; DEM, Deutschemark; ECU, European Currency Unit; EUR, euro; FRF, French franc; GBP, British pound; JPY, Japanese yen; NLG, Dutch guilder; USD, U.S. dollar.

the collapse of the Bretton Woods System, just as its further drop in 1976 reflects the balance-of-payments and currency crisis that year.[5] This is a reminder that it is important to analyze currency holdings at constant as well as current exchange rates (as in Figures 7.1 and 7.2).

Starting in the 1970s we then observe the rise of the Deutschemark and its successor, the euro. The lines representing these currencies trend upward until the outbreak of the euro crisis in 2010.[6] We also see the rise and fall of the Japanese yen, whose share in global reserves peaks in the late 1980s and early 1990s, coincident with the end of the "bubble economy," the onset of the Japanese economic and financial crisis, and the rise of new subsidiary reserve currencies.[7]

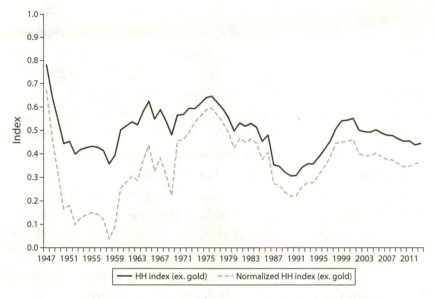

FIGURE 7.3. Currency Concentration of Globally Disclosed Foreign Exchange Reserves, 1947–2013. Source: Authors' calculations based on IMF data and sources.
Note: The basic and standardized Hirschman-Herfindhal (HH) indices calculated for the currency breakdown of global foreign exchange reserves since 1947 (i.e., the sum of squared reserve currency shares, and also scaled by a function of the number of currency units in each year, in the case of the standardized index). An index value of 1 indicates a monopolistic market; an index value of 0 indicates a perfectly competitive market.

Figure 7.3 plots the Hirschman-Herfindhal (HH) index for the concentration of foreign exchange reserves from 1947 through 2012. Two versions of the index are displayed: the simple HH index and the index adjusted for the number of currencies in the global reserve portfolio.[8] Both confirm the high concentration of reserves in one currency (sterling) immediately after World War II, the subsequent rapid fall in concentration as sterling is liquidated and dollars are earned, the growing concentration of reserves in dollars in the 1960s and 1970s, and finally very gradual movement in the direction of less dollar-dominated reserve portfolios.

Specification

Our basic specification relates foreign currency holdings to issuing-country size, exchange rate appreciation, and lagged currency holdings. The lagged currency holdings capture persistence or inertia effects; following Triffin (1960), we interpret these in terms of custom and tradition.[9] Relative size can be motivated by theoretical models of random matching games that see the emergence of international currencies as the solution to a "double-coincidence-of-wants" problem where an agent's incentive to accept a nation's currency depends on how often he or she trades with a national from that country (Matsuyama, Kiyotaki, and Matsui 1993). We measure relative size as the share of the reserve-currency-issuing country in global GDP, taking data from Maddison (2010).

This is a good place to highlight the distinction between network effects and persistence and to emphasize that one does not imply the other. Persistence can have other sources besides network effects that give rise to first-mover advantage. Examples include habit formation and the absence of low-cost alternatives to the dominant unit for providing reserves on the scale demanded. Conversely, network effects may increase the attractions of a particular standard (in this case, a currency standard) at some point in time without preventing market participants from shifting to another standard at a later point in time, assuming that mechanisms promoting lock-in are weak and agents can coordinate (as argued by David 1986).[10] The success with which open standards for personal electronics have been developed in recent years, weakening lock-in and facilitating shifts between operating systems, illustrates the point (see West 2007).

The credibility term is motivated by the idea that exchange rate depreciation makes holding a currency unattractive and discourages its international use, as in Devereux and Shi (2013). Currency fluctuations affect credibility, because reserve holders prefer reliable stores of value and may be reluctant to hold reserves in units that tend to depreciate too much for too long. We proxy credibility by the average rate of currency appreciation vis-à-vis Special Drawing Rights over the preceding 5 years (in the spirit of Chinn and Frankel 2007).[11]

By focusing on the lagged dependent variable, country size, and trend exchange rate appreciation, we follow the existing literature (see, e.g., Chinn and Frankel 2007, 2008 and Li and Liu 2008). Similarly, when we interpret these variables in terms of persistence, network externalities, and policy credibility, we build on analytical models emphasizing these effects. Whether country size is an adequate measure of these network effects can be disputed, of course. Below we consider alternatives such as the volume of the issuing country's exports and financial market liquidity (as in, e.g., Portes and Rey 1998 and Papaioannou and Portes 2008).[12]

Similarly, persistence effects reflecting habit formation have been considered in the earlier literature (see, e.g., de Vries 1988). Again, whether our lagged dependent variable is in fact capturing habit formation, as opposed to serially correlated omitted variables, can certainly be questioned. In early econometric work on partial adjustment models, Griliches (1961) suggested instrumenting the lagged dependent variable as a way of addressing this problem. We implement a version of his approach later in the chapter.

Analogously, it can be questioned whether contemporaneous exchange rate changes are a good measure of policy credibility. To address these concerns, we also consider annual CPI inflation rates, exchange rate volatility, the level of public debt, bond yields, and the current account of the balance of payments as additional measures of policy credibility.[13]

Finally, we assemble information on policy measures taken by potential reserve currency issuers (the United States, the United Kingdom, Germany, and Japan) to encourage or discourage use of their currencies as international reserves. These include whether the capital account was open or closed, whether the stated position of the authorities in the issuing country was supportive or opposed, and whether exchange rate arrangements and agreements were conducive in a sense we define below.[14]

We include time effects throughout. These capture changes in the structure of the international monetary and financial system as well as other changes in the world economy.[15] In addition, we estimate the resulting equations with random country effects to account for unobserved country-specific variation.[16]

This is an unbalanced sample by currency and year, raising the question of how to treat the missing observations. One option is to proceed with the unbalanced panel, because these are the data provided by official sources. Another is to fill in zero for the missing observations, since the IMF presumably saw no need to report reserves held in French francs and Deutschemarks before 1970; or guilder, Swiss francs, and yen before 1973; or Australian dollars before 2012 because such holdings were so small (effectively zero by the standards of reserves held in the form of U.S. dollars).[17] We report results using both procedures.

To test for shifts around the time of the collapse of Bretton Woods, we interact these variables with a post-1973 dummy variable. We test for changes in the overall relationship and in the sign and magnitude of the individual coefficients. In robustness checks, we also run rolling Chow tests to investigate whether years other than 1973 qualify as breaks. All the variables are standardized.

Results

Table 7.1 shows the results when the dependent variable is the share of identified foreign exchange reserves held in a particular currency with valuation effects removed. Columns 1 and 2 report results with the three basic explanatory variables. Columns 3 and 4 are for the pre-1973 period, and columns 5 and 6 show results for 1973 on. Column 7 includes interaction terms with a post-1973 dummy variable to test for post-1973 structural shifts. In other estimates, we substitute zeroes for missing observations of the dependent variable in Table 7.1.[18]

The results are consistent with the findings of previous studies for the recent period. Persistence is strong; a coefficient of 0.9 on the lagged dependent variable indicates a half-life of roughly 7 years. This value suggests that to adequately understand the evolution of currency shares, it is important to consider medium-term evolutions, as we do here. But this point estimate also indicates that the share of a currency in global reserves can be halved in less than a decade, which is what sterling experienced from the mid-1960s to the early 1970s. The coefficient on size is also important, consistent with the emphasis of previous authors on network effects. The full sample estimates in column 2 of Table 7.1 suggest that a one-standard-deviation increase in issuing-country size increases the share of its currency in global foreign exchange reserves by

TABLE 7.1. Demand for Reserves: Basic Estimates

	(1) Full sample	(2) Full sample	(3) Pre-1973	(4) Pre-1973	(5) Post-1973	(6) Post-1973	(7) Full sample
Inertia	0.992***	0.927***	0.997***	0.758***	0.989***	0.954***	0.886***
	(0.002)	(0.021)	(0.003)	(0.037)	(0.004)	(0.009)	(0.024)
Network effects		1.538***		5.808***		0.819***	3.036***
		(0.471)		(0.807)		(0.173)	(0.570)
Credibility		0.172**		−2.007***		0.145*	−1.279***
		(0.072)		(0.109)		(0.079)	(0.307)
Post-73 dummy							2.921***
							(0.943)
Inertia × post-73 dummy							0.045**
							(0.023)
Network effects × post-73 dummy							−1.722***
							(0.534)
Credibility × post-73 dummy							1.436***
							(0.388)
Currency effects	Yes	Yes	Yes	Yes	Yes	Yes	Yes
Time effects	Yes	Yes	Yes	Yes	Yes	Yes	Yes
Observations	288	271	54	42	234	229	271
No. of groups	8	8	4	4	8	8	8
R^2 (overall)	0.987	0.993	0.964	0.988	0.995	0.995	0.993
R^2 (within)	0.899	0.881	0.900	0.767	0.831	0.836	0.887
R^2 (between)	1.000	1.000	0.998	1.000	1.000	1.000	1.000

Notes: Random effects estimates of baseline equation where reserve currency shares purged of valuation effects are regressed on their standard determinants over selected sample periods, namely: the full sample (in columns 1 and 2); 1947–1972 (in columns 3 and 4); 1973–2013 (in columns 5 and 6) and the full sample allowing for a structural break in the estimated coefficients (in column 7). Standard errors in parentheses are robust to heteroskedasticity and clustered heterogeneity; ***, $p < 0.01$; **, $p < 0.05$; *, $p < 0.1$.

1.5 percentage points in the same year and by 21 percentage points in the long run. A one-standard-deviation appreciation in a currency's exchange rate relative to trend increases its share of global foreign exchange reserves by about 0.2 percentage points in the short run and 2 percentage points in the long run.

The effects of policy credibility as measured by the rate of appreciation of the exchange rate are more complex. Previous studies reported mixed results for this variable, and our results are mixed as well. In Table 7.1, policy credibility shows up as positive after 1973, as expected, but negative prior to that. When we add the zero observations, however, the policy credibility measure for the pre-1973 period turns positive, though it is insignificantly different from zero.[19] A cautious interpretation is that policy credibility had weaker effects before 1973 than after.[20]

We can compare our results for the full period with those of Chinn and Frankel (2007, Table 8.4, p. 303), where theirs are estimated on a shorter period. Our estimates of the size effect (designed to capture network effects) are about twice as large as theirs (although they are the same when we restrict the period to post-1973, as they do). Estimates of the lagged dependent variable, designed to capture persistence effects, are again the same. And our estimate for the change in the exchange rate is essentially identical to theirs, except that in our case, this variable is statistically significant.[21]

But there are noticeable differences between sub-periods. The coefficient capturing network effects in Table 7.1 is smaller in the second period than in the first.[22] At the same time, there is evidence of an increase in persistence. The coefficient on this variable is larger after 1973 than before, and the difference is statistically significant.[23] That inertia is stronger after Bretton Woods reflects the fact that the post-1973 period has not seen a rapid shift from one currency to another comparable to the shift from sterling to the dollar between 1947 and 1973. Before 1973, serious doubts about the prospects for sterling as a reserve currency caused reserve managers to question their habits and move away from the currency; because the United States has for the most part avoided creating equally serious doubts about the dollar, the persistence effects have, well, persisted.

That network effects are less strong is similarly intuitive. Progress in facilitating interoperability among currency units and declining switching costs argue for replacing the traditional (or "old") view of international currencies—according to which sufficiently strong network increasing returns lead to a natural monopoly in international currency status—with the new view with very different empirical implications. As explained in Chapter 1, the new view builds on the literature on information technology and systems engineering of open systems. It builds on work in which switching costs can be overcome by effective coordination mechanisms and large shocks (see, e.g., David and Bunn 1988, Clark 2003, and Farrell and Klemperer 2007).[24] Examples of forces that have reduced switching costs include advances in financial and transactions technologies, the development of currency swap markets, new hedging instruments, and increased availability of information about foreign exchange markets. These developments have allowed central banks and others to engage in international transactions and hold reserves against associated contingencies in currencies other than the dominant unit or units, without incurring costs as large as before.

The alternative to using historical information and priors as a basis for hypotheses about structural shifts in the relationship between reserves and their determinants is to let the data speak. Rolling Chow tests for the coefficients on persistence, issuing-country size as a proxy for network effects, and policy credibility produce the largest test statistic in 1960 (Figure 7.4). This was the year when U.S. official foreign monetary liabilities first exceeded U.S. gold reserves, and Triffin (1960) warned that a run by official foreign creditors was possible. There is then evidence of another structural break in 1966, 1 year prior to the second post–World War II devaluation of sterling, a currency already of great concern to investors; the devaluation itself was followed by another discrete decline in sterling reserves. The year 1966 was also immediately before France's withdrawal from the Gold Pool, under which European countries holding dollar reserves agreed to reimburse the United States for a portion of the gold it lost when other countries converted their dollars.[25] It was also a period of heightened concern over the future of the Bretton Woods System and hence the dollar peg.[26]

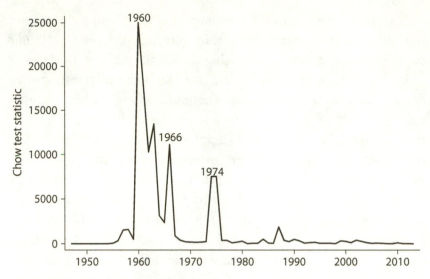

FIGURE 7.4. Time-Varying Structural Break Tests.
Source: Authors' calculations.
Note: The time-varying Chow test statistic (i.e., of the restriction test that the three coefficients on persistence, size, and credibility interacted with a step dummy are insignificant) obtained when the step dummy is allowed to vary across all years of our sample. The critical value of a $\chi 2$ (3) distribution at the 1 percent level of confidence is 11.34.

Dividing the sample in 1966 as opposed to the early 1970s has minimal impact on the point estimates and confidence intervals.[27] Nonetheless, the fact that the sharpest shift in the relationship between the currency denomination of foreign reserves on the one hand, and persistence, issuing-country size, and policy credibility on the other occurs in the 1960s rather than in 1971–1974 highlights how contemporaries may have overestimated the extent to which the actual collapse of Bretton Woods would tarnish the attractions of the dollar. It suggests that they may have overestimated the extent to which the demand for and composition of reserves would be altered by the actual shift from fixed to flexible exchange rates, as opposed to anticipations thereof.[28]

But regardless of whether one places the shift in 1960, 1966 or the early 1970s, our results are consistent with the fact that the determinants of the demand for and composition of international reserves fundamentally changed with the breakdown of Bretton Woods.

Our data, while disaggregated by currency, are aggregated across countries, where decisions regarding the currency composition of foreign reserves are made at the country level. We therefore estimated the same relationships on country-level data for a subset of advanced economies for which foreign reserve data disaggregated by currency are available.[29] These data provide annual foreign exchange reserves divided into dollar and non-dollar holdings. We used the share of the dollar in total foreign exchange reserves as the dependent variable and estimated the same basic specification using panel-data methods.

The results, shown in Table 7.2, are again broadly similar to those described above. Again there is evidence of significantly stronger inertia effects and weaker network effects after the collapse of Bretton Woods. The results also show evidence of stronger credibility effects, although this change was not statistically significant.[30]

Policy Variables

One potential explanation for the continued dominance of the dollar is the reluctance of other countries to permit international use of their currencies. In the 1960s and 1970s, Germany used capital controls to limit access to the Deutschemark. It sought to discourage central banks from holding Deutschemark reserves on the grounds that their doing so might undermine the Bundesbank's ability to control inflation. From the 1950s through the early 1980s, Japan similarly used controls and regulatory restrictions to limit official foreign holdings of yen on the grounds that such holdings would complicate its pursuit of industrial policies.

We consider measures to support and discourage international use of their currencies by these two countries and, in addition, by the United States and the United Kingdom.[31] The United Kingdom, as noted, took steps in the 1940s and 1950s to limit the liquidation of sterling reserves; subsequent policy initiatives, such as the City of London's financial "Big Bang" liberalization in 1986, can be seen as supporting sterling's international role. The United States adopted policies to support the dollar's international role, such as the Interest Equalization Tax in 1963 and the Voluntary Credit Restraint Program in 1965, to limit capital outflows, stem gold losses, and foster confidence in the convertibility of the dollar.

TABLE 7.2. Demand for Reserves: Country-Level Estimates

	(1) Full sample	(2) Full sample	(3) Pre-1973	(4) Pre-1973	(5) Post-1973	(6) Post-1973	(7) Full sample
Inertia	0.898***	0.897***	0.471***	0.471***	0.935***	0.935***	0.484***
	(0.029)	(0.029)	(0.115)	(0.115)	(0.022)	(0.023)	(0.107)
Network effects		6.743		1.789***		6.784	27.536+
		(12.880)		(0.439)		(13.190)	(17.285)
Credibility		1.326		−4.777***		1.339	−1.309
		(1.676)		(1.821)		(1.734)	(3.329)
Inertia × post-73 dummy							0.450***
							(0.111)
Network effects × post-73 dummy							−20.752+
							(13.609)
Credibility × post-73 dummy							2.648
							(4.794)
Currency effects	Yes	Yes	Yes	Yes	Yes	Yes	Yes
Time effects	Yes	Yes	Yes	Yes	Yes	Yes	Yes
Observations	540	530	120	120	420	410	530
No. of groups	10	10	10	10	10	10	10
R^2 (overall)	0.867	0.865	0.363	0.363	0.893	0.891	0.876
R^2 (within)	0.834	0.832	0.168	0.168	0.846	0.844	0.844
R^2 (between)	0.997	0.997	0.967	0.967	0.999	0.999	0.999

Notes: Random effects estimates of baseline model where the share of the U.S. dollar in the reserve holdings of a subset of advanced economies is regressed on the standard determinants of foreign reserve currency choice over selected sample periods, namely: full sample (in columns 1–2); 1960–1972 (in columns 3–4), 1973–2014 (in columns 5–6), and full sample allowing for a structural break in the estimated coefficients (in column 7). Standard errors in parentheses are robust to heteroskedasticity and clustered heterogeneity; ***, $p < 0.01$; **, $p < 0.05$; *, $p < 0.1$; +, $p < 0.16$.

The individual measures making up the dummy variables are described in Table 7.A in Appendix 7A.

The estimates, shown in Table 7.3, confirm that policies matter, but not all in the same way. It is evidently easier to discourage than to promote reserve currency use. Policies that aim to support currency use are often unsuccessful, with a few notable exceptions. Some evidence suggests, for example, that financial openness helped strengthen the importance of a particular currency as a reserve currency. The estimates in column 4 of Table 7.3, for example, suggest that a one-standard-deviation increase in a country's financial openness (i.e., about 21 index points) is associated with an increase in the share of its currency in global reserves of roughly half a percentage point in the short run and 6 percentage points in the long run. But other supportive policies appear less important. Their effect is typically insignificant.

In contrast, policies discouraging currency use often have had significant effects. This is the case of unsupportive official positions, unsupportive exchange rate regime measures (i.e., devaluing one's currency, in the manner of the repeated devaluations of sterling between 1947 and 1976 and of the U.S. dollar in the early 1970s), and other unsupportive measures that may have dented confidence (e.g., the collapse of the Gold Pool and discussions of an IMF

TABLE 7.3. Demand for Reserves: Estimates with Policy Measures

	(1)	(2)	(3)	(4)	(5)	(6)
	Full sample	Pre-1973	Post-1973	Full Sample	Pre-1973	Post-1973
Inertia	0.917***	0.789***	0.940***	0.916***	0.801***	0.952***
	(0.010)	(0.078)	(0.018)	(0.015)	(0.087)	(0.016)
Network effects	1.855***	6.513***	1.305***	1.969***	5.392***	1.097***
	(0.273)	(1.130)	(0.331)	(0.347)	(1.572)	(0.323)
Credibility	0.021	−0.746	0.046	0.127***	−1.238	0.104*
	(0.059)	(1.760)	(0.045)	(0.043)	(1.244)	(0.056)
IMF Article VIII compliance	0.036***	−0.068	0.030*			
	(0.007)	(0.065)	(0.016)			

Continued on the next page

TABLE 7.3. (*continued*)

	(1)	(2)	(3)	(4)	(5)	(6)
	Full sample	Pre-1973	Post-1973	Full Sample	Pre-1973	Post-1973
Capital flow restrictions				0.023*** (0.004)	−0.012 (0.039)	0.008 (0.007)
Official position (*supportive*)	−0.368 (1.222)	0.000 (0.000)	−0.592 (1.160)	−0.294 (1.217)	0.000 (0.000)	−0.559 (1.159)
Official position (*restrictive*)	−3.044*** (0.885)	−3.424 (3.693)	−2.112*** (0.592)	−3.298*** (0.860)	−4.637 (4.414)	−2.164*** (0.561)
Exchange rate regime (*supportive*)	−0.073 (0.827)	0.000 (0.000)	0.487 (0.818)	−0.060 (0.871)	0.000 (0.000)	0.564 (0.844)
Exchange rate regime (*restrictive*)	−2.053** (0.936)	−2.597 (4.922)	−2.588*** (0.536)	−2.058** (0.924)	−2.194 (4.795)	−2.644*** (0.510)
Other measures (*supportive*)	−0.098 (0.384)	−1.794** (0.844)	0.839+ (0.600)	−0.180 (0.368)	−1.874* (1.025)	0.694 (0.630)
Other measures (*restrictive*)	−5.755*** (0.824)	−10.644** (4.337)	−3.969*** (0.425)	−5.769*** (0.847)	−10.006** (4.121)	−3.880*** (0.422)
Currency effects	Yes	Yes	Yes	Yes	Yes	Yes
Time effects	Yes	Yes	Yes	Yes	Yes	Yes
Observations	271	42	229	271	42	229
No. of groups	8	4	8	8	4	8
R^2 (overall)	0.994	0.991	0.996	0.994	0.991	0.996
R^2 (within)	0.904	0.828	0.864	0.902	0.828	0.863
R^2 (between)	1.000	1.000	1.000	1.000	0.999	1.000

Notes: Random effects estimates of baseline model where reserve currency shares purged of valuation effects are regressed on their standard determinants over selected sample periods, namely: the full sample (in columns 1 and 4); 1947–1972 (in columns 2 and 5), 1973–2013 (in columns 3 and 6) controlling for policy measures that aim to support or restrict international currency use of the U.S. dollar, pound sterling, Deutschemark, and Japanese yen. Standard errors in parentheses are robust to heteroskedasticity and clustered heterogeneity; ***, $p < 0.01$; **, $p < 0.05$; *, $p < 0.1$; +, $p < 0.16$.

substitution account for the dollar).[32] The estimates in column 4 suggest that devaluations are typically associated with a decline in the share of a country's currency in global reserves of roughly 2 percentage points in the short run and 24 percentage points in the long run.[33]

Conclusion

In this chapter we analyzed the composition of international reserves from the late 1940s to the turn of the twenty-first century. In so doing, we utilized newly assembled data spanning the second half of the twentieth century on the currency composition of reserves, its determinants, and policy measures encouraging or discouraging the internationalization of currencies.

We find evidence of shifts in the determinants of currency shares around the time of the breakdown of Bretton Woods. In particular, the effects of inertia and the credibility of policies became stronger after the demise of Bretton Woods, while those associated with network effects weakened.

That the effects of inertia have strengthened may be seen as favoring the leading currency (the dollar), a fact underscored by the resilience of its share in global reserves since the financial crisis of 2008–2009 (a period encompassed by our data). In contrast, the weakening of network effects works against the dollar's first-mover advantage. To be sure, persistence can have other sources besides network effects, such as habit formation and the absence of alternatives. That said, the observation that persistence is not guaranteed by network effects suggests that its existence—and the dollar's continued dominance—should not be taken for granted.

The policy toolkit to discourage international currency use contains a range of effective instruments, from official announcements to exchange-rate-regime-related measures. In contrast, policy tools to encourage reserve currency status and overcome inertia have been more limited; this toolkit has been dominated by two instruments: macroeconomic stabilization policy and capital account liberalization. Our results suggest that the first set of tools has been more effective than the second: it is typically easier to discourage use of a national currency in international transactions than it is to promote its use.

These last findings have implications for China's earlier policies of discouraging international use of the renminbi and now for its efforts to promote it. They are consistent with the effectiveness of China's capital controls in limiting international use of the currency and with the evidence of Huang, Daili, and Gang (2014) that the renminbi still punches below its weight as a reserve unit. There is ample precedent for the effectiveness of such restrictive measures. At the same time, our findings suggest that, while capital account liberalization may be necessary for renminbi internationalization, it will not suffice, and that the success of the other policy initiatives needed to achieve this goal cannot be taken for granted. We revisit these issues in Chapter 11, which focuses on the renminbi.

Overview of Policy Measures to Support/Discourage International Currency Use, 1947–2013

We distinguish policies related to (a) financial openness, (b) official positions and verbal interventions on internationalization, (c) reform and regulation of the exchange rate system-cum-regime, and (d) other miscellaneous measures. Financial openness is measured using the two de jure indices of Quinn and Toyoda (2008), which capture, on the one hand, how compliant a country is with its obligations under the IMF's Article VIII to free from government restrictions the proceeds from international trade of goods and services and, on the other hand, restrictions to capital outflows and inflows by residents and nonresidents.[34] In each category we further distinguish measures to encourage international use of the currency from measures to discourage it. This gives us a total of six dummy variables capturing six categories of potential policy effects.

TABLE 7.A. Overview of Policy Measures to Support/Discourage International Currency Use, 1947–2013

A. U.S. DOLLAR

Capital Account Measures		Official Position and Verbal Interventions (U.S. Treasury)	
Supporting International Currency Use	Discouraging International Currency Use	Supporting International Currency Use	Discouraging International Currency Use
1963 Interest equalization tax created		1987 Baker talks the dollar up	1977 Blumenthal talks the dollar down
1965 Voluntary credit restraint program		1995 Rubin's "strong dollar" policy	1985 Baker talks the dollar down
1974 Interest equalization tax lifted			1986 Baker talks the dollar down

Exchange Rate Regime-Related Measures		Other Measures	
Supporting International Currency Use	Discouraging International Currency Use	Supporting International Currency Use	Discouraging International Currency Use
1987 G6 (Louvre) agreement	1971 Dollar convertibility suspended	1947 Start of Marshall Plan	1967 France leaves "Gold Pool"
	1973 Dollar allowed to float	1951 End of Marshall Plan	1968 Collapse of "Gold Pool"
	1985 G5 (Plaza) agreement	1961 Creation of "Gold Pool"	1969 Creation of the SDR
	1989 Unraveling of Louvre agreement	1963 Creation of the G10	1978 Substitution Account discussed

TABLE 7.A. (*continued*)

B. POUND STERLING

Capital Account Measures		Official Position and Verbal Interventions	
Supporting International Currency Use	Discouraging International Currency Use	Supporting International Currency Use	Discouraging International Currency Use
1954 De facto convertibility	1948 Restrictions to convertibility		
1961 Acceptance of IMF Article VIII			
1986 City of London's Big Bang			
1990 Intra-EU capital movements fully liberalized			

Exchange Rate Regime-Related Measures		Other Measures	
Supporting International Currency Use	Discouraging International Currency Use	Supporting International Currency Use	Discouraging International Currency Use
	1947 Sterling convertibility crisis	1961 Bilateral concerté	
	1949 Sterling devaluation	1964 End of bilateral concerté	
	1967 Sterling devaluation	1966 BIS group arrangement I	
	1971 End of Bretton Woods	1968 BIS group arrangement II	
	1973 Generalized floating	1971 End of BIS group arrangement I	
	1976 Sterling crisis (IMF SBA)	1974 End of BIS group arrangement II	
		1977 BIS group arrangement III	

Continued on the next page

TABLE 7.A. (continued)

C. DEUTSCHEMARK

	Capital Account Measures				Official Position and Verbal Interventions (Bundesbank)			
	Supporting International Currency Use		Discouraging International Currency Use		Supporting International Currency Use		Discouraging International Currency Use	
1961	Acceptance of IMF Article VIII	1968	D-Mark bond-issues managed by German banks only	1985	D-Mark to remain "competitive"	1971	Diversification of the international monetary system "everything but positive"	
1974	Cash-deposit requirement lifted	1971	Nonresident money market purchases restricted					
1975	Foreign deposit interest payment freed	1972	Nonresident bond market purchases restricted					
1980	Nonresident bond purchases allowed	1973	Nonresident equity market purchases restricted					
1981	Nonresident security purchases allowed							
1985	D-Mark bond-issues managed by foreign banks							
1986	Nonstraight fixed rate bonds allowed							
1989	Minimum maturities for public placements reduced							
1990	Intra-EU capital movements fully liberalized							

TABLE 7.A. (*continued*)

	Exchange Rate Regime-Related Measures		Other Measures	
	Supporting International Currency Use	Discouraging International Currency Use	Supporting International Currency Use	Discouraging International Currency Use
1961	Revaluation of the D-Mark	1987 G6 (Louvre) agreement	1979 Creation of the EMS	
1969	Revaluation of the D-Mark		1990 Germany monetary unification	
1971	D-Mark allowed to float			
1973	D-Mark re-allowed to float			
1981	EMS realignment			
1982	EMS realignment			
1983	EMS realignment (and D-Mark "dominance" theory)			
1985	G5 (Plaza) agreement			
1987	EMS realignment			
1992	ERM crises			
1993	ERM crises			

D. JAPANESE YEN

Capital Account Measures		Official Position and Verbal Interventions (Ministry of Finance)	
Supporting International Currency Use	Discouraging International Currency Use	Supporting International Currency Use	Discouraging International Currency Use
Overseas accounts for banks 1949	1st FX and Trade Control Law 1983	Yen 's role as "policy objective" 2001	Yen's role has changed "little"
1972 Yen accounts for nonresidents	1985 Capital controls strengthened	2003 Yen's role to be "promoted"	Yen's role capped by Japan's decline

Continued on the next page

TABLE 7.A. (*continued*)

	Capital Account Measures		Official Position and Verbal Interventions (Ministry of Finance)	
	Supporting International Currency Use	Discouraging International Currency Use	Supporting International Currency Use	Discouraging International Currency Use
1964	Acceptance of IMF Article VIII		1999 Study group on yen's role	
1972	Private FX holdings allowed			
1973	Inward FDI allowed			
1979	Bond purchases by nonresidents allowed			
1980	New FX and Trade Control Law			
1981	Foreign trade finance in yen			
1982	Long-term foreign lending in yen			
1983	Liberalization of "Samurai" bond issuance			
1984	FX conversion limits lifted, euro-yen bond issuance liberalized, etc.			
1985	Witholding tax on foreign interest payments lifted, etc.			
1986	Offshore market opened			
1987	Restrictions on euro-yen CP issues lifted			
1988	Other restrictions lifted			
1989	Yen deposits by nonresidents facilitated			

TABLE 7.A. (*continued*)

1996	Announcement of "big bang"
1998	New FX and Control Law
1999	New measures to enhance bond market liquidity

| | Exchange Rate Regime-Related Measures | | Other Measures | |
	Supporting International Currency Use	Discouraging International Currency Use	Supporting International Currency Use	Discouraging International Currency Use
1970			First "Samurai" bond issue	
1971	Yen allowed to float			
1972			Interbank FX transactions allowed	
1973	Yen re-allowed to float			
1977			First euroyen bond	
1983			Yen/Dollar committee created	
1985	G5 (Plaza) agreement			
1987		G6 (Louvre) agreement		

Sources: Authors' compilation based inter alia on Fukao (1990), Tavlas (1991), Takeda and Turner (1992), Henning (1994), Schenk (2010), and Takagi (2011).

Notes: EMS, European Monetary System; ERM, Exchange Rate Mechanism; FDI, foreign direct investment; FX, foreign exchange; SDR, Special Drawing Rights.

Robustness Checks

We subjected the results in this chapter to an extensive series of robustness tests. First, we examined the impact of financial market development and liquidity emphasized by Portes and Rey (1998) and Papaioannou and Portes (2008). Following Chinn and Frankel (2007, 2008) we added the logarithm of foreign exchange market turnover in billions of U.S. dollars.[35] The new variable entered with a positive coefficient indistinguishable from zero, although it is hard to say whether this reflects the absence of an effect or a more limited sample size.

An alternative is to use stock market capitalization relative to GDP as a measure of financial market liquidity and development.[36] We constructed estimates of stock market capitalization using data from Rajan and Zingales (2003) and Beck, Demirgüç-Kunt, and Levine (2009).[37] The estimates again showed market development and liquidity as entering with an insignificant coefficient and adding little to the variation explained.[38]

Next we controlled for some additional determinants of reserve currency choice, such as the public debt-to-GDP ratio, fiscal balance-to-GDP ratio, current account balance-to-GDP ratio, volume of exports in goods, long-term bond yields, exchange rate volatility (as estimated from GARCH(1,1) models, which can be thought of as alternative measures of policy credibility), as well as reserve-currency-country exports of goods (which can be thought of as an alternative measure of network effects). The main results were again robust to these changes. The coefficients on persistence, network effects and credibility were little different from those obtained with our basic model in Table 7.1. There was similarly little change in the estimated structural shifts pre- and post-1973. Of the additional controls, only public debt and the fiscal balance enter significantly. This is consistent with the observation by Frankel (2011) that the two periods when the downward trend in the dollar's share starting in the mid-1970s paused—namely, the 1990s and the most recent few years—are also the two periods when the U.S. budget balance improved.

Insofar as finance theory suggests that covariances matter, it could also be argued that if a currency has a "negative beta" (i.e., it appreciates in times of crisis), it will be regarded as attractive to hold as reserves. We hence estimated time-varying currency betas which we included as an additional control variable.[39] Our findings again remained the same.

In addition we estimated the same equation excluding the euro and replacing the exchange rate trend with CPI inflation as still another measure of policy credibility (results are not reported for sake of brevity). The main findings are robust to these changes as well.[40]

We used panel tobit estimates to control for the boundedness of reserve currency shares, which may lead to censoring, because several units have values close to zero and only a few are closer to the distribution's center.[41] The results were again unchanged from those for our basic model. The estimates where we allowed for the possibility of a structural break in 1973 were, in fact, virtually identical to those in Table 7.1.[42]

We adjusted for possible endogeneity using the generalized method of moments. The estimation results were obtained with a collapsed set of instruments, as suggested in Roodman (2009), to minimize instrument proliferation bias.[43] The results were again very close to those obtained with our baseline specification.

Since reserve currency shares are persistent, we estimated error-correction models. The long-run estimates suggest that the elasticity of currency shares with respect to a one-standard-deviation increase in economic size is about 21, and it is 1 in the case of a one-standard-deviation appreciation in exchange rate, similar to the elasticities in the baseline model. The single-equation error-correction model estimates further suggest a speed of adjustment of 6 percent per year. In other words, half of the deviation from equilibrium is eliminated after 7 years, again consistent with the baseline estimates.

We controlled for unobserved continent effects. We grouped currency units by continent: North America (Canadian dollar, U.S. dollar), Asia-Pacific (yen, Australian dollar), and Europe (all other units). The full model estimates are again similar to those of the baseline model in sign, statistical significance, and economic magnitude. They again suggest that network effects became weaker and credibility effects stronger after the breakdown of Bretton Woods. They also suggest that inertia effects tended to become stronger.[44]

Finally, we considered a logistic transformation of the dependent variable in the spirit of Chinn and Frankel (2007, 2008).[45] We again find significantly stronger credibility effects following the breakdown of Bretton Woods, as in the baseline specification. Some evidence suggests that inertia effects became stronger and network effects weaker after the breakdown of Bretton Woods, but in this case the change is not statistically significant. [46]

8

The Retreat of Sterling

A striking fact discussed Chapter 7 is the numerical dominance of sterling in international reserves after World War II. But, as we saw in Chapter 4, that numerical dominance was not as pronounced, or even evident, in the 1930s. The situation in the late 1940s was entirely the product of World War II. Nor did it last. All this makes it important to understand how this peculiar situation came about.

The Starting Point

Sterling's numerical dominance of foreign exchange reserves in 1946, the first postwar year, is striking, given the situation in the 1920s, when the pound and the dollar were coequals. In the aftermath of World War II, in contrast, sterling accounted for upward of 80 percent of total identified reserves, the dollar for less than 20 percent. Then reserve portfolios rebalanced toward the dollar. The dollar first matched sterling, as measured by the two currencies' respective shares of global exchange reserves, in the first half of the 1950s.[1] After some further decline, sterling's share of global reserves leveled off at 25–30 percent. This was followed next by a further sharp fall following devaluation in 1967.[2] From this time on, there was no question about the dollar's predominant role in the operation of the international system and the status of sterling as a subsidiary international currency.

Foreign central banks, not excluding those of the Sterling Area, had sought to replace their foreign balances with gold with the approach of World War II, questions having arisen in those unsettled circumstances about whether sterling was as good as gold. Sterling depreciated from $4.86 to $4.03 on the eve of hostilities.[3] Gold was a better bet, and non-Commonwealth members of the Sterling Area in particular sought to obtain it where they could.[4]

Thus, the United Kingdom's net external liabilities, in practice mainly liabilities to foreign central banks and governments, fell from some £800 million at the end of 1937 to just £542 million mid-1939. The exchange reserves of Sterling Area countries other than the United Kingdom itself (the so-called Outer Sterling Area) accounted for roughly half this total.

Members of the Commonwealth and Empire and other suppliers of foodstuffs and matériel to British forces accepted large amounts of sterling for goods and services rendered during the war.[5] One might reasonably ask whether these balances should be counted as reserves or simply as an inadvertent and undesired by-product of hostilities. Did central banks and governments hold sterling after World War II as an international unit of account, means of payment, and store of value—that is to say, to finance transactions, to preserve their savings, and as insurance against shocks? Or did they hold it out of loyalty, because the British government compelled them to do so, and because liquidating it might destabilize financial markets? The answer, unsurprisingly, is a bit of both.

The Working of the Sterling Area

The context for these developments was the Sterling Area that had developed in the 1930s. The motivations for membership were several. Linking to sterling was attractive for countries that did a significant share of their international business with Britain and for members of the Commonwealth and Empire on a sterling standard.

It was attractive insofar as the alternatives of a gold or dollar standard implied deflation, prior to 1933–1934, at least, when the dollar was devalued and then repegged to gold, and insofar as floating the national currency without an external anchor was perceived as risky. Linking to sterling was attractive also because the unit was still convertible, unlike a growing number of other European currencies subject to exchange control.

Finally, linking to sterling was attractive because Britain exhibited a modicum of economic, financial, and political stability, relative in particular to gold bloc members like France. Starting in mid-1932, with the advent of the policy of "cheap money," the United Kingdom put in place a monetary regime that delivered price stability. As part of the 1932 Ottawa Economic Conference, Britain and its Commonwealth and Empire reiterated their collective commitment to stable prices, to the pursuit of economic recovery, and to the maintenance of trade among themselves—goals that they hoped might go together. Stable exchange rates were needed for their achievement and for the promotion of trade in particular. The economies represented at Ottawa therefore encouraged still other countries to join them in their arrangement so that exchange rate stability could be maintained over a still wider area.

The members of the Sterling Area shared a natural complementarity with one another. When commodity prices rose, Britain's import bill rose, causing the Bank of England and the Exchange Equalisation Account to lose gold and foreign exchange reserves.[6] But the members of the Outer Sterling Area, being commodity exporters, saw their trade balances strengthen, causing them to accumulate reserves, which they held as deposits in London. When the Outer Sterling Area responded to increased incomes by importing more, it drew many of its imports from the United Kingdom, reflecting the influence of history and now of the commercial preferences extended to the country by members of its Commonwealth and other Sterling Area countries. Thus, not only were the sterling reserves of the entire area more stable than the reserves of any one member, but Britain's own reserves were more stable owing to these preferential trade arrangements.

The grouping was informal. There was no application to join the Sterling Area and no collective governance. Central banks and governments chose to peg to sterling and held assets denominated in the currency of their own volition. Some countries held the largest part of their reserves in sterling, while others held only a fraction. Some moved quickly to establish a sterling link, but others took their time. While some maintained that link rigidly, others allowed their currencies to fluctuate.[7]

The composition of the Sterling Area evolved as additional countries joined (Argentina, Uruguay, Yugoslavia, and Greece, for example). Some countries that might have been candidates for membership, like Canada and Newfoundland, stayed out because of economic ties to the United States or for other reasons. Some countries met certain criteria for membership (seeking to keep their currencies stable against sterling) but not others (not holding substantial sterling reserves), creating disagreement about how they should be classified.[8] That there is less than full agreement on which countries were members is itself indicative of the amorphous nature of the grouping.[9]

These arrangements were then formalized with the outbreak of World War II. The borders of the Sterling Area became coterminous with those of the British Empire and Commonwealth, as non-British countries abandoned their sterling pegs and liquidated their London balances. Britain imposed a comprehensive system of exchange control in September 1939, and other Commonwealth members followed suit.

As a result, controls were effectively erected around the entire group of sterling countries and not just the United Kingdom. While each member, aside from the colonies, operated its own system of exchange control, they cooperated with one another.[10] Governments prohibited or limited transactions on capital or financial account and subjected transactions on current account to licensing requirements. What defined the Sterling Area was that those import licensing systems favored imports from other members of the Sterling Area that could be settled through transfers of the currency while limiting purchases from "hard currency countries" (what came to be known as the Dollar Area). Members of the Sterling Area held their reserves in London and allowed the British government, through its agent, the Bank of England, to transfer them between accounts.

This practice of accepting sterling for transactions when possible was a "gentleman's agreement."[11] It reflected the solidarity fostered by the war. It was facilitated by Allied control of shipping, which posed obstacles to private parties that might have otherwise sought to use their sterling to purchase commodities from the Dollar Area. But this last fact also pointed to the likelihood of problems when hostilities ended and such obstacles were removed.[12]

Initially British exchange control was relatively lax, the authorities fearing that draconian measures would have adverse implications for the postwar period. Too strict a system might cause foreign holders to shift their business toward New York and the dollar. It soon became apparent, however, that the only way of preserving London's position was by winning the war and that a comprehensive system of control was an essential means to that end. Thus, a new, stricter system was introduced in July 1940.[13]

Members of the Commonwealth and Empire, in particular, acquired very extensive sterling claims through the operation of this system. Dollar receipts earned by Malaya for exports of rubber, by India for exports of jute and tea, and by Egypt for services rendered to the U.S. military were exchanged in London for sterling. In contrast, payments to local forces and for the construction of airfields, port facilities, roads, and barracks were made in local currency obtained from central banks and other note-issuing authorities in exchange for sterling. As a result of such transactions, India and Egypt emerged from World War II as the two largest holders of sterling balances. They were followed by Britain's African colonies, by Palestine and Transjordan, and by Malaysia in descending order of numerical importance. In all, the London balances of the Outer Sterling Area increased tenfold between early 1939 and 1945.

Sterling in Decline

After the war, the question became what to do about these balances. Britain was a declining power, a fact symbolized by its withdrawal from Greece in 1947. Military power and international currency status went hand in hand, and the British military was no longer as imposing as it had been. The country was now a less important trading power than the United States. When members of the Outer Sterling Area imported more, they were less prone to draw those additional imports from the United Kingdom. Thus, the post–World War II Sterling Area no longer displayed the built-in stability of its 1930s predecessor.

Britain's external debts were also heavier, and a significant fraction of its external assets had been liquidated.[14] The security provided by the government's official reserves was questionable; they would prove to be inadequate in the crises of 1955 and 1956.[15] Having been slower to adopt modern mass-production methods and having inherited a set of militant but decentralized trade unions, there were questions about whether British industry could meet the challenge from the United States and Continental Europe. The possibility of sterling devaluation was in the air. When the currency was devalued once in 1949, this only excited talk that it might be devalued again. Fewer countries now pegged to sterling than in the 1930s.

All these events were grounds for rebalancing reserve portfolios toward the dollar. There were no questions about U.S. military strength and export competitiveness. The dollar was freely convertible into gold for official foreign holders, and no one doubted the adequacy of U.S. reserves.[16] The direction in which the dollar was likely to move against sterling was clear. This was the period of the so-called dollar shortage, when scarcity made greenbacks dear.

But the conversion of sterling into dollars was subject to regulation. British restrictions limited the conversion of sterling balances held in London by overseas official and private holders. Some sterling balances blocked in this way could be used for purchases of merchandise or other assets in the Sterling Area but not elsewhere. Specifically, they could not be used for purchases of dollars or payments to the Dollar Area. Sterling reserves were also held by members of the so-called Transferable Account area. Its members, mainly European countries, were permitted to use their sterling reserves for payments between Transferable Accounts and Sterling

Area accounts but not for payments to so-called American account countries (members of the Dollar Area).

The effect was to limit opportunities for converting sterling into dollars and using it to purchase merchandise in the Dollar Area. Sterling could be redistributed among Sterling Area countries, but residents could liquidate their sterling reserves only by using them in settlements with the United Kingdom itself. The British government fostered the practice by maintaining trade and capital controls.

Economies were only bound by these regulations if they entered into agreements with Britain. Not all holders had a choice: Britain's East and West African possessions followed the dictates of the Colonial Office. But Egypt had a choice, despite the presence there of British troops through 1954. Australia and New Zealand had long since gained the autonomy to manage their exchange rates and foreign reserves. India, Pakistan, and Sri Lanka acquired this prerogative with independence in 1947, although they remained members of the British Commonwealth.

How consequential was Commonwealth status for these portfolio decisions? That loyalty to the Commonwealth significantly affected the maintenance of sterling balances after World War II is questioned by Schenk (2010) in her influential history of the period. The sense of collective responsibility felt during World War II, she suggests, no longer operated as powerfully in its wake. That said, to some extent the independent members of the Sterling Area now substituted a sense of collective responsibility for the maintenance of a stable and smoothly functioning international monetary system. They were aware that if they precipitously sold off their sterling balances, the international monetary system, denied an important source of liquidity, could come crashing down. They understood that if Britain was again forced to devalue and to tighten exchange controls, confidence would be damaged, and holders of sterling might only end up inflicting losses on themselves.

But the orderly rebalancing of reserve portfolios that was in the collective interest might not be in the individual interest. Individual countries still had an incentive to liquidate their balances if they could get away with it. Given the extent of the problem (given

the number of countries that were part of this collectivity), the or-
derliness of the process is impressive.[17]

Some observers pointed to custom and tradition as explanations
for sterling's continued role.[18] In addition, however, there remained
fundamental reasons for holding sterling reserves. Britain was one
of the few countries other than the United States with a significant
history of international banking business.[19] Pegging to pound was
attractive insofar as doing so provided a modicum of exchange rate
stability without requiring the costly acquisition of dollar reserves.
Britain was still the second leading trading nation (after the United
States), accounting for more than 10 percent of world merchandise
trade at the beginning of the 1950s. Although that share declined
subsequently, the United Kingdom was still third, behind only the
United States and West Germany, as late as the 1960s. The point is
strengthened if one considers not just Britain but the Sterling Area
as a whole.[20]

In addition, sterling still accounted for half of global trade settlements and invoicing, down only slightly from the 1930s.[21] It retained
a consequential unit-of-account function; when on September 18,
1949, the pound was devalued by 30.5 percent against gold and the
dollar, a variety of other countries—Austria, Egypt, Finland, Indonesia, Israel, the Netherlands, Norway, and Sweden—devalued their
currencies by the same amount. Although this was a smaller number
than did so in 1931 (reflecting the diminished economic and financial
stature of the currency and its issuer), it was still significant.[22] To be
sure, the colonies continued to borrow in London; in the course of
so doing, they accumulated additional sterling. Schenk concludes on
this basis that sterling was still "vital" to the operation of the international monetary system in the 1950s, which explains the willingness
of other central banks and governments to hold it.[23]

It can be argued that sterling was more a regional than an international currency, where the relevant region was the Commonwealth
and Empire, newly independent former colonies with an inheritance
of sterling pegs and reserves, and countries where Britain had troops
on the ground and where its oil companies had an extensive presence
(Iran and Kuwait). As Conan observed, "the overwhelming majority

of international transactions carried out using sterling are transactions in which a sterling area resident is either buyer or seller."[24]

London's Response

The question for the British authorities was whether to seek to maintain sterling's international position and tailor policy accordingly. The Bank of England, preoccupied by London's status as an international financial center, attached high priority to this objective. Other branches of government, by comparison, were more concerned with the strength of the economy generally.[25] Strengthening the economy generally meant maintaining controls to create room for domestic demand-management policies. In contrast, maximizing sterling's international role, as the Bank of England sought to do, implied eliminating restrictions on its use as quickly as possible.

The Articles of Agreement of the IMF, negotiated in 1944, required the United Kingdom, like other countries, to remove restrictions on transactions on current account within 5 years of the Fund's coming into operation. The 1946 Anglo-American loan required the country to do so even faster, by July 1, 1947. Much as Federal Reserve Bank of New York Governor Benjamin Strong had seen Britain's return to gold in 1925 as the key step toward restoring a global system of stable exchange rates conducive to the growth of U.S. exports, U.S. Treasury Secretary John Wesley Snyder and other members of the Truman Administration now saw the restoration of current account convertibility by the United Kingdom as a key step toward opening foreign markets, including those of the Sterling Area, to U.S. goods.

The restoration of current account convertibility on July 15, 1947, was a disaster. Two-thirds of the Anglo-American loan already had been used up prior to the event. As soon as the capital account was opened, the remaining balance quickly leaked out of the country. Controls were restored on August 20, and the Americans agreed that, henceforth, British policy makers could move more deliberately.

But efforts to encourage freer international use of sterling persisted. The 1949 devaluation against the dollar strengthened the competitiveness of British exports, allowing the resumption of cautious steps in the direction of current account convertibility. When Britain then negotiated clearing arrangements with the countries of Continental Europe in preparation for joining the European Payments Union in 1950, sterling could be used in settlement for transactions throughout the Union.[26] In this context Britain could continue to liberalize its exchange control apparatus at a measured pace.

The postwar adjustment difficulties of the British economy would have been ameliorated, some argued, had the government quickly moved to write down the sterling balances and devalued by a larger amount in 1949. But a larger devaluation could have fanned inflation, and 30 percent was already enough to anger the French. Alternatively, the challenges of external payments management might have been met by moving to a floating exchange rate, as contemplated in 1952, when the British balance of payments again came under pressure.[27] But the desire to maintain sterling's role as an international currency and London's status as an international financial center militated against this option. Writing down overseas liabilities would have done nothing to enhance the currency's attractions to foreign holders, to put an understated gloss on the point. Floating might have eroded sterling's unit of account function, or so policy makers feared.[28]

These international considerations were never the only factors shaping policy on the sterling balances. Repudiating obligations to the colonies was seen as reprehensible on political and moral grounds. Currency depreciation, its opponents warned, would give rise to a self-defeating wage-price spiral. Above and beyond these other factors, however, was the desire to preserve sterling's international position. Some critics of policy argued that Britain would have been better off pursuing these alternatives and, more generally, maintaining stricter capital and exchange controls, thereby creating additional room for maneuver to adjust fiscal policy so as to stabilize the economy and stimulate growth.[29] In the event, this was not to be.

In the second half of the 1940s, the independent members of the Sterling Area already had begun moving to limit their exposure to the currency. Egypt threatened to demand dollars in payment for supplies for British troops and in this way exacted agreement to liquidate some of its sterling balances.[30] Australia accumulated dollars whenever its reserves rose while liquidating sterling when they fell, quietly rebalancing its portfolio.[31] Britain's balance-of-payments problems encouraged these countries to redouble their efforts to diversify out of sterling. The surprise shock of the 1949 devaluation and the payments deficit associated with rearmament in 1951–1952 also contributed to this shift.

In 1956 the country's botched intervention in the Suez Canal Zone, in concert with France and Israel, fanned tensions with the United States and disrupted oil markets, forcing the government to seek a standby loan from the IMF—not the kind of action expected of the issuer of a stable reserve currency. Then 1957 saw yet another crisis, as speculators bet that the Deutschemark would be revalued against sterling, reflecting the strength of the German balance of payments, and the British authorities were forced to tighten exchange controls, banning U.K. residents from buying foreign securities—even from residents of other Sterling Area countries—without prior authorization.

All this made for a gradual decline in the share of global foreign exchange reserves held in the form of pounds. This trend is evident in Figure 7.1 in the previous chapter, which shows the share of foreign reserves held in sterling declining inexorably over the 1950s.

By the end of the 1950s, then, a growing share of sterling balances was held by Britain's colonies, current and former. This reassured British policy makers insofar as these holders were unlikely to abruptly liquidate their balances. But this tendency was also indicative of sterling's declining importance as an international currency. The British economy no longer possessed the health or the economic scale for its currency to rival (or even significantly supplement) the dollar.

The 1960s saw the continuation and, indeed, acceleration of this trend. One balance-of-payments crisis followed another. U.K. productivity growth remained slow by the standards of Continental Europe, making for chronic competitiveness problems. British governments insisted on running the economy under high pressure of demand, depressing interest rates in an effort to goose growth and keep unemployment in the low single digits. Inevitably, however, strong domestic demand spilled over into deteriorating balances of trade and payments, forcing the authorities to raise interest rates, taxes, or both in what were critically referred to as "stop-go policies." This reluctance to put on the brakes forced those authorities to resort to special expedients—a temporary 15 percent import surcharge, restrictions on travel abroad, and additional recourse to the IMF—and further undermined confidence in sterling.

The final nail in the coffin was the 1967 devaluation, which was the culmination of more than 2 years of balance-of-payments problems. Harold Wilson, the Labour prime minister who reluctantly presided over the devaluation, conveniently blamed the Arab-Israeli War (which led to closure of the Suez Canal) and British dock strikes (which also disrupted exports), but to no avail.[32] Devaluation against the dollar not only reduced the value of sterling reserves at a stroke but also signaled that the British authorities had higher priorities than the maintenance of sterling's international position. The consequences are clearly evident in Figure 7.1, which shows the accelerating decline in the share of sterling reserves in the global total after 1967.

Conclusion

The numerical dominance of the pound sterling in the foreign balances of central banks and governments after World War II is widely cited as evidence of the inertia and persistence that characterize international currency status. The United States already had overtaken Britain as the world's largest economy in the 1870s. America already had surpassed the United Kingdom as an exporter on the eve of World War I. Yet some 30 years later, the sterling reserves of central banks and governments still vastly exceeded their holdings of dollars.

In this chapter we have argued that sterling's position after World War II was more an artifact than a regularity. The accumulation of sterling balances by British allies was almost entirely a product of the war. It reflected the imperatives of that conflict rather than any optimizing economic calculus.

After 1945 these holders moved as quickly as possible to dispose of the bulk of their sterling balances. But as quickly as possible did not always mean quickly. The British government used capital controls, moral suasion and geopolitical influence to manage and, in practice, slow the adjustment.[33] It succeeded in preventing the abrupt liquidation of sterling balances and averting a collapse of the currency. The result was a gradual, ongoing decline in the share of foreign exchange reserves worldwide held in the form of pounds and serial devaluations in 1967 and the 1970s. If there was inertia in the reliance on sterling of central banks, governments and other holders, this reflected no intrinsic attractions of what had once been the leading international and reserve currency but instead the British authorities' success, however limited, in managing its decline.

9

The Rise and Fall of the Yen

The rapid growth of Japan—the "Japanese economic miracle," as it is commonly known—was one of the signal economic events of the third quarter of the twentieth century, much as the Chinese economic miracle was one of the key events of the fourth. By the early 1970s, two decades of near-double-digit growth had vaulted Japan into second place in the GDP league tables, after only the United States, and transformed it into the second largest exporter of goods and services.

Given Japan's economic status, the fact that the yen played virtually no international role was an anomaly—not unlike how the dollar, the currency of what was already the world's largest economy, played virtually no international role prior to 1914. As of 1970, no international trade, not even the trade of Japan itself, was invoiced in yen. Purchases and sales of yen on the foreign exchange market were de minimis. No foreign government or corporation issued yen-denominated bonds. Until 1975 the share of identified global foreign exchange reserves in yen was too small even to be distinguished by the IMF, the official arbiter of such matters, even though it was already some years since Japan had surpassed Germany as the second largest economy.[1]

Financial Repression with a Vengeance

As had been true of the United States a half century earlier, this anomaly reflected the underdevelopment, if not the absence, of the institutions needed to support an international currency. U.S. officials then had made a conscious decision not to create a central bank capable of providing liquidity to markets in internationally traded financial instruments. The National Banking Act that preceded the Federal Reserve era was designed to limit the cross-border operations of commercial banks. In practice this meant limiting both cross-state and transnational operations, which in turn circumscribed the international role of the dollar.

In the case of post–World War II Japan, limits on international financial transactions and domestic financial markets were even more severe. Aramaki (2014) describes the postwar Japanese financial system as organized around three principles. First was the principle of "general prohibition with liberalization for exceptions." Financial transactions were restricted except where expressly authorized. Funds were channeled so as to advance the authorities' developmental objectives through the maintenance of prohibitions on alternative uses.

Second was the principle of "foreign exchange concentration." All foreign exchange receipts were centrally controlled and allocated by the authorities. The objective of the policy was to husband foreign exchange for use in sourcing parts, machinery, and technology from other countries so as to support the rapid growth of the Japanese economy and its manufacturing sector in particular. The effect was to restrict the exchange of yen for other currencies even more severely than other financial transactions.

The third principle was reliance on the "authorized foreign exchange bank system." Only banks with express authorization were permitted to deal in foreign exchange. The banks in question were closely monitored and required to follow the government's instructions when managing foreign currency and capital account transactions. This reinforced principle number two.

These principles can be thought of as constituting a strategy of economic development by financial repression.[2] That strategy was successful, because Japan was in the catch-up phase of growth, emulating the modern mass-production methods of the economic leader, the United States. Starting out far behind America but having already industrialized significantly before World War II, postwar Japan possessed the capacity—in the form of education, experience, and bureaucratic competence—needed to catch up. Bureaucrats could simply look to U.S. technology, rendering them as well placed as anyone to make allocation decisions. Once the allocation problem was solved, growth depended only on capital formation, making a repressed financial system that could maximize the investment rate ideal.

Financial repression at the national level is only feasible if there are limits on international financial flows; otherwise, investors denied higher returns at home will seek more attractive opportunities abroad—hence the second and third principles of the postwar financial system. Only in 1960 was external current account convertibility permitted for nonresidents, and only in 1964 was full current account convertibility finally restored, consistent with the requirements of the IMF's Articles of Agreement. Capital controls limited outward foreign investment.[3] This, in combination with growing current account surpluses, prevented foreigners from accumulating yen balances. Given the currency's limited financial utility, it was used only to a very limited extent, if at all, in international trade— not just by foreign firms but, revealingly, by Japanese companies as well. As late as 1970, less than 1 percent of Japanese merchandise exports were invoiced in yen, and only 0.3 percent of imports were so invoiced.[4]

The 1970s then saw the tentative liberalization and opening of Japan's financial system. The rate of GDP growth came down with the end of catch-up and the first OPEC oil-price shock in the 1970s, suggesting that changes in financial strategy were now required. Japan experienced even higher inflation than did other advanced economies, as high as 30 percent in 1972. Tavlas and Ozeki (1991, 7) suggest that this experience with high inflation encouraged policy makers to contemplate the transition from a monetary policy implemented through credit controls and regulated interest rates to a "more conventional system with market determined interest rates geared toward achieving price stability." As in China today, this shift toward more market-determined interest rates was a prerequisite for thoroughgoing capital account liberalization and other steps to foster currency internationalization.

Meanwhile, the government's budget deficits of the post-oil-shock period led to the expansion of primary and secondary bond markets and pressure from the financial sector for improvements in their efficiency.[5] Improvements in efficiency, in this context, meant the development of repurchase agreements (repos) for government bonds (the so-called Gensaki market) and a market in certificates of deposit, these being the two most important instruments for supplying liquidity to a money market with market-determined interest rates. The development of this market was yet another necessary condition for currency internationalization.

In addition, some controls were relaxed, first on outward foreign direct investment and then on selected international financial transactions. The collapse of the Bretton Woods System encouraged Japanese policy makers to think twice about their country's reliance on the dollar in international transactions and to at least contemplate the possibility of encouraging more widespread use of their own currency in the cross-border transactions of Japanese banks and firms.[6]

But the shift toward a more open financial system was glacial. The authorities' position was one of studied neutrality, not active promotion. The Foreign Exchange Law of 1980 established the principle that all external transactions could be freely conducted, but it still allowed the government to use controls for balance-of-payments and exchange-rate-management purposes, as it did. Authorized foreign exchange banks and designated securities companies were permitted to undertake international transactions without advance approval by the government, but they were still actively monitored by the Ministry of Finance, which continued to limit the banks' open positions in foreign exchange and impose other prudential limits in the interest of systemic and, more controversially, exchange rate stability.[7]

The Political Economy of Financial Liberalization

Vested interests opposed more rapid financial liberalization and opening. Exporters feared that capital inflows would drive up the exchange rate and damage their competitiveness. Along with their governmental champions (mainly the Ministry of Finance), they feared that the increase in capital flows permitted by external liberalization would heighten exchange rate volatility, complicating the export trade. In effect, they favored the retention of capital controls as an instrument of exchange rate policy. Japanese banks, for their part, feared competition from foreign financial institutions.[8] While recognizing the need to move toward a more market-led financial system, government officials shared these private sector concerns. As Frankel (2011) puts it, whereas domestic politics was actively opposed to currency internationalization, government policy was at best neutral.

External pressure, notably from the United States, helped tip the balance.[9] The first half of the 1980s saw a sharp rise in the value of the dollar, mainly due to America's own policies: the high interest rates imposed in pursuit of disinflation by the Federal Reserve under Paul Volcker and the budget deficits of the first Reagan Administration.[10] These policies were associated with U.S. current account deficits and competitiveness problems in America's industrial heartland. Japan, the principal current-account-surplus country, was accused of compounding these problems by limiting capital inflows, barring its door to U.S. banks, and holding down the value of the yen.

To be sure, subsequent developments were not attributable to foreign pressure alone. There was also the 1985 report of the Council on Foreign Exchange and Other Transactions, an advisory body to the Ministry of Finance, which endorsed the principle of yen internationalization and advocated domestic financial liberalization as a means to this end. This was indicative of a body of technocratic opinion in Japan favoring liberalization and internationalization. But acknowledging this fact is not to dismiss entirely the role of foreign pressure.

The U.S. government campaign to force Japan to liberalize more quickly culminated in the Yen-Dollar Agreement of 1984. As foreseen in that agreement, the conversion of foreign currencies into yen was finally decontrolled. The Japanese government moved to establish new markets in short-term financial instruments (banker's acceptances in 1985, short-term bonds in 1986), to admit American securities companies to the Tokyo Stock Exchange, and to relax restrictions on the share of foreign securities that could be held by Japanese insurance and trust companies. In 1988 the Bank of Japan shifted its market interventions toward short-maturity securities, leading to a significant increase in the size and liquidity of treasury bill markets.[11] This in turn spurred the development of a repurchase market in treasury bills analogous to the previously established repo market for bonds.[12]

Each of these steps was a milestone of sorts. But the creation of markets in banker's acceptances and short-term treasury bills and subsequent steps to enhance their liquidity were particularly important from the point of view of currency internationalization, since banker's acceptances are used in financing merchandise imports and exports, while treasury bills are a preferred habitat of central banks holding foreign reserves.

The Rise of the Yen

These steps led to a noticeable increase in international use of the yen and, predictably, to talk that the currency might rival or even "dethrone" the dollar. The share of Japan's own exports invoiced in yen rose from less than 30 percent in 1980 to nearly 40 percent in 1991. Although this was an impressive increase, the level was still far lower than in countries like Germany, 80 percent of whose exports were invoiced in its own currency, and even in France and the United Kingdom, the majority of whose exports were also invoiced in their national currencies. The share of Japan's imports invoiced in yen was even lower, reflecting the importance of energy and raw materials in the national import basket and the fact that these commodities were and still are traditionally invoiced in dollars. But the yen share of imports rose as well, from less than 3 percent in 1980 to more than 15 percent in 1991.[13]

Meanwhile, the share of the yen in total identified foreign exchange reserves rose from 4.1 percent in 1982 to a bit more than 8 percent in 1991, encouraged by the greater availability of liquid yen-denominated assets but also by expectations that the currency would continue to appreciate, as it had for much of the 1970s and 1980s. The share of the yen in global gross foreign-exchange-market turnover rose to 27 percent in 1989, according to the Bank for International Settlements.[14] The share of the yen in global cross-border bank positions rose from negligible levels to just over 10 percent in the course of the 1980s.

Along none of these dimensions, admittedly, did the yen begin to approach the importance of the U.S. dollar as an international currency. But Japan's currency nonetheless appeared to be acquiring a consequential international role.

Why wasn't that role even more extensive? Fukuda and Cong (1994) point to the still-small size, compared to other countries, of markets in short-term debt instruments of a sort that are attractive to private and official foreign investors. In particular, the treasury bill market remained considerably smaller—only one-seventh the size—that of the United States. Not only were these markets small, but they were illiquid, as emphasized by Garber (1996). The Japanese government continued to levy a tax on transactions in government securities partly to raise revenue, partly to encourage buy-and-hold investors, and partly because it had always taxed them in the past. In addition, the Bank of Japan was reluctant to negotiate currency-swap arrangements and act as banker for foreign central banks. This would change in the wake of the Asian financial crisis of 1997–1998, with negotiation of the Chiang Mai Initiative and Bank of Japan swap agreements with other Asian central banks, but not yet.

In attempting to explain why the yen's role was not more expansive, Fukuda and Cong pointed also to the importance of large trading companies for Japanese exports, arguing that large companies have a comparative advantage in managing currency risk and are therefore willing to invoice their sales in dollars, even if their costs are denominated in local currency. They noted that raw materials continued to account for 40–50 percent of total imports, a higher share than in other advanced economies, and that prices on global commodity markets are quoted in dollars.

Sato (1999) pointed in addition to the structure of supply chains in East Asia. This was the period when a growing number of Japanese corporations established assembly operations elsewhere in the region while continuing to sell their final products predominantly into U.S. and European markets. Because their final products were exported to, inter alia, the United States and consequently priced in dollars, it made sense, the argument ran, for headquarters to similarly price components exported from Japan to its East Asian assembly platforms in dollars, thereby obtaining a kind of natural hedge.

Finally, Ogawa (2000) noted, rightly or wrongly, the roles of inertia and network effects—first-mover advantage, in other words—in accounting for the dollar's continued dominance of international financial markets and the subsidiary role of the yen.

The Fall of the Yen

The early 1990s, as it turned out, was the high-water mark of the yen's international role. With the onset of the Japanese financial crisis and "lost decade," the yen lost market share along virtually every dimension. The share of yen in total identified foreign exchange reserves worldwide fell from 8.3 percent in 1991 to 7.3 percent in 1993, 6.2 percent in 1995 and just 4.8 percent in 1997. The currency's share of global foreign-exchange-market turnover declined after 1989. Its share of identified global foreign exchange reserves peaked in 1991 before heading steadily downward. The share of Japanese exports invoiced in yen fell from 40 percent to barely 30 percent over the course of the 1990s. The number of foreign companies listed on the Tokyo Stock Exchange fell from 127 in 1991 to a mere 38 in 2001.[15]

The explanation for this retreat was, as noted, first the banking crisis, then the lost decade, and finally Japan's failure to keep pace with other economies after the turn of the century. Japanese banks lost their position in global top-ten rankings. The number of foreign companies listed on the Tokyo Stock Exchange slid from 127 in 1991 to only 11 in 2012. Japan's share of global GDP fell from 18 percent in 1994 (as the onset of the lost decade is typically dated) to 8 percent in 2011. Its share of global exports fell from 10 percent in 1986 to 5 percent in 2010. The dependence of other Asian countries on trade with Japan declined continuously. To be sure, some of these trends were heavily influenced by developments in other countries, first and foremost China. But they also reflected Japan's own failure to right the economic and financial ship.

The causes of the banking and financial crisis and then the lost decade are too complex to be fully analyzed here. But it is relevant to ask whether they were linked to efforts to foster currency internationalization directly or indirectly.

The argument runs as follows. The creation of more liquid bond and bill markets, which was part of the internationalization push, allowed big Japanese corporations to utilize securities markets to fund their operations. The banks, having lost many of their big corporate customers, out of necessity turned to other lines of business. In particular, they resorted to lending to customers outside the manufacturing sector against equity and real estate collateral. Risk taking was encouraged by the expectation that banks developing problems would be bailed out by the Ministry of Finance, since they had always been bailed out in the past. Given a regulatory system geared toward channeling funds into particular uses and not toward preventing excesses, prudential supervision and regulation did little to restrain this behavior. This is a simple explanation for the stock market and real estate bubbles that culminated in a crash and then a wave of nonperforming loans, one in which currency internationalization ambitions played at least a subsidiary role.[16]

But if it is possible to link efforts to foster currency internationalization with the banking crisis, the same is not true of the economic and financial policy decisions that transformed the banking crisis into a deflationary crisis and a lost decade.[17] These started with the failure to close down bad banks and require others to more quickly raise additional capital. This failure reflected the continuing influence of a powerful bank lobby and the reluctance of policy makers to acknowledge that Japan was now overbanked.[18]

Next was the failure of the authorities to ease monetary and fiscal policies more forcefully in 1992–1993 to offset the impact of collapsing asset prices on spending and bank balance sheets. Here the authorities, their views shaped by past experience, continued to anticipate the spontaneous recovery of the economy, even when bank distress and collapsing asset prices continued to drag it down. When, in the mid-1990s, they finally acknowledged that policy action was required to initiate recovery, the authorities relied excessively on monetary policy, the Ministry of Finance remaining focused on the budget deficit and hesitant to make active use of fiscal policy. Supplementary budgets, such as they were, were on-again, off-again.

But monetary policy was constrained by the zero lower bound on interest rates, resulting in too little macroeconomic policy support for the resumption of growth. And among the side-effects of this mix of loose monetary and tight fiscal policies was a weak yen, which did not encourage foreign central banks to diversify their reserve portfolios in the direction of yen-denominated assets.

If the authorities did not manage to address Japan's deflation and depression challenges, then at least they could divert attention from them by focusing on structural issues and objectives, including the yen's international role. The economic stagnation of the 1990s had the side effect of weakening the power of vested financial interests, in turn allowing successive governments to commit to comprehensive deregulation of financial markets.[19] In 1996 the Hashimoto government announced plans for comprehensive financial liberalization, leading to the financial "Big Bang" of 1998. Cross-entry regulations were relaxed with the goal of promoting competition among different types of previously specialized financial institutions. Cross-border financial transactions were completely liberalized through the final removal of prior approval and notification requirements, and authorized-foreign-exchange-bank and designated-securities-company status were finally abolished.

The Asian financial crisis of 1997–1998 then created another opportunity for Japanese policy makers to advance their international ambitions. Vice Minister of Finance Eisuke Sakakibara ("Mr. Yen") proposed the creation of an Asian Monetary Fund, under which countries in the region, with Japanese leadership, would provide emergency loans to neighbors in need, where a substantial fraction of these loans would presumably be denominated in yen. The Council on Foreign Exchange and Other Transactions, the same advisory body that endorsed yen internationalization in 1985, published a new report in 1999, "Internationalization of the Yen for the Twenty-First Century," arguing that the yen should play a role in Asia comparable to those of the dollar and the euro in the Western Hemisphere and "Greater Europe," respectively (Ministry of Finance 1999). Following issuance of this report, the government took a number of additional steps to expand the market for Japanese government bonds and bills and improve the usability of the yen (Subacchi 2013).

These initiatives were intended to elevate the status of Tokyo as an international financial center. In practice, they did have the effect of encouraging foreign financial firms to establish subsidiaries in Japan. Their presence led to a decline in the cost of transacting in yen, as reflected in the narrowing of bid-ask spreads and narrowing differentials between the spreads quoted by Japanese and non-Japanese financial institutions.[20] As a result, foreign participation on the Japanese stock market increased.

But the share of global foreign exchange reserves denominated in yen continued to fall. Tokyo continued to lag behind not just New York and London but now also other Asian financial centers, such as Hong Kong and Singapore, on the standard rankings. Foreign exchange market turnover in yen was barely a quarter of that in dollars in 2013, and it lagged turnover in the euro as well.

Nor did the ambition to transform the yen into the leading international and reserve currency for Asia bear fruit. In the wake of the Asian financial crisis of 1997–1998, the effort to create a yen-based, Tokyo-led Asian Monetary Fund foundered on opposition from the United States, China and the IMF.[21] When Asian countries moved in 2000 to create a regional safety net (the Chiang Mai Initiative), the weights attached to the yen and the Chinese renminbi were carefully calibrated to match each other. There was no special status for the yen, in Asia or elsewhere, analogous to that accorded the dollar at Bretton Woods in 1944. Although the Bank of Japan then proceeded to negotiate a series of bilateral swap agreements under the umbrella of the Chiang Mai Initiative, these were never activated in the course of the subsequent decade, not even during the global crisis of 2008–2009. The yen continued to punch below its weight even in Asia, when its share of trade invoicing and international reserves and its weight in its neighbors' exchange rate baskets is compared with Japan's share of trade and financial transactions in the region.

Conclusion

That Japan did not succeed in elevating the yen to the rank of a first-tier international currency reflects not so much the dollar's first-mover advantage or lack of room in the international monetary system for more than one consequential international currency as it does the country's history and home-grown problems. That history resulted in a late start in internationalizing the yen, not unlike the situation of the United States and the dollar at the turn of the twentieth century. It also bequeathed a set of institutions, attitudes, and policies that served Japan well during the high-growth era, but which Japanese officialdom found difficult to jettison subsequently. Most obviously, Japan was late to liberalize its financial markets and, specifically, foreigners' access to them.

No sooner did it finally begin doing so than the country succumbed to a crisis. Ultimately that crisis, extending over more than a decade, finally forced officials to abandon earlier policies, to complement a market-led system with strong supervision and regulation, and to commit to currency internationalization. By then, however, the high-growth period was over, and other potentially more attractive candidates for international currency status, such as the Chinese renminbi, had arrived on the scene.

Thus, Japan's experience serves as a cautionary tale, not just for Japan itself but also for China and other aspiring reserve-currency countries.

10

The Euro as Second in Command

At its birth in 1999, the euro, as the successor to 11 European currencies (including some, like the Deutschemark, that already played significant international roles), immediately became the second-most important international currency after only the U.S. dollar. Initially the euro's position as an international currency developed positively. This was true of its use as a form in which to hold international reserves, its share in global foreign exchange market turnover, as a vehicle in which to denominate international bonds, as a unit in which to invoice and settle merchandise transactions, and as an anchor currency for the exchange rates of other countries. In all these respects, the euro took on a more important role, quantitatively and qualitatively, than the Deutschemark in the pre-1999 period. In all of them other than share of foreign exchange market turnover, it took on a more important role than previously assumed by the so-called legacy currencies as a group.[1] (Foreign exchange market turnover was different, because creation of the single currency necessarily eliminated transactions in the former, separate currencies of what were now euro area members.) None of this is to deny that the dollar remained the international currency primus inter pares. That investors rushed to the safety and liquidity of the greenback in 2008 following the failure of Lehman Brothers—a *U.S.* investment bank—epitomizes the point.[2]

But then, with the outbreak of the euro area sovereign debt crisis in 2009, the gap in international usage relative to the dollar widened further. [3] As the heretofore orderly convergence of spreads on sovereign bonds issued by different euro area countries was reversed, concerns developed over the liquidity of European financial markets.[4] With the euro's post-2014 depreciation against the dollar, its share in global foreign exchange turnover and identified foreign exchange reserves both declined.

Yet despite the global financial crisis and then the euro area's sovereign debt crisis, and the setbacks they entailed, the euro remains the second most important international currency even today, behind only the dollar. Although its use has a strong regional dimension—it is used more widely in Europe's neighborhood than globally—the rise of the euro provides more evidence that international currency status is no longer a natural monopoly (if it ever was). The euro's position is yet another indication that multiple international currencies can coexist.

Great Expectations

The immediate motivation for establishing the euro was not, of course, so much to create a rival to the dollar as to meet the European Union's own internal needs. [5] The euro was intended to help complete the Single European Market agreed to in the 1980s and to secure its four freedoms: free movement of goods, services, labor, and capital. Volatile fluctuations between separate national currencies might lead to capricious changes in national competitive positions and disrupt transactions in the single market, but holding their exchange rates stable might be impossible without controls on capital flows—controls that were incompatible with the Single Market. Such were the perceived lessons of the 1992 European currency crisis.[6] A single currency was the obvious solution to this dilemma. But, in addition, some European leaders (French President François

Mitterrand, for example) saw the possibility of creating a potential rival, or at least supplement, to the dollar as an important ancillary benefit of a single European currency.[7]

Once that single currency came into existence, it was quickly adopted in transactions between the euro area and other economies and, in addition, in cross-border transactions not involving the euro area directly. Beneath this development lay an obvious economic logic. The euro area and the United States were roughly equal in economic size, and the two accounted for broadly comparable shares of global merchandise trade.[8] Some observers hailed the euro as "the most important development in the international monetary system since the adoption of flexible exchange rates in the early 1970s" and predicted that the dollar would now have "its first real competitor since it surpassed the pound sterling as the world's dominant currency during the interwar period."[9]

Not everyone subscribed to this optimistic forecast, however. Skeptics cautioned that international currency status is predicated on more than just economic size and the magnitude of trade connections. They pointed to the incumbency advantage of the dollar and to institutional factors, such as the jurisdictional separation between monetary policy (assigned to the European Central Bank) and prudential regulation (still the responsibility of national authorities under the provisions of the Maastricht Treaty, the founding document of the euro area).[10] They questioned whether the European Central Bank (ECB) would be an active lender and liquidity provider of last resort, backstopping markets in debt securities so as to render them attractive to international investors.

To the extent that a key determinant of international use of the euro would be the evolution of transaction costs in foreign exchange and securities markets, much would hinge, these skeptics cautioned, on the success of euro area member states in integrating their national capital markets, a process whose outcome remained uncertain.[11] Still others warned that lack of real economic convergence (very different levels of income and economic structures in different euro area member states), together with historically rooted differences in economic policy preferences among these nations, might create tensions that would weigh on the new European currency's international standing.[12]

The ECB, the institution most immediately tasked with managing the euro, did not take a side in this debate. Wim Duisenberg, the ECB's founding president, noted in his inaugural speech only that "the Eurosystem [would] accept the international role of the euro as it develops as a result of market forces. To the extent that the Eurosystem is successful in meeting its mandate and maintaining price stability, it will also automatically foster the use of the euro as an international currency." This signaled that while the ECB would not pursue the internationalization of the euro as a formal policy goal, neither would it hinder that development.[13]

This institutional neutrality reflected a compromise between those who were open to promoting the euro area's role in global monetary and financial affairs and others who worried about the downside of currency internationalization. The latter view was in turn informed by Germany's experience during and immediately following the collapse of the Bretton Woods System, when the country experienced large capital inflows. In this earlier era the German authorities worried that Deutschemark internationalization might complicate the Bundesbank's efforts to exercise monetary and inflation control. They therefore introduced controls to stem capital inflows, a policy that in turn worked to limit use of the Deutschemark by residents of other countries, as described in Chapter 7.[14]

Another basis for the ECB's position of studied neutrality was the difficulty of quantifying the benefits and costs of currency internationalization. As the central bank put it, "the list of potential benefits and costs for euro area residents is for the time being of a rather speculative, forward-looking nature. Many benefits are difficult to measure with precision."[15] Perhaps the most obvious potential benefit was seigniorage (i.e., interest-free loans from nonresidents holding euros). The single currency might provide the euro area with an "exorbitant privilege" analogous to that enjoyed by the United States—namely, the ability to place debt with nonresidents at lower interest rates and to invest the proceeds in higher-yielding foreign assets.

But efforts to quantify those seigniorage benefits universally led to the conclusion that they were far from large. One study conducted a few years after the launch of the euro found that in practice, the main component of this seigniorage income (the yield differential) was actually quite small.[16] If anything, the environment of low interest rates prevailing since the global financial crisis has made them smaller still.

Be this as it may, historical experience, notably that of Great Britain and the United States in the nineteenth and twentieth centuries, suggested that the extent of currency internationalization—and hence the magnitude of any benefits accruing to the issuer—would depend to a significant degree on the depth and liquidity of that issuer's financial markets. Among the expectations of the euro's champions was that the new currency would encourage the development of new financial market segments denominated in euros. In line with these expectations, the market for euro-denominated corporate bonds developed quickly in the single currency's initial years, as European companies capitalized on the elimination of exchange risk to tap what was now a continent-wide security market free of exchange risk. Before long, non-euro area companies joined them as active issuers of euro-denominated bonds, contributing further to financial market depth and liquidity.

A second potential benefit of euro internationalization was thus lower borrowing costs for European banks and firms. But any such benefits again had to be balanced against the potential costs. Chief among these was the traditional German concern that an increase in the euro's international use could make monetary control more difficult. It could make monetary developments harder to interpret insofar as shifts in nonresidents' demands for euros could impact exchange rates and money aggregates. These concerns suggested that the ECB and other euro area authorities should proceed cautiously in promoting international adoption of the euro. The revolution in international monetary relations predicted by the single currency's most enthusiastic champions might therefore take a considerable period of time to materialize.

The Record So Far

And that, not surprisingly, is how events transpired. As a result, the dollar unquestionably remains the leading international currency, accounting for half or more of international transactions, depending on the criterion (Figure 10.1). But the euro is the undisputed second, accounting for roughly a quarter of these same transactions. Notwithstanding the outbreak of the euro area sovereign debt crisis, it remains far ahead of all other units, including the Chinese renminbi, which are sometimes spoken of in the same breath.[17]

Strong support for the euro's international standing is found in developments in international debt securities markets, as already noted. The share of the euro in the value of outstanding international debt securities peaked at nearly 42 percent in 2007, up from 27 percent for its earlier legacy currencies (Table 10.1). The market depth

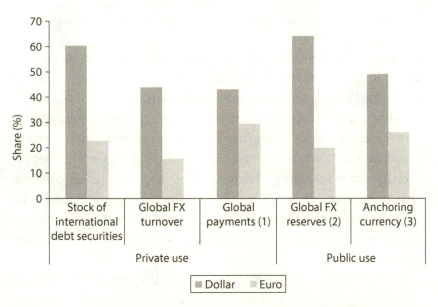

FIGURE 10.1. Comparison of the Dollar and the Euro (percentage of total unless otherwise noted).
Source: Data from Bank for International Settlements, European Central Bank, International Monetary Fund, and national sources.
Note: Data as of 2015 (or latest available). (1)According to SWIFT. (2) According to the IMF COFER data base. (3) Number of economies using either the dollar or the euro as their de facto anchor according to an IMF classification.

TABLE 10.1. Selected Indicators of the International Use of the Euro, 1998–2015 (Share of the euro at market exchange rates as a percentage)

	1998	2001	2007	2015
Global holdings of foreign exchange[1]	14.5	19.2	26.1	19.9
Global foreign exchange turnover[2]	46.7	37.6	37.0	31.3
Stock of international debt securities ("narrow" measure)[3]	19.6	23.0	32.2	22.7
Stock of international debt securities ("broad" measure)[4]	27.3	24.8	41.5	32.8

Sources: European Central Bank (1999), Detken and Hartman (2002), and Mehl (2015).
Notes: BIS, Bank for International Settlements; DEM, Deutschemark; ECU, European Currency Unit; FRF, French franc; NLG, Dutch guilder.
[1]Sum of holdings in DEM, FRF, NLG, and ECU, not net of intra-euro area holdings. Data for 1998 not revised after changes to the International Monetary Fund methodology in 2005.
[2]Data for 1998 not net of intra-euro legacy currency turnover. Data for 2015 refer to April 2016.
[3]Bonds and money market security issues in foreign markets based on the residence principle, including home currency issuance and excluding intra-euro area issuance. Data for 1998 not revised after changes to BIS methodology in 2012.
[4]Bonds and money market security issues in foreign markets based on the residence principle, excluding home currency and intra-euro area issuance. Data for 1998 not revised after changes to BIS methodology in 2012.

and liquidity resulting from the creation of a large single, integrated market in euro-denominated securities reduced the costs of underwriting and issuing euro-denominated bonds.[18]

Following the eruption of the euro sovereign debt crisis in 2009, these same measures of market liquidity then went into reverse. In addition, sharp interest rate cuts by the U.S. Federal Reserve, taken in response to the global financial crisis, made dollar issuance more attractive. These events led to sharply higher issuance of dollar-denominated securities by emerging market economies in particular, resulting in a decline in the share of international debt securities denominated in euros.

The introduction of an asset purchase program by the ECB in 2015 then brought about an increase in euro-denominated issuance. Seeking to take advantage of historically low interest rates in the euro area, internationally active corporations, including many headquartered in the United States, became active issuers of euro-denominated bonds, the proceeds of which they swapped back into dollars. Emerging markets also took advantage of low financing costs

in the euro area, with the government of Mexico, for example, issuing a euro-denominated bond with a maturity of no less than a
century in the spring of 2015.

In the foreign exchange market, by comparison, change has been
less rapid, even glacial. The share of the dollar in foreign exchange
market turnover remained at 80–85 percent of the global total over
the euro's first 15 years.[19] In other words, only 10–15 percent of foreign exchange trades do not involve the dollar on one side of the
transaction. The share of the countries in question actually fell with
the advent of the single currency, since this eliminated trades between the earlier legacy currencies, as already noted. Where trading
in euro legacy currencies had accounted for half of global foreign
exchange turnover in 1998, by 2016 this share had fallen to less than
one third.

To be sure, these summary statistics, based on a survey of
1 month of trading undertaken by the Bank for International Settlement (BIS) every 3 years, are not without potential biases. In 1998
arbitrage trading between the currencies of the future members of
the euro area (bets that interest rates in other euro area members
would converge to the lower levels prevailing in Germany) was
widespread. This resulted in an unusually high level of trading in
the currencies in question.[20] Similarly, in April 2016, when the BIS
again conducted its triennial survey, transactions in sterling were
unusually high, because investors were betting on the outcome of
the referendum on British exit from the European Union ("Brexit"),
which took place on June 23, 2016. Again, the result might have been
to understate the relative importance of trading in the euro. As a
result, whether there actually has been a trend decline in the share
of the euro in global foreign exchange turnover remains somewhat
uncertain.

Turning to currency use by governments and central banks, the
euro accounted for about 20 percent of global foreign exchange
reserves at the end of 2015, compared to 19 percent in 2001 and
15 percent for its legacy currencies in 1998. The share of the euro
then peaked prior to the outbreak of the European sovereign debt
crisis in 2009 at a bit less than 28 percent. However, one should

not rush to the judgment that the subsequent decline in the share of euro reserves is indicative, necessarily, of mistrust on the part of official holders of the euro's role as a store of value. In large part this declining share reflects valuation effects, insofar as the euro depreciated by about 25 percent against the dollar in the 6 years to 2015.[21] It reflects changes in reporting practice, since China first disclosed to the IMF the composition of a fraction of its foreign exchange reserve holdings, which are known to be heavily dollar dominated, in the second half of 2015.

The euro also remains less important than the dollar, numerically, as an anchor for the currencies of additional countries. Again, the evidence on this question should be interpreted cautiously. The number of currencies pegged to the euro will be a declining function of the number of countries joining the monetary union, other things being equal, and additional countries continue to join. Since their accession to the EU in 2004, seven new member states that previously limited the movement of their national currencies against the euro (that used the euro as an anchor) adopted the single currency.[22] As of 2015, some 50 other countries and territorial communities still use the euro as a reference currency for exchange rate management, a number broadly comparable with that prevailing by the time the euro was established. Many of the countries in question neighbor the euro area, as in the case of countries in Central and Eastern Europe. Others have long-standing institutional links to one of the euro area members, such as the western and central African countries of the former French franc zone. This again underscores the regional and political dimensions of the euro's international role.

Conclusion

The euro crisis exposed weaknesses in the governance of Europe's monetary union. The rules of the game, such as they were, did not prevent the emergence of economic imbalances and stability risks. Policy responses did not mitigate the concerns of market participants about bank solvency and sovereign debt sustainability.

The crisis also revealed the extent to which financial integration in the euro area was incomplete. Cross-border financial links were heavily dominated by short-term interbank debt rather than equity or direct cross-border lending to firms and households. And that short-term interbank debt was prone to evaporate quickly. Finally, the crisis exposed weaknesses in the euro area's fiscal framework, the provisions of which had not been adequately enforced in the preceding period.[23]

Insofar as international use of a currency rests fundamentally on two ingredients, confidence and deep and liquid financial markets, it is unsurprising that the crisis weighed on the euro's international standing. But once policy measures were taken at the European and national levels to restore stability, there were signs of a stabilization in some aspects of the international use of the currency.[24] In particular, the share of the euro in global official holdings of foreign exchange reserves stabilized around 20 percent. But in other dimensions the euro continued to lose some ground.

In addition to implementing immediate policy measures, European leaders committed to pursuing a set of further initiatives designed to complete their economic and monetary union. These initiatives were outlined in the 2015 report of the EU's "Five Presidents" (the presidents of the EU, the European Commission, the European Parliament, the Eurogroup, and the European Central Bank).[25] While the immediate aim was to address Europe's economic and political challenges (as had been the case of the decision to go ahead with the single currency in the 1990s, as noted earlier in the chapter), these initiatives, if enacted, would have important implications for the euro's international status as well. "Capital markets union" (more liquid and deeply integrated capital markets that would channel funds to small and medium-sized enterprises and finance infrastructure projects) coupled with banking union (the creation of a single-supervisor, single-resolution mechanism and a European deposit insurance scheme) would lay the groundwork for a genuine financial union. The latter would foster the euro's international role by enhancing the depth, stability, and liquidity of euro area banking and capital markets alike.

Looking further ahead, more ambitious initiatives could further buttress the euro's international standing. These include a common macroeconomic stabilization function to deal with asymmetric shocks that are not easily managed at the national level, unified external representation of the euro area in international financial institutions like the IMF (to remedy a situation where the euro area's fragmented voice means that it punches below its economic weight), and a euro area treasury.

A stronger international role for the euro in the years ahead would therefore be an indicator not only of the confidence of the rest of the world in the single currency, but also of the success of Europe in completing its monetary union and in containing political risks in euro area countries. Whether and how this will happen, only time will tell.

11

Prospects for the Renminbi

China's renminbi is widely regarded as a potential candidate to supplement the dollar in the international sphere. One can imagine rapid adoption of the renminbi as an international unit of account, means of payment, and store of value, to the point where it quickly comes to be used widely in cross-border transactions, similarly to the rapid adoption of the dollar between 1914 and 1924. But one can also imagine Beijing's efforts to internationalize the renminbi coming to grief as in the case of Japan and the yen. Specifically, one can imagine them being derailed by a sharp economic slowdown and financial instability compounded by the very same policy measures designed to encourage wider international use of the currency.

But a third scenario is possible. Chinese policy makers could cautiously and deliberately implement, over an extended period, reforms that pave the way for a slow but sustained increase in the use of renminbi for cross-border transactions. There will then be no "big bang" like with dollar internationalization between 1914 and 1924. But neither will the process of currency internationalization go into reverse, as happened with the yen between 1984 and 1994.

For the renminbi to be successfully internationalized, China will have to undertake more far-reaching policy reforms than did

America in 1914 or Japan in 1984. Those extensive reforms will not be completed overnight. Chinese policy makers understand that this process will take a considerable period. But it is important that they remain committed to seeing these challenges through.

The Conventional Narrative

The conventional narrative starts by pointing to the large and rapidly rising value of China's cross-border transactions and to the growing use of its currency in that connection. China is already the world's largest exporting nation, due to the very rapid growth of its trade over the past decade. China is the single largest trade partner for upward of 75 countries.[1] This creates an opening for Chinese officials seeking to promote cross-border use of their currency, who can use moral suasion and other means to encourage Chinese enterprises to finance and settle their transactions in renminbi. In 2015 fully 25 percent of China's trade was settled in the country's own currency.[2] According to the Society for Worldwide Interbank Financial Telecommunication, the renminbi has now surpassed the euro as the second-most widely used currency in global trade finance.[3] These figures are doubly impressive, given that it was only in 2009 that select Chinese companies were first authorized to settle trade-related transactions with counterparties in Hong Kong, Macau and the Association of South East Asian Nations (ASEAN) in renminbi, and only in 2010 that they were permitted to so settle their transactions with the rest of the world.[4]

The presumption is that wider use of the renminbi in trade-related transactions will lead to the currency's wider use in cross-border investment and international financial transactions generally, as in the case of the dollar in the 1920s. Exporters to China with renminbi exposure will hedge by purchasing currency swaps and futures on the foreign-exchange-derivatives markets. Corporations, private financial institutions, and central banks with renminbi-denominated receipts will invest them on Chinese financial markets. The renminbi will become a consequential currency in due course, not only for

trade finance and settlement but also for cross-border financial transactions generally.

None of this has happened yet. For the time being, the renminbi
plays a smaller role in international financial markets than in merchandise trade. In overall transactions related to not just trade but
also finance, the currency accounted for just 2 percent of global
payments in September 2014 according to SWIFT (2015), far behind
not only the dollar but also the euro, sterling and the yen. The renminbi is the currency of denomination for less than 1 percent of international bonds, notwithstanding a few high-profile international
issues, such as placement of RMB 3 billion of international bonds
by the British government.[5] Although as many as 50 central banks
are reported to have added the currency to their reserve portfolios,
it still accounts for only about 1 percent of global foreign exchange
reserves.[6] The renminbi is the currency of denomination of only a
small fraction of international bank liabilities, no more than $500
billion in absolute amount.[7] To put this in perspective, recall that the
dollar accounts for upward of $7 trillion of bank liabilities.

Similarly, whereas the dollar accounts for more than 85 percent of
turnover on global foreign exchange markets, the renminbi accounts
for barely 2 percent.[8] Bid-ask spreads on purchases and sales of renminbi for dollars are wider than spreads on purchases and sales of
dollars for sterling, euros, yen, and the Indonesian rupiah.[9] Compared
to sterling and the euro, the two currencies other than the dollar that
are traded most widely, renminbi spreads are four times as large.

Thus, while China has made substantial progress in encouraging
importers and exporters of commodities and merchandise to invoice
and settle their transactions in renminbi, it still faces a long march
on the financial front.

Chinese policy makers are seeking to address these issues with
two sets of initiatives. First, they are liberalizing the access of nonresidents to Chinese financial markets and the access of residents
to markets offshore. This process dates from 2002, when Qualified
Foreign Institutional Investors, initially Hong Kong–based subsidiaries of mainland asset managers, were first permitted to buy and

sell a limited range of renminbi-denominated securities in China. In 2004, residents of Hong Kong and Macau were authorized to open renminbi-denominated deposit accounts. The year 2006 saw the creation of a Qualified Domestic Institutional Investor Program permitting Chinese asset managers to sell overseas stock and bond funds to local investors. The first renminbi-denominated bonds issued in Hong Kong, known as dim sum bonds, were floated in 2007. In 2010 offshore banks involved in cross-border trade settlement were allowed to invest renminbi funds in the Chinese interbank bond market, where most Chinese bonds are traded. Since then, Qualified Foreign Institutional Investor and Qualified Domestic Institutional Investor quotas have been increased, and the range of assets that can be purchased has been expanded. In 2014 China opened a link between the Hong Kong and Shanghai stock markets (the Shanghai–Hong Kong Stock Connect), giving Chinese savers a channel through which to invest in overseas stocks and Hong Kong residents greater scope for investing in Shanghai. In 2015 foreign central banks were allowed to trade on China's onshore foreign exchange market.

This list provides a clear sense of the gradual nature of Chinese capital account liberalization. But it is also a reminder that the country has a long way to go before it has a fully open capital account. That said, this history leaves no question that the authorities are committed to moving, slowly but surely, in the direction of further liberalization.

Second, Chinese officials are negotiating a network of central bank currency swap lines. They are working with foreign regulators to designate Chinese financial institutions as official clearing banks for foreign financial centers. These measures are intended to encourage regulators in other countries to permit the financial institutions under their aegis to engage in a range of renminbi-related transactions. Regulators in Europe and other advanced economies allow banks in their jurisdictions to fund themselves in (that is to say, to borrow) dollars, because if their dollar funding unexpectedly dries up, the authorities can obtain dollars from the Federal Reserve via its standing swap arrangements with foreign central banks. This enables them to act as lenders of last resort in dollars to local financial institutions.

People's Bank of China swap lines with foreign central banks similarly encourage foreign regulators to permit their banks to borrow and lend renminbi. The People's Bank has negotiated 29 bilateral swap agreements with foreign central banks at last count.[10] Eleven of these are with Asian countries, ten are with European countries, and eight with countries in other regions, indicative of the renminbi's global reach. The largest single swap line is with the European Central Bank, befitting the fact that China is the euro area's third largest export market after the United States and the United Kingdom.

Designating an official clearing bank enables financial institutions in a foreign financial center to trade renminbi for local currency directly without having to go through the dollar—without having to first exchange renminbi for dollars and then trade those dollars for local currency. Paying only one bid-ask spread, rather than two, makes the currency more attractive. For the decade ending in October 2013, only Hong Kong had an official offshore renminbi clearing bank. Since then more than a dozen official clearing banks have been designated for financial centers, from Seoul and Qatar to London and New York.

In addition to its bilateral swaps, China has negotiated a set of multilateral swap arrangements with a range of regional partners. Since 2000 it has offered to loan reserves, in dollars or renminbi, to the ASEAN countries, Japan and South Korea (all of which are members of the ASEAN+3 grouping) through the Chiang Mai Initiative Multilateralization (CMIM). China's CMIM swaps with Japan, Korea, and the Philippines are all specified in the partners' local currencies.[11]

China's foreign investment projects are a final channel through which payment can be made in renminbi and foreigners can acquire the currency. China is now one of the largest foreign direct investing countries in the world. It has agreed to the creation of a BRICS Bank, through which members will lend for development projects, where much of that money will presumably be denominated in the currency of the lender—and China will be the most important lender.[12] Beijing has advanced a Silk Road Initiative to promote trade and economic integration in Central Asia, again to be implemented through a program of long-term foreign investment.[13] One school of thought about international currency status argues that strategic considerations, and specifically diplomatic and military leverage, are as important (or even more important) than purely pecuniary motives in influencing the decision of other countries to use a foreign currency in cross-border transactions.[14] If so, the Silk Road Initiative, China's aircraft carrier program, and the country's island-building strategy in the South China Sea all work in this direction.

These, in the conventional narrative, are the elements of a coherent, multi-prong strategy to encourage wider cross-border use of the renminbi.

Out of Their Depth

Encouraging trade settlements in renminbi, relaxing capital controls, and negotiating central bank swap lines are one thing, but building deep and liquid financial markets is another matter. A key condition for a currency to be widely used internationally is the existence of deep and liquid markets in securities denominated in that unit. The United States in 1914 lacked a lender of last resort, a liquid acceptance market, and commercial banks with international reach. But it had more than a century of financial development under its belt, 50 years under the National Banking System alone. In China, in contrast, development of a market-based financial system did not really get under way until the twenty-first century. There are few things international investors value more than market liquidity. For China, providing such liquidity will be a challenge.

To be sure, China has the fourth-largest financial system in the world, behind only those of the United States, the euro area, and Japan.[15] But this reflects little more than the country's singular size. When scaled by GDP, its financial depth lags not just the advanced countries but also emerging markets like Brazil, Korea, Malaysia, Taiwan, and Thailand. Richer countries (as measured by income per capita) tend to have deeper and better-developed financial markets, and Brazil, Korea, Malaysia, and Thailand, not to mention the advanced economies, all remain richer than China for the time being. When bond and equity market capitalization is arrayed against Asian countries' per capita incomes, China is not a particularly prominent outlier in either the positive or negative direction (see Figures 11.1 and 11.2). But its financial market capitalization as a share of GDP is relatively low, because its per capita income is relatively low. Information on corporate and government finances is limited, so only the most reputable and creditworthy enterprises and governments are able to access the bond market. In the Chinese case, this means state-owned enterprises, banks, and local governments whose issuance is effectively guaranteed by the central authorities.

What is true of market capitalization is also true of turnover on bond markets, a straightforward measure of liquidity. Here China compares unfavorably even after adjusting for per capita GDP. Most Chinese bonds are held by banks. Since banks are buy-and-hold investors, transactions on Chinese bond markets are relatively limited.

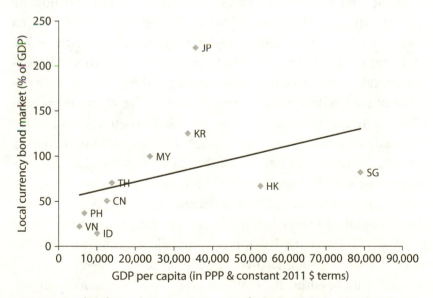

FIGURE 11.1. Bond Markets and GDP per Capita at Purchasing Power Parity, 2014. Source: Asian Development Bank, International Monetary Fund, and World Bank.
Note: CN, China; HK, Hong Kong; ID, Indonesia; JP, Japan; KR, Korea; MY, Malaysia; PH, Philippines; SG, Singapore; TH, Thailand; VN, Vietnam.

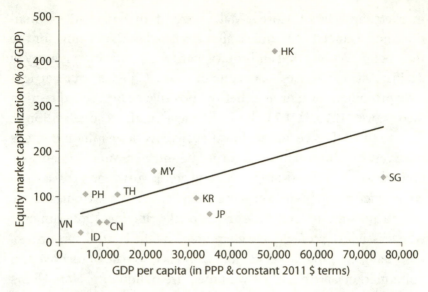

FIGURE 11.2. Equity Market Capitalization and GDP per Capita at Purchasing Power Parity, 2012. Source: World Bank.
Note: CN, China; HK, Hong Kong; ID, Indonesia; JP, Japan; KR, Korea; MY, Malaysia; PH, Philippines; SG, Singapore; TH, Thailand; VN, Vietnam.

In the case of equity markets, in contrast, turnover is not the problem. In mid-2015 combined turnover in Shanghai and Shenzhen was as high as $400 billion a day, half again as high as the value of shares traded in the United States, a country with stock market capitalization more than twice as large. The problem, from the point of view of international investors, lies elsewhere, namely in Chinese markets' lack of transparency, high volatility, and heavy government involvement. The Shanghai Composite index rose by nearly 250 percent between October 2014 and May 2015, for example, and then lost nearly a third of its value over the subsequent month. In the summer of 2015 and again at the beginning of 2016, the Shanghai and Shenzhen markets repeatedly rose and fell by as much as 5–10 percent a day. This volatility did not render the market attractive to international investors eyeing Chinese assets.

The Chinese authorities initially responded to the spike in volatility in the summer of 2015 by providing investors with more liquidity to be used as margin credit. They injected funds into the China Development Bank and the Export-Import Bank, so that these entities could provide more credit to the economy. They encouraged the country's banks, state-controlled insurers, and pension funds (the so-called national team of state-directed investors) to buy shares as a way of supporting the market. They imposed a ban on short selling, which did not reassure observers that prices would be allowed to find their own levels. The China Securities Regulatory Commission tightened its control of new listings in a further effort to support prices.

To investors, these measures smacked of desperation. They suggested that the authorities were responding to problems that had not yet been revealed to the markets. Worries mounted about disclosed and undisclosed problems in banks, trust companies, and other investment vehicles that had made loans to property developers or had guaranteed loans extended to property developers by other lenders. These worries precipitated capital outflows, reportedly at rates as high as $100 billion a month.

This was nothing that couldn't be handled by a central bank and government with more than $3 trillion of foreign reserves. But it raised questions about what might happen if capital flight accelerated further. It was a reminder of how far China still had to go in developing deep, liquid, and transparent financial markets on which prices are influenced by government at arm's length, if at all.

Developing financial markets that are deep (in the sense of being well capitalized), sufficiently liquid that investors can buy and sell blocks of securities without significantly moving prices, and stable rather than prone to volatility will require far-reaching policy reforms. Creating a liquid market means allowing prices to change in response to supply and demand, in turn requiring the authorities to limit their intervention. The actions of traders should be guided by information about the financial condition and prospects of the governments, banks, and corporations issuing securities, which in turn requires transparency and rigorous disclosure. This allows prices to adjust smoothly as information percolates to the surface, and it discourages investors from herding in and out of markets on the basis of rumor. Permitting investors to differentiate among issuers according to their credit risk means allowing troubled bond issuers to default rather than being bailed out by the government.[16] This in turn means more strongly capitalizing and truly commercializing banks and insurers, so that the financial system can survive defaults and still provide liquidity to traders through the interbank bond market.

Until now, financial development in China has been state led. Banks and insurers have been told when to lend. Information has been suppressed. Debt issuers and insurers have been implicitly or explicitly guaranteed. All this can be seen as part and parcel of a tradition of state direction of the economy that developed over more than 50 years. It will have to change for China to develop deep and liquid financial markets.

British financial markets in the nineteenth century and U.S. financial markets in the twentieth were not exactly paragons of depth, stability, and liquidity, as we have seen in previous chapters. That said, both countries made considerable progress in building the financial infrastructure needed for the development of deep and liquid markets, so as to render their currencies attractive to international investors. China still has a long way to go before it can claim analogous status for its financial markets. Reaching that goal will take more than just time. It will take a change in the fundamental approach pursued until now to develop and regulate the financial sector. Policy reform in China proceeds gradually. If history is a guide, this suggests that Chinese financial development will proceed gradually as well.

Credible Commitments

One can ask whether the prerequisites for the emergence of the renminbi as an international and reserve currency require changes in not only Chinese economic and financial policies but also in the institutional arrangements through which those policies are made.[17] The principal international and reserve currencies of the nineteenth and twentieth centuries, the pound sterling and the dollar, were the currencies of political democracies. Fan et al. (2006) argue that constraints on arbitrary action by the executive are critical for reassuring foreigners contemplating investment in a country.[18] Britain and the

United States limit arbitrary action by the executive via contested elections and developed political systems. If one considers the Dutch guilder as the leading international currency prior to sterling, then one can point to the fact that the Dutch Republic had a federal structure, with a "States General" of representatives of delegates from different provinces to similarly limit the scope for opportunistic behavior by the central authorities while encouraging competition for financial resources.

Some argue that China can constrain executive action in a different, "Chinese way." Observers like Naughton (2011) argue that the powers of the general secretary of the Chinese Communist Party are increasingly constrained by the institutions of the party. Other key decision makers in the bureaucracy are similarly constrained by requirements of transparency and disclosure. If Naughton is right, then policy making in China is moving in a direction where key decision makers are bound by law and where checks and balances on members of the administrative hierarchy are more effective.

Or maybe it will be necessary to move further. The argument that democracy is associated with financial development—and through that channel, with international currency status—is based on the idea that democratically elected governments are best able to make the credible commitments needed to develop financial markets. North and Weingast (1989) and Schultz and Weingast (2003) argue that democracies are better able to develop markets in the benchmark asset, government bonds, whose existence is a prerequisite for reserve currency status. "Representative institutions make it easier for those with a stake in the repayment of debt to punish the sovereign in the event of default," as the second set of authors summarize the point.[19] When creditors are able to make their dissatisfaction known at the polls, the threat of adverse electoral consequences prevents democratically elected governments from reneging on their financial commitments. And because debt contracts are enforced and financial obligations are met, financial deepening and development, in the benchmark asset and more generally, ultimately follow.

Using nineteenth- and twentieth-century historical data, Bordo and Rousseau (2006) find that contested elections, universal suffrage, and few irregular changes in government are positively associated with financial deepening and development. Focusing on data for recent years, Girma and Shortland (2007) similarly conclude that democracy is positively and significantly associated with financial development.[20]

This view has not gone unchallenged. The principal historical challenge to North and Weingast's view that democratic political institutions are necessary and sufficient for financial development is, ironically, North and Weingast's own case: England in the seventeenth and eighteenth centuries. The authors argued that the Glorious Revolution of 1688, by strengthening Parliament, created checks, balances, and sanctions that forced the Crown to meet its financial obligations, in turn creating the confidence necessary for the development of an active market in government debt. But Clark (1996) shows that there was little sign that interest rates on the sovereign's debt fell in the wake of the Glorious Revolution. Reviewing a longer period, Stasavage (2002, 2007) finds evidence of that interest rate decline but argues that it was not democratic political institutions but, rather, who dominated those institutions that mattered for interest rates and financial development. In England, it was the dominance of a Whig Party that was closely aligned with the creditors.

Foreign investors do not vote in domestic elections, and it is not obvious that any favorable treatment enjoyed by domestic creditors, via their influence over political decision making, will be extended to foreigners. It could be that when governments are led to change their attitudes toward domestic investors, they change their attitudes toward investors more generally. Another reason governments choose to respect their debts to foreigners may be the risk that doing otherwise will jeopardize their trade relations. Rose and Spiegel (2004) show that countries that trade extensively with the rest of the world, and with their creditors in particular, are less likely to default on their debts. China certainly qualifies as a country that trades extensively. Others suggest that countries are reluctant to default on their obligations to their alliance partners. China is certainly actively at work building diplomatic alliances with other countries.

Conclusion

Alternatively, a federal structure may be the key institutional variable that instills confidence in foreign investors. Weingast (1995) observes that a federal political structure that checked opportunistic autocratic rule is observed in two of our reserve currency cases: the Netherlands in the seventeenth century and America in the twentieth. In a federal system, the representatives of the constituent states will push for protection against arbitrary action by the central executive, and the benefits of that protection may also accrue to foreign investors. Invoking the experience of the United States, Sylla (2005) suggests that competition among local governments in a federal system will encourage those units to adopt measures designed to attract footloose banks and firms, fostering financial development. In the U.S. context, that competition took the form of free banking laws, legislative measures to promote activity on regional stock exchanges, and a variety of similar initiatives. In the Chinese context, one can think of the competition between Shanghai, Beijing, and Hong Kong for financial-center status as providing impetus for financial development.

Or maybe it is political stability, as opposed to federalism or democracy.[21] That the American, British, and Dutch political systems have been stable for long periods is consistent with this view. McGuire and Olson (1996) argue that a regime's willingness to invest in public goods diminishes as its horizon shortens—that is, with regime turnover. In this connection, one can think of internationalization of the renminbi as providing Chinese banks and firms with a public good. One can similarly conceive of financial development as requiring a range of public goods from reliable contract enforcement to effective supervision and regulation.[22] That China's political system is relatively long lived and stable is supportive, in this view, of its efforts to develop its financial markets and internationalize its currency.

Finally, it can be argued that it is not the structure of the political system but the result—the efficiency of administration and its success at controlling corruption—that matters for financial development and for foreign investor participation in those markets. An extensive empirical literature on the determinants of foreign direct investment

(FDI) investigates the point. Neither Oneal (1994) nor Alesina and Dollar (1998) found much evidence of a relationship between FDI inflows and the nature of the political system. A recent study by Yang (2007) further confirms their conclusion.

In contrast many academic studies conclude that control of corruption is important for attracting foreign direct investors. Mauro (1995), Wei (2000), and Habib and Zurawicki (2002) all document a negative association of corruption and inward foreign investment for various country samples and periods. More recently, Castro and Nunes (2013) investigate FDI inflows into 73 countries during 1998–2008 and find that where corruption is lower, FDI inflows are higher, even after controlling for other economic and political characteristics. Other investigators, such as Han (2006) and Caetano and Caleiro (2007), argue that the relationship is subject to threshold effects: relatively low levels of corruption matter little for the foreign investment decision, but high levels of corruption constitute a significant deterrent to inward FDI. No direct evidence has been reported that what deters foreign direct investors also deters foreigners from holding bank deposits and financial securities. But common sense suggests that the results carry over.

These observations suggest that it is a positive from the point of view of China's international currency ambitions that the government embarked on an ambitious anticorruption campaign following the elevation of Xi Jinping to general secretary of the Communist Party at the eighteenth National Party Congress in 2012. Observers have suggested different interpretations of the motivations underlying that campaign. Some suggest that its goal is to strengthen the role of formal institutions and suppress factionalism and networks of personal loyalty that have limited the efficiency of governance. Others argue that a successful campaign will uproot entrenched interests that have resisted more ambitious structural reforms. Still others argue that the anticorruption campaign is a way of addressing public concerns about widening income inequality and a growing concentration of wealth at the top. But whatever the rationale, the resulting reforms, if and when completed, promise to enhance the attractions of the renminbi for international investors.

12

Conclusion

Multiple considerations point to a future in which several national currencies will serve as units of account, means of payment, and stores of value for transactions across borders. Other countries and not just the United States will have deep and liquid financial markets open to the rest of the world. Other countries like China and potentially India and Brazil will have an economic size and volume of cross-border transactions comparable to America's. Financial technology will continue to evolve in directions that facilitate the use of several national currencies in those transactions, reducing network effects, impediments to switching, and costs of information in the international monetary and financial sphere.[1]

As we have shown in this book, the world has been here before. These international currency functions were broadly shared by sterling, the French franc, and the German mark before World War I. They were shared by sterling and the dollar in the 1920s. From this vantage point, it is the second half of the twentieth century that is the anomaly, when an absence of alternatives allowed the dollar to come close to monopolizing this international currency role. Figure 12.1 summarizes our evidence for one function of international currencies, namely, the provision of international reserves, but the conclusion holds more broadly.

Theory and history point to both reassuring and worrisome aspects of a world with multiple international currencies. On the reassuring side, countries will possess better diversified sources of international liquidity. In an international monetary and financial system dominated by the dollar, the United States is essentially the sole supplier of the safe and liquid assets that central banks hold as reserves and commercial banks and corporations use as the risk-free bedrock of their portfolios. If emerging markets continue growing faster than the U.S. market, as the logic of convergence suggests, then their demand for safe and liquid assets will rise faster than the

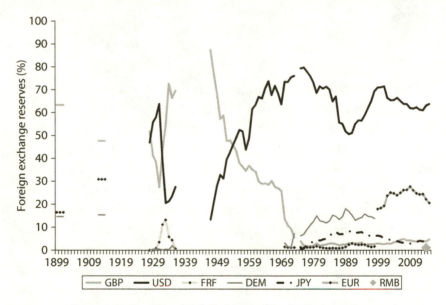

FIGURE 12.1. Currency Composition of Globally Disclosed Foreign Exchange Reserves, 1899–2015 (percentage of selected currencies at market exchange rates). Source: Lindert (1969), central bank archives.

Note: Data for 1899 and 1913 taken from Lindert (1969). Data for 1920–1938 elaborated by Barry Eichengreen and Marc Flandreau from central bank archived material; fixed composition sample of 15 countries for 1928 to 1936 (accounting for ¾ of global foreign exchange reserves); see Eichengreen and Flandreau (2009) for further details. Data for 1947–2015 elaborated by Barry Eichengreen, Livia Chiţu, and Arnaud Mehl from IMF Annual Reports (various printed issues) updated with IMF COFER data for 1999–2014; see Eichengreen, Chiţu and Mehl (2016) for further details. The estimate for the Chinese renminbi is taken from IMF (2015) and refers to the share of China's unit in global official foreign currency assets. DEM, Deutschemark; EUR, euro; FRF, French franc; GBP, British pound; JPY, Japanese yen; RMB, renminbi; USD, U.S. dollar.

capacity of the United States to supply them, where that capacity is limited by the ability of the U.S. government to raise taxes and service the government debt securities that are held as reserves and used in cross-border transactions by other countries.[2] The world will then be faced with a twenty-first century version of the Triffin Dilemma. Either the United States will limit its issuance of debt securities, in which case other countries will be starved of international liquidity, or the U.S. government will increase issuance along with foreign demand, in which case confidence in its ability to service that debt, and therefore the safety and liquidity of the latter, will be cast into doubt.[3]

But in a world of multiple international currencies, other governments can similarly issue claims that are regarded as safe and liquid, and that are willingly held as a store of value and accepted as a means of payment by central banks, private financial institutions, and nonfinancial corporations in a variety of countries. This twenty-first century version of the Triffin Dilemma will no longer bind.

More generally, other countries able to tap alternative sources of safe and liquid assets will no longer be as vulnerable to disruptions flowing from doubts about the creditworthiness of the U.S. government. In the past, the U.S. Congress has threatened not to raise the legislative limit on the amount of national debt that can be issued by the U.S. treasury (the debt ceiling). This has raised questions about which government payments will be given priority (whether interest payments to bondholders will be prioritized and in particular, whether the bondholders in question would include nonresidents). Congress in its wisdom could go down this road again, and foreign holders could liquidate their dollar balances in response or even in anticipation. There would then be a shortage of dollar balances with which to make international payments and a reluctance to accept them. In a phrase, a shortage of international liquidity would result.

One can dismiss this debt-ceiling scenario as implausible while still pointing to other situations that might create similar doubts and problems. But in a world of several international currencies, those problems would be less severe. Central banks, private financial institutions and nonfinancial firms reluctant to hold dollar balances could replace them with claims on other countries whose government debt securities were themselves regarded as safe and liquid. A shortage of international liquidity would no longer result, since the world would then possess a diversified set of national sources of safe and liquid assets.

In addition, foreign central banks and governments would no longer depend so heavily on the Federal Reserve System and the acquiescence of U.S. politicians for emergency liquidity in times of crisis. During the 2008 financial crisis, the Fed extended emergency dollar swap lines (credit facilities through which it agreed to lend dollars in return for foreign currencies) to a variety of central banks. These included $30 billion swap lines to four emerging markets: Brazil, China, Mexico, and South Korea. Given the heavy reliance of banks in these and other countries on dollar funding for their international investments, these Federal Reserve swaps proved critical when the interbank market seized up and private sources of dollar funding evaporated.[4] Only dollars were viewed as sufficiently safe and liquid to be freely lent and borrowed. At the height of the crisis, the Fed's dollar swap lines turned out to be key.[5]

Because of its leadership and status, the Fed in 2008 was aware of its role as an international lender of last resort. But its priorities were not universally shared: its provision of dollar swaps subsequently came under public and Congressional scrutiny and criticism.[6] There is no guarantee that a future Federal Reserve Board will be equally conscious of its responsibility for providing emergency global liquidity or as free to act.

In contrast, in a world where banks can fund themselves by borrowing not just dollars but also other currencies on the interbank market, their dependence on the Fed would be reduced. They might be able to obtain emergency swap lines from other central banks that were similarly issuers of currencies regarded as sufficiently safe and liquid to be widely traded on the international interbank market.[7] As a result, the Fed would no longer be the only "global lender of last resort."[8]

On the worrisome side, the existence of several international currencies, all traded in liquid markets, will create additional scope for central banks, commercial banks, and other investors to alter the composition of their foreign balances and payment practices at the first sign of trouble. In the next episode of U.S. Congressional debt-ceiling brinkmanship, these agents could bolt out of dollars and rush into other currencies that were also traded in liquid markets. One reason that no mass flight from the dollar has occurred in recent episodes of financial strain in the United States is the absence of other equally liquid assets and markets. Few other safe havens exist— there are only so many Swiss francs to go around. But this would no longer be true in a world of multiple international currencies as a matter of definition. The result could be more volatile exchange rates as investors rush out of one currency and into another. And those more-volatile exchange rates could catch important investors off balance, in the worst case precipitating a crisis.[9]

How real are these risks? Here it is important to distinguish between different holders of foreign balances and different policy environments. Central banks are conservative investors. Rather than maximizing profits and minimizing losses, they can afford to invest with longer-term objectives in mind. Rather than liquidating their holdings of a particular currency in anticipation of capital losses, they tend to replenish their holdings when a currency depreciates, with an eye toward restoring the previous balance between the value of different currencies in their portfolios.[10] In contrast, private investors are more likely to move quickly in response to considerations of profit maximization and loss aversion.

Whether central banks and other like-minded investors reconsider their behavior will depend on the policies of the countries and central banks issuing the competing international currencies. Stable policies in the countries whose currencies are widely used for cross-border transactions would minimize these risks. Unstable policies would heighten them.

History, like theory, provides examples of both possibilities. The three decades before 1913 saw a broadly stable system organized around several international currencies, because the policies of the issuers were broadly stable. Financial problems were far from absent, but none of these forced Britain, France, or Germany to suspend the convertibility of their currencies into gold or alter their exchange rates against one another. When exchange rates moved within the bands of the gold standard, they were expected to move back; as a result, extrapolative expectations were rare.[11] Sources of global liquidity grew increasingly diversified, as we saw in Chapter 2. Governments and central banks provided one another with emergency liquidity in times of crisis, not simply (or even mainly) the Bank of England but also the Bank of France and the German Reichsbank, among others.

The 1920s and 1930s are the contrasting case. American and British policies were unstable. When exchange rates moved, they encouraged the expectation that they would move further in the same direction. Google's Ngram Viewer, which can be used to search books published at different dates, reports a few references to the term "hot money" at the time of the Napoleonic Wars and the paper pound, in the late 1870s and again during World War I, but such references then rise by several orders of magnitude in the 1930s.[12] When one international currency (sterling) was devalued, expectations quickly developed that the other (the dollar) would suffer a similar fate. Global liquidity sloshed, as it were, from one side of the pond to the other. Foreign reserves were liquidated starting in 1931, as we saw in Chapter 4. Emergency liquidity assistance was miserly by the standards of 2008–2009, with political and diplomatic obstacles hindering reliable extension.[13] This was anything but a stable multiple international currency system.

Which scenario is more likely for the future? The answer is uncertain. It is for policy makers and their publics to decide.

NOTES

Chapter One

1. A famous example is Kennedy (1987).

2. See Maddison (1982).

3. Kindleberger (1973) is the locus classicus of this argument as applied to the 1920s and 1930s; he generalizes it in Kindleberger (1988).

4. See, for example, Kirshner (1996).

5. This is how Keynes memorably put it in his *Treatise on Money* (Keynes 1930). World Bank (2013) distinguishes three "ages of financial globalization;" the second half of the nineteenth century constitutes the first.

6. References include Gilbert (1968) and McKinnon (1996, 2010).

7. In the most recent round of attention, following the global financial crisis of 2008–2009, policy makers in emerging markets (Finance Minister Guido Mantega of Brazil, for example) complained first about the Federal Reserve's policy of quantitative easing, which put "undue" upward pressure on their currencies and financial markets, and then about its decision to taper its asset purchases and normalize the level of interest rates, which weakened emerging-market currencies and, these same critics argued, precipitated sharp downward adjustments in asset valuations in the developing world.

8. There is, admittedly, a decided lack of consensus about when precisely this transition will occur.

9. See, for example, the writings of Arvind Subramanian (Subramanian 2011; Subramanian and Kessler 2013).

10. See Krugman (1980, 1984); Matsuyama, Kiyotaki, and Matsui (1993); Zhou (1997); and Rey (2001).

11. Influential examples of this language in connection with problems like ours—though very different products—are Farrell and Saloner (1986) and Greenstein (1993). Shy (2010) provides a survey of the field.

12. In the text we emphasize the economic advantages of using the currency of the leading economic power, and the corresponding economic leverage that dominant power may have over the choices of decision makers in other countries. But insofar as the leading economic power also has strategic, diplomatic,

and military advantages, other countries may also see it as in their strategic, diplomatic, and military—that is to say, their political—interests to conduct the majority of their international transactions using its currency, and the leading economy may have the political leverage needed to encourage the practice. We explore these ideas also in their historical context starting in Chapter 2 (although hints already appear in the third paragraph above). Other authors exploring them include Kindleberger (1970), Strange (1971, 1988), Kirschner (1995), Williamson (2012), and Cohen (2015).

13. The earliest and still most influential formalization of the point is Arthur (1989).

14. International conferences like that at Bretton Woods, New Hampshire, in the summer of 1944, at which governments agree on a new common standard, are an alternative to decentralized decision making. In principle, they are venues for coordinating action across countries. In practice, such conferences are relatively rare, although there are several examples in history, starting with the 1867 conference in Paris, which sought to lay the basis for a concerted move to a universal gold standard. But for every successful Bretton Woods Conference there have been several unsuccessful conferences. Agreement at such conferences tends to prevail only when a dominant country has the leverage to impose it, as the United States did at Bretton Woods. More generally, strategic, diplomatic, and military leverage can be used to encourage a critical mass of countries to shift from one international monetary standard to another (or to resist the temptation to shift). We will see examples of this in the British, French, and German spheres of influence before World War I; in the various regional currency blocs of the 1930s; and in the persistence of the Sterling Area after World War II.

15. One exception is Farhi and Maggiori (2016), who propose a simple model of the international monetary system and study the global supply and demand for reserve assets under a variety of scenarios, including a hegemonic world and a multipolar world.

16. The seminal work of Lindert (1969) is discussed further in Chapter 2.

17. Even the COFER database is imperfect, since some countries do not report the currency composition of their international reserves to the IMF. China, for instance, did not report the currency composition of its reserves until the second half of 2015. On the COFER data base, see http://www.imf.org/external/np/sta/cofer/eng/. More detail on the COFER database and its limitations is provided in Chapter 7.

18. Evidence on this is presented in Chapter 2.

19. The term "new view" was evidently first applied to these analyses of international currency competition by Frankel (2011).

20. See, for example, Clark (2003) and Farrell and Klemperer (2007) .

21. David and Bunn (1988, 170). See also Braunstein and White (1985), Crandall and Flamm (1989), and David and Greenstein (1990).

22. For another closely related dispute, see David (1985) and Liebowitz and Margolis (1990).

23. Recent historical research on foreign exchange markets provides evidence of considerable sophistication in early periods, suggesting that the ability to produce market liquidity in a variety of different currencies was widely shared. Examples include Suzuki's work on the role of so-called exchange banks in dealing with "silver risk" (Suzuki 2012) and Jobst's work on the use of forward foreign exchange interventions by central banks as instruments of monetary policy (Jobst 2009).

24. See Flandreau and Jobst (2009).

25. The difference between the two questions (externalities and lock-in) is acknowledged in the theoretical literature; see, for example, Portes and Rey (1998). However, which regime obtains in practice is first and foremost an empirical question, motivating the approach taken in this book.

26. See de Cecco (1984) and the conclusion of Chapter 2.

27. More recently, Stefano Ugolini (2016) provides systematic empirical evidence to this effect.

28. A discussion of the cases for and against this hypothesis is found in Obstfeld and Rogoff (2011).

29. Triffin's original formulation emphasized that the lead country could not meet the world's international liquidity needs indefinitely, because eventually its foreign liabilities would vastly exceed its gold reserves, precipitating a run on the latter, given Bretton Wood's fixed price of gold in terms of dollars (see Triffin 1960, 1964). In the absence of a fixed price for gold, the twenty-first-century variant emphasizes instead how the foreign liabilities of the lead country, which typically take the form of government bonds, will eventually outstrip the fiscal capacity of that country to service them (Obstfeld 2013).

30. See Gourinchas and Rey (2007).

31. We also provide references to scholarly articles where it is possible to find those formal models, also as in earlier parts of this chapter.

Chapter Two

1. The term national bank of issue refers to authorization to issue banknotes, which was one of the original privileges (often a monopoly privilege) conferred on the entities that came to be known as central banks.

2. For details and discussion, see Conant (1910) and Ugolini (2011, 2012).

3. De Roover (1953); see also Usher (1914, 1934); Boyer-Xambeu, Deleplace, and Gillard (1986); Neal (1990); and Jobst and Nogues-Marco (2012).

4. Santarosa (2015) describes how bills of exchange were structured to address information problems and asymmetries.

5. This being the title of Cassis (2009).

6. Flandreau and Sussman (2005, 155–166).

7. The arrangement can be understood as an instance of "relationship banking," in which banks monitor borrowers by observing the borrower's account.

8. Their motivations are described by Flandreau (2003).

9. Gallarotti (1995) has described the process as a "scramble for gold." For more detail, see Flandreau (2004, chapter 8). Meissner (2005) estimates a model of the scramble, while Flandreau and Oosterlinck (2012) provide evidence on the emergence of the silver risk in the 1870s.

10. In contrast to a gold coin standard, under a gold bullion standard, gold was warehoused at the treasury or central bank, while notes and token coins convertible into gold at a fixed price circulated hand to hand.

11. Kemmerer described the rationale for the Philippine gold-exchange standard, in whose design he had been involved. "There was the advantage of economy, and this was a matter of great importance to a country like the Philippines, which wanted to be on a gold basis but could not afford the luxury of a gold-coin or even of a gold-bullion standard." Kemmerer (1944, 160).

12. The term in quotes is from Bordo and Kydland (1996). Patterson (1870) and Flandreau and Ugolini (2014) describe British consular efforts and their reception during the 1866 suspension.

13. Before the shock of the Franco-Prussian war there was a market in the yellow metal in Paris with liquidity that rivaled and even surpassed (if one generalizes from bid-ask spreads) that in London (Flandreau 2004).

14. Scammel (1968) dates the development of the Treasury bill market from 1877. For a discussion of the relationship between banking and monetary policy at this time, see Goodhart (1972).

15. Bloomfield (1959, 45). Others, like Wood (1939) and Clapham (1944), note that the Bank of England engaged in sporadic open market purchases and sales in earlier periods, such as the 1830s, but such operations only became commonplace at the end of the nineteenth century.

16. Bagehot (1873) is the classic statement of the principle.

17. This is the conclusion of Bignon, Flandreau, and Ugolini (2011). Flandreau and Ugolini (2014) document the Bank of England's efforts to provide liquidity to bill brokers engaged in investing in acceptance credits during this crisis.

18. The evidence here is from Flandreau and Jobst (2005).

19. White (1933) and Bazot, Bordo, and Monnet (2014) analyze Bank of France reserve management during this period.

20. An act of parliament in 1708 prohibited banks with more than six partners from issuing notes, effectively limiting partnerships to that size, a restriction that was finally relaxed in the nineteenth century.

21. As Sayers (1936, 7) puts it, "London's position as the leading free gold standard centre depended fundamentally upon the Bank's power to control interest rates in London. With that power gone, London's position could only be maintained by adoption of some radical change."

22. It did so by changing the purity of the gold in question, for example.

23. De Cecco (1984, 120). Shannon (1952, 321) goes on: "The local Currency Boards are, therefore, merely automatic money-changers: they issue legal tender locally on demand against deposits of sterling in London, they hold this sterling in cash or sterling securities, and they pay it out on demand against local coin or notes paid in. They have no discretion in the matter. Constitutionally, the rate of exchange is fixed in London by the central authorities."

24. Keynes (1913) and Kemmerer (1944) cite India as the first economy for which a fully worked out plan for a gold-exchange standard was devised, by A. M. Lindsay of the Bank of Bengal starting in 1876.

25. The Presidency Banks of Calcutta, Bombay, and Madras, established by royal charter starting in 1806, were known by that name because they were set up in the three "presidencies" that were the administrative units of the East India Company.

26. The proportions depended on "considerations of temporary convenience—recent or impending capital transactions in London, the likelihood of sterling funds being needed for the purchase of silver, and trade demands for Council Bills as a means of remittance" (Keynes 1913, 128).

27. The residual was held in silver bullion and rupees (Keynes 1913, 127).

28. It also invested in miscellaneous securities of other colonial governments and in modest amounts of gold earmarked on its behalf at the Bank of England.

29. On the dollar-based gold-exchange standards of the Philippines and Panama, see Metzler (2006).

30. See Pittaluga and Seghezza (2016).

31. Details are provided by Schiltz (2012).

32. Smethurst (2007, 146–147), Metzler (2006, 70).

33. This argument is made forcefully by de Cecco (1984). It is also evident in Lindert's figures after 1910.

Chapter Three

1. Bloomfield (1963) is the source of these estimates (see Chapter 2 in this book).

2. Trust companies set up foreign offices to gather information on foreign-currency-denominated bonds, which were obvious assets to add to their portfolios, since they matched the maturity of their liabilities to their trustees. In addition, certain state charters allowed banks to branch abroad, although few state banks ever did. There was also one specialized institution, the International Banking Corporation, set up by the Remington Arms Company to assist it in foreign sales, which operated foreign branches but was prohibited from engaging in domestic banking.

3. Kemmerer, who had previously helped establish the gold-exchange standard in the Philippines, as described in Chapter 2, wrote on the problem of seasonal instability in a study for the National Monetary Commission, whose investigation helped lay the groundwork for the Federal Reserve (Kemmerer 1910).

4. Present at the Jekyll Island meeting were Nelson Aldrich (senator from Rhode Island), Arthur Shelton (Aldrich's personal secretary), A. Piatt Andrew (assistant secretary of the treasury and former Harvard University professor), Frank Vanderlip (president of National City Bank), Henry Davison (J.P. Morgan partner), Benjamin Strong (head of Bankers Trust), and Paul M. Warburg (Kuhn, Loeb partner).

5. National banks with capital and surplus of $1 million or more could request permission from the Federal Reserve Board to establish branches abroad under Section 25 of the Federal Reserve Act. For more on the market in trade acceptances, see Chapter 5.

6. Warburg contributed the volume on the discount system in Europe to the National Monetary Commission (Warburg 1910). For a collection of Warburg's early writings on the subject, see Warburg (1930). A popular account of Warburg's career is Chernow (1993).

7. Figures are for the central and federal government, respectively.

8. Figures are from Feinstein (1972, Table T97).

9. See, for example, Goldsmith (1952).

10. United States Bureau of the Census (1975, 869).

11. The figure was 103 percent to be precise, according to the Bureau of Labor Statistics series.

12. It can be argued that the U.S. suspended the gold standard between September 1917 and June 1918 when President Wilson barred the free export of gold, invoking the provisions of the Espionage Act of 1917. All the while, however, domestic convertibility of notes into gold remained legal, so from a domestic point of view the gold standard remained in force

13. See the discussion in Moggridge (1969).

14. The fears at Brussels, as Petrescu (1920, 983) put it, were that "the Americans would not help and the Germans would not pay."

15. Traynor (1949, 65), Fink (1984, 235).

16. Cassel emphasized the potential for conflict in a background memorandum for the conference (Siepmann 1920).

17. This was the high point of Hawtrey's career as civil servant and for that matter as an economist (Davis 1981).

18. One is reminded of the decision at the Bretton Woods Conference in 1944 to allow for changes in exchange rate parities only in the event of "fundamental disequilibrium," a term that was never defined.

19. The language here is from Cassel (1925, 205–206), but he made similar arguments at the time of Genoa (see above).

20. Hawtrey (1922, 295).

21. Moreover, central bank autonomy and cooperation went together. In the words of Hawtrey (1922, 291):

> Inflationary government finance once eliminated, the real responsibility for the currency passes from the government to the central bank. The central bank may be itself a government department, or essentially subordinate to the government, but, even if it is, it has the responsibility for regulating the currency on banking principles. When, therefore, the governments of Europe pass on their monetary programme to the central banks, it is the same sort of step forward as is taken by allies in war, when the political leaders hand over the task of concerting operations to the military commanders. Broad guidance must be given by the political leaders, but it is only the military commanders who can plan and take practical action.

22. Thus the creation of the central bankers' bank, the Bank for International Settlements, in 1930 was seen as a descendent of the Genoa agreement (Traynor 1949).

23. Clarke (1967, 36–37). Clay (1957, 138–139) notes that the U.S. State Department initially approved Federal Reserve participation but hints that Benjamin Strong had developed second thoughts.

24. An account of the activities of the Financial Committee is in Clavin (2013).

25. Nurkse (1944, 30–31).

26. Chandler (1958, 263), Schuker (2003, 62).

27. Sayers (1976, 199).

28. For more on Kemmerer's activities, see the introduction in Flandreau (2003).

Chapter Four

1. As of June 1927, as quoted in Federal Reserve Board (1928, 392).

2. See Nurkse (1944, chapter 2 and appendix).

3. Until its devaluation in 1936, the Swiss franc was a gold currency whose gold content was equivalent to that of the pre-1914 French franc (a result of the monetary standardization that prevailed under the 1865 Latin Union). It was the accounting unit of the Bank for International Settlements, as noted by Einzig (1931).

4. That the dollar was used by the League for valuation purposes is presumably already telling us something about the currency's international unit-of-account role.

5. The League of Nations' *Memoranda* do not cover 1926–1928, nor do they say anything about currency composition. Before 1925 they provide data for "foreign accounts" and "foreign bills." After 1929 they also occasionally record "foreign government securities."

6. It provides total gold holdings in U.S. dollars (Federal Reserve Board 1943).

7. Albania, the United States and the United Kingdom (no foreign exchange reserves) are included in the Bank for International Settlements' tables but not in those of the League of Nations. Nurkse appears to have added some corrections to the BIS figures. This is suggested by the correction he made for France for which foreign exchange holdings registered in 1926–1927 with other items under the heading "divers" have been incorporated, appropriately, into foreign exchange reserves.

8. Banca d'Italia (1993, Tables 1–2; 51–64). Even in this case, the figures need to be reworked in order to replace book values by market valuations. In the 1920s, for instance, Italian foreign-currency reserve decomposition uses prewar parities, which were out of line with actual market exchange rates.

9. Nor is it always clear what price was used when valuing gold.

10. For example, suppose that the central bank holds foreign exchange for the account of the government, perhaps because the treasury has deposited foreign currency at the central bank intended for the service of the external debt.

11. Initially, there appears to have been very little tendency to "mark to market." That is, more than a few central banks continued to value gold and, often, foreign exchange reserves at the 1914 parity long after the pre–World War I gold standard had collapsed. This tendency then diminished over time. In contrast, no effort was made to adjust the price of foreign securities to market, since the number and type of securities held were typically not reported.

12. The members of the British Commonwealth (such as Australia, New Zealand, and Ireland) are omitted here, since their political or monetary autonomy from Britain was limited. Archival materials point strongly to the conclusion that their foreign exchange reserves were entirely in sterling. Adding them would only reinforce our picture of sterling making a comeback in the 1930s. Important foreign exchange holders for which we have not been able to get material for this period include Germany, Mexico, Canada, and Argentina.

13. In terms of missing countries, next in order of importance is Belgium, which probably split its reserves between London and New York. (If it was a typical member of the gold bloc it would have held, say, 55 percent of its exchange reserves in dollars and 45 percent in pounds). The Belgians subsequently complained of large capital losses due to the depreciation of sterling in 1931, which may indicate larger reserve holdings. But the impact on our estimates would in any case be of second-order importance, since Belgium foreign exchange reserves accounted for less than 0.5 percent of the global total.

14. The economics of the Poincaré stabilization continue to be debated. For an influential rendering see Sargent (1983).

15. The Bank of France's sales of sterling caused problems for the Bank of England, leading its governor, Montagu Norman, to pay an emergency visit to Paris at the end of May. See Clarke (1967, 117–118).

16. Their efforts are recounted by Myers (1936).

17. This lack of data is not surprising, given the chaotic political and financial circumstances of this period.

18. The "under the harrow" quote is from Montagu Norman. Comments by the governor of the Bank of France during the summer of 1929, quoted by Accominotti (2009), are indicative of the worries about the future of the pound, leading to the growing dominance of the dollar. Einzig (1931) disputes the point, but then he was an unrepentant supporter of sterling. Future developments would vindicate his prejudices, but at the time of his writing, Einzig was deeply wrong.

19. The Canadian case was more complicated, given the economy's close ties to the United States. We have not been able to find comparable information for that country, which created its central bank only in 1935. Gold reserves held by the government to back Dominion notes and those held by the chartered banks to back their borrowings from the government were transferred to the Bank of Canada that year; revaluation profits were used to create a fund to purchase foreign exchange reserves. Circa 1936 most of these reserves (nearly 90 percent) were held in U.S. dollars, with the remainder split between sterling and funds of other countries on a gold standard. Starting in 1937, the Bank's balance sheet lumped sterling and dollar funds together in one account.

20. The divergent evolution of Spanish exports and imports and growth of the trade balance between 1929 and 1932 are studied by Gimenez and Montero (2012).

21. This response of Central European central banks was commented on by Coste (1932).

Chapter Five

1. This is according to Williams (1968). America's dependence on London for trade credit was well known. Myers (1936) comments on France's all but complete reliance on Britain for trade finance prior to World War I.

2. The same is of course the case of virtually all merchandise imports of the United States itself. Gopinath's (2015) estimates of the dollar share of global trade is lower, but she too finds that the share invoiced in dollars exceeds by a factor of five the share of imports drawn from the United States.

3. As a matter of definition.

4. This interpretation is the best way, some will say, of understanding the patterns evident in Chapter 4.

5. Jacobs (1910, 13).

6. Parrini (1969, 105).

7. As in Warburg (1910). Of course the metaphor was flawed: British bankers financed American trade more cheaply than New York bankers would have (Phelps 1927, p. 102). The actual amount involved was a small fraction of U.S. trade and GDP. In 1927, by which time U.S. banks had secured a large share of the global market for acceptances, the *Acceptance Bulletin* estimated the annual saving to have been a "material" $5 million, this in a year when U.S. GDP is estimated to have been $95 billion.

8. See King (1936).

9. The banks could also secure advances from the central bank against the parcels.

10. The relevant legislation lacked provisions explicitly authorizing banks to engage in this business, but the courts, channeling long-standing American suspicion of concentrated financial power, ruled against their efforts to do so. While other forms of short-term credit emerged, they were less liquid than European style acceptances. One short-term negotiable security that played some domestic role was single name "commercial paper" (single name in the sense that the security was endorsed and therefore the obligation of a single signatory). Commercial paper was issued by industrial and commercial enterprises of substantial standing and traded in organized markets. But while commercial paper paid with "clockwork regularity," it was relatively illiquid (Foulke 1931, 80, 84– 86; James 1995, 224).

11. As recalled by James (1995, 227), the Federal Reserve Act was defined as "An Act to provide for the Establishment of Federal Reserve Banks . . . and to afford means of rediscounting commercial paper." Thus, the Federal Reserve Act was intended in part to address the liquidity problems in the commercial paper

market alluded to in the preceding endnote. For dollar acceptances, the editors of the *Acceptance Bulletin* constructed monthly series from material submitted by reporting banks. The resulting series is available from January 1917 to April 1936, when the *Bulletin* was discontinued. From 1917 on, the *Bulletin* distinguished acceptances created to finance exports, imports, shipments, and goods stored in foreign countries, domestic shipments, domestic warehouse credits and dollar exchange. Federal Reserve reports and bulletins provide information on acceptances between 1936 and 1939.

12. As noted in Chapter 3, trust companies were partially exempted from earlier prohibitions on originating foreign business and in some cases possessed foreign connections even before 1914.

13. The bank complained, however, that the acceptances it originated failed to find ready buyers, forcing it to hold them on its own account.

14. The figures we report are for the sub-period 1927–1937. Truptil (1936, 159 ff) used material from the Committee on Finance and Industry (1931) to impute missing information. Baster (1937) then extended Truptil's estimates. We have also drawn on unpublished estimates by the Bank of England. Starting in the 1930s, the Bank provided estimates of the volume of acceptances (Bank of England Archive EID4/86). We thank Olivier Accominotti for this material. Because domestic trade could also be financed by domestic drafts, attempting to disentangle domestic and foreign drafts is hopeless. Statisticians of British acceptances typically sought to identify acceptances from banks' balance sheets, as did the editors of the *Acceptance Bulletin* for the United States.

15. This resemblance is unsurprising, since foreign exchange reserves mostly comprised bills (or acceptances), deposits and government bonds. In the Fed's case foreign deposits were often reinvested in acceptances.

16. We discuss this pattern later in the chapter.

17. See the Federal Reserve Board's *Annual Report for 1915* (Federal Reserve Board 1916).

18. The report also mentions that 7 banks in the area had entered the acceptance business (Federal Reserve Board 1916, 136).

19. Federal Reserve Archival System for Economic Research, Federal Reserve Open Market Investment Committee (Open Market Policy Conference), Excerpts, 1923 to 1928. Quote taken from "Excerpts of the Federal Open Market Investment Committee during 1923," p. 5.

20. Sayers (1976) discusses the conflicts created by the multiplicity of policy objectives in the 1920s and partial remedies for dealing with them.

21. See Battilossi (2006) and Briones and Villela (2006). Most of these banks were specialized financial institutions controlled by or affiliated with the Great Banks that were the pillars of the German banking system (Deutsche Bank, the Discontogesellschaft, and the Dresdner Bank, for example). Such arrangements were not specific to Latin America; for instance, the Deutsche-Asiatische Bank was active in China during this period.

22. In 1914, the Allies forced the Deutsche-Asiatische Bank to terminate its operations in China. These branches were barely able to resume their operations after 1918. See King (1989) and Horesh (2008).

23. Parrini (1969, 129).

24. Inflation also played a role in the reduction in the capital base of the German banks, but wartime dislocations were, in our view, decisive. Had shareholders of German overseas banks felt that recapitalization would bring revenues, they presumably would have supplied the needed resources.

25. The data come from the Baker Library at Harvard University, Columbia University's Online Digital Collection, the British Library, and the Graduate Institute of International and Development Studies' collection of banks' balance sheets. See the chapter appendix for details.

26. The Federal Reserve Act authorized national banks to purchase or discount acceptances up to 50 percent of capital. The ceiling was raised to 100 percent subsequently.

27. It could be, of course, that branching does not add more acceptances, but that banks that offered other services to originate acceptances had to branch to meet customers' needs. However, considering this would weaken the case for branches, and given our later finding, it would only strengthen our conclusions.

28. Introducing capital and total assets together creates a problem of multicollinearity, as one would expect.

29. Again, multicollinearity is an issue.

30. In Tables 5.3 and 5.4, we continue to cluster the standard errors.

Chapter Six

1. The reluctance of foreign investors to purchase bonds denominated in the currency of the issuer in more recent periods is similarly emphasized by Eichengreen and Hausmann (2005).

2. This source also contains data on outstanding amounts of *domestic* public debt in some 50 countries during the interwar period, compiled from national sources, data that have been used by Reinhart and Rogoff (2008, 2009ab, 2010) and Reinhart (2010) and in subsequent work on public debt (e.g., Ali Abbas et al. 2011; Fratzscher, Mehl, and Vansteenkiste 2011). Data on domestic public debt were not broken down by currency, which is why we focus in this chapter on foreign debt.

3. Since we exclusively consider non-U.S. and non-U.K. debt, it is the international financing role of sterling or the dollar that is captured by our data.

4. For instance, a bond issued in French francs in London might be payable in dollars. An illustration of these practices is the case of Norway. As the UN authors explain (United Nations 1948, 107), "The loans raised [by Norway] in France were originally issued in francs [i.e., the currency of the country in which the bond was issued as well as its currency of issuance], but are also payable in several currencies at fixed rates of exchange, including sterling at 25.25 francs = 1 sterling [i.e., currency in which the bond was redeemed]. After the devaluation of the French Franc in 1928, these bonds were paid, beginning with 1933, in sterling in Paris, rather than in French francs." The authors adjust the data correspondingly: "The outstanding amounts have therefore, up to 1932 inclusive, been converted at

par rates of exchange, but beginning with 1933 the francs have been converted in sterling at 25.25." In cases where the currency of denomination was not specified (e.g., for Canada, Australia, New Zealand, and South Africa), we determined this from other sources. Where it was not possible to determine this on the basis of other sources, we excluded the country.

5. Names could change over time. The Austro-Hungarian guilder was replaced by the crown (krone) in 1892 as part of the introduction of the gold standard. However, the name florin was used on Austrian coins, while forint was used on post-1867 Hungarian banknotes and coins.

6. Borchard (1951) describes this in more detail.

7. There were, however, gold clauses specifying payment in dollars of constant gold content in U.S. Treasury liabilities issued domestically. Those gold clauses were thrown out by the U.S. Supreme Court following the 1933 devaluation of the dollar (Kroszner 1999).

8. These rates are taken from the UN volume, "Global Financial Data" (https://www.globalfinancialdata.com/), and the "Measuring Worth" database (https://measuringworth.com/). A further distinction is between fiscal and calendar years. A few countries have fiscal years that start on April 1 of year t and end on March 31 of year $t + 1$. Some countries (e.g., Brazil, France, Romania, and Poland) changed from calendar to fiscal year at some point in our sample. We follow the UN convention by assigning data for fiscal year April 1 t to March 31 $t + 1$ to calendar year $t + 1$. Three exceptions were France, Poland, and Romania, where we assigned the data to calendar year t so as to avoid gaps in the time series.

9. For instance, Brazil's debt in gold francs (issued in 1914) is converted to its equivalent U.S. dollar amount using the 1914 franc germinal (5.095 gold francs per dollar). We use currency shares at current exchange rates in our empirical model, allowing us to compare our results with those of earlier studies. To account for valuation effects, we also calculate currency shares at constant exchange rates, which we consider in robustness checks. Considering the evolution of currency shares in both constant and current market exchange rates is similarly the practice in studies of the currency composition of foreign exchange reserves (e.g., Truman and Wong 2006; European Central Bank, various issues).

10. Germany's reparations-related debts are also excluded, since they were excluded by the UN statisticians on whose compilation we draw. Including them would only reinforce our principal conclusion that the dollar quickly came to rival sterling as a currency of denomination for international bonds in the 1920s, insofar as Germany borrowed heavily in the United States.

11. This compares with 39 percent of world GDP for both the United States and the United Kingdom.

12. This amount corresponded to some 4 percent of world GDP. It is a bit larger than the amount of global reserves (in gold and foreign exchange, with 24 countries) for that year, namely about $10 billion (see Chapter 4 for details). By comparison, as of the end of 2010, the stock of international debt securities accounted for 17 percent of world GDP and 114 percent of world reserves, according

to data from the ECB's *International Role of the Euro* (2011 edition) and the IMF's "World Economic Outlook" database (September 2011 edition).

13. Amounts borrowed from the UK by the French government were slightly smaller (Moulton and Pasvolsky 1926, p. 45). The relatively even breakdown of French debt between sterling and dollars in the 1920s is evident in Figure 6.7.

14. Of the $245 million of war loans floated abroad by the Japanese government in 1904–1905, $192 billion were sold in the United States (Lewis 1938, 340). It appears that, unlike Japanese borrowing in New York in the 1920s, these earlier bonds were not all dollar denominated.

15. That India, as a British colony, issued debt exclusively in London is unsurprising. While the Thais maintained their independence by playing the British and French off against each other, their dependence on the London market (with their foreign debt consisting "entirely of sterling obligations," as stressed in United Nations (1948, 129) is evidence of the continuing importance of sterling and of the secondary status of the French franc in international bond markets (see above).

16. The sovereignty of these countries remained subject to limitations at least until the statute of Westminster in 1931 which declared self-governing dominions within the British Empire to be equal.

17. Lewis (1938, 376).

18. Notwithstanding this setback, the dollar then permanently overtook sterling in the early 1940s—and not only after World War II, as suggested in earlier accounts.

19. We focus on the sample of 28 countries, unless explicitly stated otherwise.

20. Again we use market exchange rates in this computation. Moreover, many of these countries borrowing exclusively in one of the two major currencies were members of the British Empire that essentially had no choice.

21. And by 1919 in the case of Poland, after it gained independence in 1918.

22. Lewis (1938, 377).

23. Calculated using data from the Groningen Growth and Development Centre (founded by Angus Maddison). See http://www.ggdc.net/databases /hna.htm.

24. These are again taken from "Global Financial Data."

25. King and Levine (1993) also analyze the impact of financial deepening, where financial depth is proxied by such variables as credit to GDP or money to GDP and has been found to have strong causal effects on domestic growth.

26. Trade data are from Mitchell (1998abc). This results in a number of missing observations and a smaller sample size, which is why we limit use of this variable to the section on robustness checks.

27. We take short-term nominal interest rates from Michael Bordo's multi-country dataset on financial crises (http://sites.google.com/site/michaelbordo /home4).

28. The full sample of 33 countries is considered in robustness checks.

29. Note that Chinn and Frankel also provide panel logit estimates; when we ran regressions with this estimator, convergence of the likelihood function to a global maximum was not obtained.

30. When one does not control for size and credibility, financial depth is significant at the 13 percent confidence level.

31. This assumes that other factors remain constant. In fact the bank-asset ratio continued to increase in the United States through 1931–1932, even though bank assets declined (GDP declined faster). After that, however, the trend reversed.

32. Regime shifts occurred between 1918–1919, when the United States had double-digit inflation, 1921–1922, when it experienced double-digit deflation, and the remainder of the 1920s, when prices were broadly stable.

33. More precisely, financial deepening, along with inertia, is the most important *identified* contributor to the decline in the share of sterling, given that the contribution of the residual is larger in absolute value.

34. An alternative hypothesis is the dollar's departure from the gold standard led to the decline in its share of global foreign public debt. This is unlikely, however. Sterling left the gold standard 2 years earlier than the dollar, but its share actually increased over the 1930s.

35. This method will yield consistent, albeit inefficient, estimates, inefficient because the adjustment does not correct for error autocorrelation.

36. These are not always the same, as already noted.

37. This estimator also addresses residual autocorrelation, like the Griliches (1961) and Liviathan (1963) estimator and that of Hatanaka (1974) in Table 6.A1. The instruments here are based on moment equations constructed from lagged levels of currency shares and of the first-differenced errors, along with the ratios of broad money, private credit, and narrow money to GDP as additional instruments. Given our large T context (33 years of data), the number of instruments is large relative to the number of groups N (350 vs. 54). This is unlike the standard Arellano and Bond (1991) context, where N is large and T small. It is at odds with a standard rule of thumb, according to which the number of instruments should not exceed N. The Sargan statistic does not reject the null that our overidentifying conditions are valid. Moreover, there is evidence of first-order serial correlation in the first-differenced disturbances, as expected, but not of second-order correlation.

38. Fisher-Phillips-Perron tests for unbalanced panels also reject the presence of a unit root in financial depth, both with and without a time trend, according to the Z and L^* statistics of the tests.

39. The results are not reported here to save space but are available from the authors upon request.

Chapter Seven

1. The franc, Deutschemark, guilder, and ECU were then succeeded by the euro starting in 1999.

2. For part of the period, there is a small residual category of claims in other currencies. Before 2005 the IMF did not distinguish between reserves in "other currencies" (reserves whose currency of denomination was reported but was

other than one of the currencies distinguished in its reports) and reserves whose currency of denomination was not reported to the Fund. In 2005 the IMF revised its data back to 1994, distinguishing the two "others." Since we do not have information on the distinction prior to 1994, we do not analyse the "other currencies" category prior or subsequent to 1994.

3. See Truman and Wong (2006), Dominguez, Hashimoto and Ito (2012) and Ouyang and Li (2013).

4. This is the case for eurodollar assets, which are included along with U.S.-issued reserve assets denominated in dollars.

5. See Cairncross and Eichengreen (1983) and Burk and Cairncross (1992), as well as Chapter 8.

6. The impact of the crisis on the euro's international role is analyzed by European Central Bank (2013).

7. We discuss the abortive rise of the yen as a reserve currency in Chapter 9.

8. This number rose with time, most notably in the 1970s, when the two lines in Figure 7.3 converge.

9. See also Krugman (1980, 1984) and Rey (2001).

10. And as discussed in Chapter 1.

11. We calculate trend appreciation using data from the IMF's "International Financial Statistics" (http://data.imf.org/?sk=5DABAFF2-C5AD-4D27-A175-1253419C02D1).

12. It can also be argued that economic size may, in fact, strengthen credibility—for example, because larger countries have greater fiscal capacity. Our results remain unchanged when we control for the public-debt-to-GDP and fiscal-balance-to-GDP ratios.

13. Data are from the IMF's "International Financial Statistics," "Global Financial Data" and Fratzscher, Mehl and Vansteenkiste (2011). URLs for both of these data bases are provided above.

14. To construct these measures, we draw on a range of sources, including Fukao (1990), Tavlas (1991), Takeda and Turner (1992), Henning (1994), Schenk (2010), and Takagi (2011).

15. Including an entire vector of year effects would absorb all time series variation common to all currency units and introduce a large number of additional coefficients. We therefore included instead a vector of nonoverlapping 5-year effects.

16. Earlier studies have similarly used random country effects (e.g., Ouyang and Li 2013). Estimates obtained with fixed effects yield economically implausible coefficients for the size variable and may be distorted by the time-fixed effects (insofar as the estimates become close to those obtained with random effects, once we do not include time effects). A Hausman test rejects random effects relative to fixed effects at the 10 percent confidence level only. We also correct for heteroskedasticity and clustering when computing panel-consistent standard errors. One might also wish to correct for left-censoring of the estimates that include values of zero with tobit estimates (which also means dropping the correction for heteroskedasticity and clustered heterogeneity, implying inefficient standard

errors). We report tobit estimates in robustness checks, together with system generalized method of moments estimates to account for possible endogeneity arising from, for example, the dynamic specification of our model.

17. Just as reserves held in other currencies were even smaller throughout the period and are therefore not reported.

18. This substitution will be evident from the increase in the number of observations.

19. Arithmetically, the negative coefficient on the credibility-related exchange rate term for the pre-1973 period reflects depreciation of sterling on two occasions when the share of sterling reserves was relatively high; it also reflects the appreciation of the Deutschemark in the early 1970s, when the share of Deutschemark reserves was low.

20. Most of these results carry over when we instead compute currency shares without adjustment for valuation effects. The main difference is that the interaction term for policy credibility and the post-1973 period dummy in column 4 of Table 7.1 is now insignificantly different from zero. These changes are not surprising, since allowing for exchange rate effects in the dependent variable creates the potential for spurious correlation with the exchange rate when the latter is included as an independent variable. We are therefore more inclined to trust the estimates of credibility effects in Table 7.1.

21. One needs to use the unstandardized variables to compare our estimates with theirs. Note what we compute the exchange rate as SDRs per national currency unit, whereas Chinn and Frankel compute it as national currency units per SDR, which explains the difference in the sign of this effect.

22. The change in magnitudes is statistically significant at the 1 percent confidence level.

23. This difference is significant at the 5 percent confidence level. In practice, the large coefficient on the lagged dependent variable (evidence of significant—but not insurmountable—persistence effects) may reflect the obstacles to the quick liquidation of sterling reserves discussed earlier in the chapter.

24. Open standards like Linux, Apache, or TeX are interoperable by design, with no specific cost or benefit for any user (in our context the foreign reserve holder) for selecting one product (or currency) over another on the basis of standardized features. "Products" (in our context, currencies) compete on an array of factors, such as performance, price, user friendliness (in our context, reliability as a store of value, liquidity, etc.) while keeping users' data intact and transferable, even if the user decides to switch to a competing product (in our context, to another currency unit). See the related discussion in Chapter 1.

25. The Gold Pool is the subject of Eichengreen (2007, chapter 3).

26. One indication of this concern is a sharp local peak around 1966–1968 in the number of books citing Bretton Woods, according to Google's Ngram Viewer. In turn, 1968 was a key year in the negotiations to create SDRs as a possible alternative to dollar reserves; an amendment to this effect to the IMF's Articles of Agreement was drafted and ratified by a growing number of countries in the course of the year, although the amendment only came into effect in 1969, and ac-

tual SDRs were only issued (in small numbers) starting in 1970. Note that the only other chi-square statistics that come close to rivaling the 1960 and 1966 values are in the first years of the floating rate era.

27. Note also that dividing the sample in 1960 leaves too few observations for meaningful estimates for the preceding period.

28. See, for example, Frenkel (1978) and Heller and Kahn (1978).

29. This subset of economies is also considered in Committee on the Global Financial System (2010) and Kubelec and Sá (2012).

30. The increased credibility effects may reflect the fact that we could not adjust the dependent variable for exchange rate valuation effects in the absence of information on the currency composition of non-dollar reserve holdings. These results are available from the authors upon request.

31. We are not aware of similar measures adopted by other countries in our data set.

32. In general, the effect of unsupportive official positions and unsupportive exchange-rate-regime-related initiatives is economically smaller than that of other unsupportive measures.

33. As mentioned, these estimates are obtained with currency shares already purged of exchange rate valuation effects.

34. The indices run from zero (complete financial autarky) to 100 (complete financial openness) and are available for all the currencies in our sample.

35. This required us to limit the sample to the period since 1973 due to the unavailability of earlier data on turnover. Turnover was taken from the BIS Triennial Surveys of global foreign exchange market activity back to 1986 and from G30 and national central bank reports for 1973–1986, as in Chinn and Frankel (2007, 2008). Following the practice of these other authors, the series was linearly interpolated.

36. Chen, Peng, and Shu (2009) use stock market capitalization as a measure of financial development and find that it is economically important and statistically significant in the recent period. Another alternative would be to use bond market capitalization, but then the data would have an insufficiently long time span.

37. We used the Rajan and Zingales (2003) data for 1950–1999 (linearly interpolated) and the data in Beck, Demirgüç-Kunt, and Levine (2009) for 1999–2013. Nominal GDP was taken from the IMF's *International Financial Statistics*.

38. Yet another alternative is to substitute the log level of market capitalization for country size. In this case, stock market capitalization enters positively (but insignificantly) before 1973, while the interaction term for the post-1973 period is negative (but also insignificant). This echoes the pattern found in the baseline model. Hence it is hard to know whether results obtained using this specification are in fact capturing the effects of market development and liquidity, or those of country size (with which market capitalization is correlated). This causes us to prefer the results in Table 7.1.

39. The time-varying betas were constructed as 5-year rolling estimates where the dependent variable is log currency i returns and the independent variable is the weighted average of the log returns in all other currencies of our sample (a

proxy for world currency returns minus currency i itself, to avoid spurious correlation), where the weights are time-varying country shares in world exports in year t.

40. An exception was the credibility of policies as measured by inflation rates, which was found to have weakened post-1973. This likely reflected the correlation between relatively high British inflation and the falling share of sterling in international reserves. U.S. inflation in the later period, evidently, had a smaller and less significant effect.

41. As noted, one then has to forgo robust standard errors adjusted for clustering.

42. The reason is that we have no right/left-censored variables, so that tobit estimation is actually not needed. When we obtain estimates without missing observations, the standard errors become quite large, however, which may be because they are not robust to heteroskedasticity.

43. When constructing the instrument matrix, we treated persistence, size, and credibility as endogenous and year dummies as exogenous. The very high p-value of the Hansen statistic (which overwhelmingly suggests that the instruments are orthogonal) likely indicates that the number of instruments still remains large relative to the number of currency units despite the Roodman (2009) correction. Moreover, there is evidence of significant dynamic effects only at the 25 percent level of confidence, as measured in the first-order serial correlation of the first-differenced disturbances of the estimated models (and evidence of second-order serial correlation in two specifications).

44. Although the change was not statistically significant.

45. Where the logistic transformation is defined as log [share/(1 − share)].

46. It could be argued that a logistic transformation of the dependent variable is not practical here, because such a nonlinear transformation may lead to inconsistent estimates (especially when reserve currency shares are close or equal to zero). See Santos Silva and Tenreyo (2006) for further details.

Chapter Eight

1. "It took ten years following the end of the war (and a 30 percent devaluation of the pound) before the share of dollar reserves exceeded that of sterling. This rather contradicts Chinn and Frankel's assertion that 'by 1945 the dethroning [of sterling] was complete.'" Schenk (2010, 30).

2. Much of this slide was valuation effects, but by no means all. When currency shares are constructed on a constant-exchange-rate basis, the step down in 1967–1968 disappears, but the subsequent downward trend remains.

3. The currency was then held at that level through a combination of controls and actions by the Bank of England until 1949, when it was devalued (see below).

4. Bareau (1948, 8).

5. The United Kingdom had few other means with which to make payment and preferred to use scarce gold and dollars to source commodities and matériel

from the Dollar Area, where sterling was less likely to be accepted (for more on the Dollar Area, see below).

6. The latter being the Treasury's vehicle for intervening in the foreign exchange market (see Howson 1980).

7. A few adjusted the sterling parity significantly in response to events, for example, New Zealand in 1933. New Zealand was reacting to the depression in the farm sector and to competition from other countries with depreciated currencies, such as Denmark.

8. France after 1936, for example, falls under this heading.

9. Day (1954) similarly disputes that Argentina and Greece qualified, while including the Scandinavian and Baltic states, Egypt, Iraq, Portugal, and Siam.

10. Ironically, it was partly distrust of the managed pound sterling that led to the feasibility of these arrangements. That distrust was part of what led members of the Commonwealth, such as Canada and Australia, which had not previously established central banks, to do so in the 1930s; those central banks then became the agents of wartime control.

11. In the words of Bareau (1948, 9).

12. Thus, in the second half of the 1940s, holders were able to exchange their "cheap sterling" for dollars on the black market and use the dollars to purchase merchandise from the Dollar Area, now that the authorities no longer controlled shipping.

13. Conan (1952, 43–44).

14. Britain's total external liabilities roughly doubled between the outbreak of the war and the end of 1941, with close to 100 percent of the change accounted for by the British Empire. They then tripled between the end of 1941 and the end of 1945 (Cohen 1971, 90). On the asset side, all marketable British investments in the United States were requisitioned by the government in 1940–1941, their previous owners being compensated in sterling. Britain still earned net interest income abroad in the second half of the 1940s, because foreign assets bore higher rates of interest. However, these earnings declined absolutely and as a share of the current account deficit.

15. A third factor was instability of reserve position. Kenen (1960, 14–15) notes that the United Kingdom lost 20 percent of its reserves in the second half of 1955 and a third of its reserves in late 1956.

16. No questions, at least, until U.S. foreign monetary liabilities exceeded U.S. monetary gold reserves starting in 1960.

17. Schenk (2010) notes that there was similarly no sudden rush out of sterling by British colonies when they gained their independence in the late 1950s and early 1960s.

18. See, for example, Conan (1952, 54–56).

19. For more on the openness, or otherwise, of British financial markets, see below.

20. In the first half of the 1950s the area as a whole accounted for nearly 40 percent of world trade. The United Kingdom in this period was party to some two thirds of the area's trade. See Kenen (1960, 9).

21. This estimate leaves aside what became the Soviet bloc in the 1950s (Clarke 1965, 211). Invoicing and settlement in sterling then fell to no more than a third by the early 1960s and perhaps 22 percent by 1967 (this last estimate is from Cohen 1971). On the situation in the 1930s, see Chapter 5.

22. The 1949 devaluation of sterling also had implications for the stature of the newly created International Monetary Fund. Where the IMF's Articles of Agreement stated that a country seeking to devalue its currency by 10 percent or more should give the Fund 72 hours' notice and seek its assent, the British government gave it only 24 hours' advance warning and announced the move as a fait accompli. Nor did the government consult with its major non-Commonwealth trading partners, which did little to endear it to these large holders of sterling balances. The only consequential advance negotiations were with the U.S. government, which is revealing of where the real economic and financial power now lay. The story of the 1949 devaluation is told in Cairncross and Eichengreen (1983, chapter 4).

23. Schenk (2010, 84).

24. Conan (1952, 116).

25. Fforde (1992, 221).

26. That is to say, it could be used up to the limits prescribed by that system.

27. This was the so-called ROBOT plan described by Burnham (2003).

28. Officials in the Bank of England dissented from the majority view, arguing that floating and the early resumption of full current account convertibility (as needed to preserve sterling's international role) might go together (Fforde 1992, 221).

29. Schonfield (1958, 218).

30. Fforde (1992, 250–251).

31. Changes in the relative importance of members of the Sterling Area also occurred, as countries like India that held a large proportion of their reserves in sterling grew more slowly than others with more widely diversified portfolios.

32. Cairncross and Eichengreen (1983, 192–193).

33. Schenk (2010) is a book-length treatment of these efforts.

Chapter Nine

1. Angus Maddison dates the cross-over point as occurring in 1967, when GDP is expressed in purchasing-power-parity-adjusted terms (Maddison 2010).

2. Importers and exporters also applied pressure; as Aramaki (2014) notes, commodity and merchandise imports were also initially subject to an approval system, and current account transactions were only even partially liberalized with the "Basic Plan for Liberalization of Trade and Foreign Exchange" in 1960.

3. Some relaxation of restrictions on inward foreign investment started in 1967 (Aramaki 2014).

4. Fukuda and Cong (1994, 512). The comparable shares for the U.S. dollar were 90 and 80 percent, respectively.

5. Tavlas and Ozeki (1991, 11).

6. As the Japanese Ministry of Finance (nd) puts it on its website, "Interest in the international role of the yen was first sparked by the discussion seeking a new international monetary system in the wake of the collapse of the Bretton Woods System, that is the adoption of a floating exchange rate system in March 1973 following the 'Nixon shock' of August 1971." The Ministry then goes on to explain how interest was further encouraged by the fact that during this period, "the United States continued to suffer a secular decline in its global economic standing, provoking a further decline in international confidence in the dollar," while Japan "emerged from these shocks with renewed vigor."

7. In addition, under the 1980 law, the Ministry of Finance could prohibit authorized foreign exchange banks from paying interest on yen deposits held by nonresidents (Takagi 2011).

8. The banks did tend to push for financial liberalization at home, since under the country's repressed financial system, they received low interest rates on the government bonds that constituted an increasingly large share of their investment portfolios; see Dominguez (1999).

9. This is the conclusion of Frankel (1990).

10. On the role of U.S. policy in these dollar swings, see Sachs (1985).

11. Dominguez (1999, 138).

12. This occurred with a lag of several years, as described by Moreno (1996).

13. Fukuda and Cong (1994, 512). See also Taguchi (1994) for further details.

14. See Bank for International Settlements (1995). Note that shares of exchange-market turnover sum to 200 percent, since two currencies are involved in every trade.

15. The one exception was samurai bonds (international bonds denominated in yen), which gained market share. Developing countries were attracted to issuing yen bonds by the low yen-denominated interest rates prevailing in Japan owing to depressed economic conditions there. See Packer and Reynolds (1997) for discussion.

16. A more extensive analysis can be found in Hoshi and Kashyap (2000).

17. A compact summary of this experience is Patrick (1998).

18. See Cargill (2000).

19. This is argued by Takagi (2011).

20. See Ito and Melvin (2001).

21. Foreign reactions to the Asian Monetary Fund proposal are described in Blustein (2001, 166–190).

Chapter Ten

1. "Legacy currencies" is the name assigned to the former national currencies of what were now the members of the euro area.

2. As noted in Chapter 1.

3. See Bénassy-Quéré and Coeuré (2014) for an analysis of post-crisis developments in the euro's international role.

4. See International Capital Market Association (2014). In addition, the Association cites the new bank regulation as a factor in declining secondary-market liquidity.

5. See also the discussion in Bénassy-Quéré and Coeuré (2010).

6. This thesis has been argued by many authors, including one of us: see Eichengreen (1994).

7. See the discussion in Martin and Ross (2004, 79–80)

8. We follow here the arguments presented in Bergsten (1997).

9. Bergsten (1997, 83). This goal—and not that of completing the single market—was among the key objectives of the founders of the euro, according to Feldstein, who stressed that "French officials have been outspoken in emphasizing that a primary reason for a European monetary and political union is as a counterweight to the influence of the United States both within Europe and in international affairs" (Feldstein 1997, 72–73).

10. See Eichengreen (1998).

11. This point was stressed by Portes and Rey (1998), who deemed both (de) regulation and policy harmonization across Europe to be important in this respect, together with private market initiatives (e.g., in establishing benchmark interest rates and securities).

12. See Feldstein (1997). For more on these questions, see also Bénassy-Quéré, Mojon, and Schor (1998).

13. This neutrality was further elaborated in an ECB document released in the summer of 1999, which discussed the costs and benefits of currency internationalization along with its implications for monetary policy and indicated that the ECB and the Eurosystem (the ECB together with its network of member-country central banks) would "neither hinder nor foster the international use of its currency" (European Central Bank 2001, 45).

14. The Swiss franc faced similar safe haven flows both in the early 1970s and again following the global financial crisis of 2008–2009, forcing the Swiss National Bank to push policy interest rates into negative territory following the collapse of Bretton Woods and again in 2015.

15. European Central Bank (1999, 43).

16. For the euro area countries, the study considered the period 1999–2007 (see Habib 2010).

17. See Chapter 11.

18. This underappreciated potential impact of the euro was emphasized by Ronald McKinnon in a series of articles (see inter alia McKinnon 2001). A subsequent study by Papaioannou and Portes (2008) suggested that this was the main factor in the development of the euro as an international financing currency in its first years of existence.

19. Since two currencies are involved in each foreign exchange transaction, the global total, recall, is 200 percent.

20. See Detken and Hartmann (2002) for details.

21. Adjusting for such valuation changes arising from exchange rate movements, the decline in the share of the euro between 2009 and 2015, at 3 percentage points, is similar to that of the U.S. dollar over the same period.

22. These countries are Slovenia (which joined the euro area in 2007), Malta and Cyprus (which joined in 2008), Slovakia (in 2009), Estonia (in 2011), Latvia (in 2014), and Lithuania (in 2015).

23. Hence governments had limited fiscal space with which to absorb exceptional shocks, and confidence in the medium-term soundness of public finances was not sufficiently anchored.

24. See European Central Bank (2013, 2014).

25. See Juncker (2015).

Chapter Eleven

1. China has signed free trade agreements not just in Asia but also as far afield as Chile, Costa Rica, Peru, Iceland, and Switzerland.

2. European Central Bank (2015, 21). An important qualification is that a disproportionate share of renminbi settlements are for trade between China and Hong Kong.

3. The crossover point was in 2013, as cited in BRICS Post (2015) and Wilson (2015).

4. Moreover, authorization to settle commercial transactions in renminbi was extended to the entire Chinese economy only in 2011.

5. The pioneering U.K. government issue was in October 2014. There have also been a handful of other foreign government bonds issued in RMB, such as the Canadian province of British Columbia issuing a RMB 3 billion bond in China's domestic market in January 2016.

6. The estimate is from International Monetary Fund (2015) and refers to the share of China's currency in global official foreign currency assets.

7. The $500 billion estimate is from Fernandez (2015).

8. The Chinese currency is thus behind not only the dollar but also the euro, the yen, sterling, the Australian and Canadian dollars, the Swiss franc, and the Mexican peso.

9. And also the Canadian and Australian dollars, as well as the Swiss franc.

10. As of 2015.

11. The other CMIM swaps are specified in dollars. China has also committed to pooling up to $100 billion of reserves in a Contingent Reserve Arrangement with the other so-called BRICS countries (Brazil, Russia, India, and South Africa). It is not clear whether Contingent Reserve Arrangement lending by China will be in dollars or renminbi (the initial BRICS Contingent Reserve Arrangement treaty refers to dollars, but this may simply denote the unit of account).

12. "BRICS" is the standard acronym for the founding member states: Brazil, Russia, India, China, and South Africa.

13. The plan envisages enhancing connectivity within Asia and between Asia, Europe, and Africa via land and adjacent sea routes, although it appears to be centered on Central and Southeast Asia. The Silk Road Economic Belt will run along the historic Silk Road trade route, which stretches from coastal China through Central Asia, while the Maritime Silk Road will connect the China's south

with Southeast Asia. Although focused on transport and other forms of physical infrastructure, the Silk Road Initiative is also intended to encompass trade facilitation, financial cooperation, and cultural exchange. Insofar as it achieves its goal of reducing transport costs, cultural barriers, and other obstacles to exchange, it has the potential to deepen trade and financial interaction between China on the one hand and Southeast and Central Asian countries on the other, thereby enhancing the attractions of use of the renminbi in the region.

14. See Kindleberger (1970), Strange (1971, 1988), Kirschner (1995), Williamson (2012), and Cohen (2015).

15. Here we measure financial size as the sum of bank lending and the market value of outstanding bonds and equity.

16. The decision in 2014 to allow Chaori, a solar-cell company, to default was a first step in removing the implicit guarantee. A second step was then taken in April 2015, when the government of the city of Ordos, China, refused to guarantee the bonds of the troubled Sundry Group of construction companies, property developer Kaisa Group missed an interest payment on its dollar-denominated debt, and state-owned power equipment manufacturer Baoding Tianwei Group failed to make a payment on its domestic debt.

17. Some policy makers have argued that central bank independence is important in this connection. For instance Coeuré (2015) has expressed "doubt that a currency can gain international status if investors do not trust its issuing central bank to be free from political interference."

18. This idea is consistent with Gehlbach and Keefer (2009), who argue that autocracies are capable of making credible commitments to honor their financial obligations. In some autocracies the elite, which holds many of the financial claims, is protected from expropriation by membership in the institutionalized ruling party, which is a mechanism through which members, acting together, can limit the scope for opportunistic action by the autocrat.

19. Schultz and Weingast (2003, 5).

20. Quintyn and Verdier (2010) focus on periods of sustained financial deepening as captured by a rising ratio of private sector credit to GDP and show that this is more likely in countries that rank high on the polity scale of the extent of democracy, where there are significant checks on the prerogatives of the executive, and where elections are freely contested. They find less evidence that political arrangements matter for the likelihood of short bursts of financial deepening as opposed to sustained movements. But it is those sustained movements that are important for present purposes.

21. Recall, however, that the two variables may not be independent. Authors like Bienen and Van de Walle (1991) have shown that leaders of democratic states tend to have shorter tenures than the leaders of nondemocratic states.

22. Girma and Shortland (2007) provide statistical support for the notion that political stability is associated with financial development.

Chapter Twelve

1. We are conscious of having said nothing in this paragraph about when (Chapter 11 having highlighted the uncertainties that surround the timing of these developments). Recall the first rule of forecasting: "Give them a forecast or a date, but never give them both."

2. If one prefers a more expansive definition of safe and liquid dollar assets, then these can be widened to include not only U.S. government bonds but also agency bonds (securities issued by government-sponsored housing agencies) and investment-grade debt securities issued by the corporate sector, although these are generally regarded as riskier than government bonds (they are subject to the "sovereign ceiling" that they cannot be rated higher than government bonds, although they can be rated lower). In addition, foreign central banks in particular are generally reluctant to hold them. The case of subprime-linked-mortgage securities, noted in Chapter 1, suggests that such "private-label" debt securities may not be as safe and liquid as initially supposed and can be re-rated in the blink of an eye, explaining the reluctance of central banks to hold them as reserves. Be this as it may, assuming that other countries and their corporations will continue to grow faster than those of a mature economy like that of the United States, the arguments in the text continue to stand.

3. The original Triffin Dilemma tied U.S. provision of safe and liquid assets to the stock of U.S. gold reserves as opposed to the government's fiscal capacity. For elaboration see Obstfeld (2013).

4. In addition to U.S. banks, U.S. money market mutual funds were and are key suppliers of dollar funding to non-U.S. banks, as described by Baba, McCauley, and Ramaswamy (2009).

5. So it is argued, for example, in the case of Korea by Park (2011).

6. See, for example, O'Driscoll (2011).

7. The major central banks have made clear that the arrangement of swap lines should remain at their discretion and must be in line with their respective mandates (on this point, see also Coeuré 2015).

8. The phrase in quotes is from the title of Broz (2012). To be sure, it is possible for countries to obtain limited amounts of emergency dollar liquidity from the IMF. But the Fund's lending capacity is limited. It cannot print dollars but must ask its members to contribute them. Its procedures are time consuming, and only a handful of countries have signed up for quick-disbursing facilities (like its Flexible Credit Line, where they prequalify for assistance), presumably owing to stigma problems. In addition, countries can borrow dollar reserves from one another and have established several regional financial arrangements with this in mind. This assumes of course that the countries in question do not all need their dollar reserves at the same time and that they are confident that they will be paid back what they lend. Perhaps reflecting this last concern, there has been a reluctance to activate these arrangements.

9. It has been suggested that, if reserve issuers cannot commit to not inflating away their debts, worsening coordination problems might not only lead to a less stable international monetary system but also to a fall in the supply of reserve assets; see Farhi and Maggiori (2016).

10. See, for example, the evidence in Truman and Wong (2006).

11. This is the conclusion of Bordo and MacDonald (2012).

12. https://books.google.com/ngrams.

13. The comparison between emergency liquidity assistance in 1931 and 2008–2009 is developed in more detail in Accominotti and Eichengreen (2016).

REFERENCES

Accominotti, Olivier (2009), "The Sterling Trap: Foreign Exchange Reserve Management at the Bank of France during the Gold Standard, 1928–1936," *European Review of Economic History* 13, pp. 349–376.

Accominotti, Olivier, and Barry Eichengreen (2016), "The Mother of All Sudden Stops: Capital Flows and Reversals in Europe, 1919–1932," *Economic History Review* 69, new ser., pp. 469–492.

Alesina, Alberto, and David Dollar (1998), "Who Gives Foreign Aid to Whom and Why," *Journal of Economic Growth* 5, pp. 33–63.

Ali Abbas, S. M., Nazim Belhocine, Asmaa El-Ganainy, and Mark Horton (2011), "Historical Patterns and Dynamics of Public Debt—Evidence from a New Database," *IMF Economic Review* 59, pp. 717–742.

Aliber, Robert (1966), *The Future of the Dollar as an International Currency*, New York: Frederick Praeger.

Allayannis, George, and Eli Ofek, (2001), "Exchange Rate Exposure, Hedging and the Use of Foreign Currency Derivatives," *Journal of International Money and Finance* 20, pp. 273–296.

Allayannis, George, Gregory Brown, and Leora Klapper (2003), "Capital Structure and Financial Risk: Evidence from Foreign Debt Use in East Asia," *Journal of Finance* 58, pp. 2667–2709.

Aramaki, Kenji (2014), "Capital Account Liberalization: Japan's Experience and Its Implications for China," unpublished manuscript, Tokyo University (September 13).

Arellano, Manuel, and Stephen Bond (1991), "Some Tests of Specification for Panel Data: Monte Carlo Evidence and an Application to Employment Equations," *Review of Economic Studies* 58, pp. 277–297.

Arthur, Brian (1989), "Competing Technologies, Increasing Returns, and Lock-In by Historical Events," *Economic Journal* 99, pp. 116–131.

Baba, Naohiko, Robert McCauley, and Srichander Ramaswamy (2009), "US Dollar Money Market Funds and Non-US Banks," *BIS Quarterly Review* (March), pp. 65–81.

Bagehot, Walter (1873), *Lombard Street: A Description of the Money Market*, London: H.S. King.

Banca d'Italia (1993), *I bilanci degli Istituti di Emissione 1894–1990*, Rome and Bari: Laterza.

Bank for International Settlements (1932), "The Gold Exchange Standard," mimeograph, Monetary and Economic Department, Basel.

———. (1995), *Triennial Central Bank Survey of Foreign Exchange and Derivatives Market Activity*, Basel.

Bareau, Paul (1948), *The Sterling Area: What It Is and How It Works*, London: Longmans Green.

Baster, A.S.J (1937), "The International Acceptance Market," *American Economic Review* 27, pp. 294–304.

Battilossi, Stefano (2006), "The Determinants of Multinational Banking during the First Globalisation, 1880–1914," *European Review of Economic History* 10, pp. 361–388.

Bazot, Guillaume, Michael Bordo, and Eric Monnet (2014), "The Price of Stability: The Balance Sheet Policy of the Banque de France and the Gold Standard (1880–1914)," NBER Working Paper 20554 (October), Cambridge, MA: National Bureau of Economic Research.

Beck, Thorsten, Aslı Demirgüç-Kunt, and Ross Levine (2009), "Financial Institutions and Markets across Countries and over Time: Data and Analysis," World Bank Policy Research Working Paper 4943 (May), Washington, DC: World Bank.

Bénassy-Quéré, Agnès, and Benoît Coeuré (2010), "Le rôle international de l'euro: chronique d'une décennie," *Revue d'Economie Politique* 120, pp. 355–377.

———. (2014), *Economie de l'euro*, Paris: Editions La Découverte.

Bénassy-Quéré, Agnès, Benoît Mojon, and Armand-Denis Schor (1998), "The International Role of the Euro," CEPII Working Paper 1998–03 (July), Paris: CEPII.

Bergsten, Fred (1997), "The Dollar and the Euro," *Foreign Affairs* 76, pp. 83–95.

Bienen, Henry, and Nicolas van de Walle (1991), *Of Time and Power*, Stanford, CA: Stanford University Press.

Bignon, Vincent, Marc Flandreau, and Stefano Ugolini (2011), "Bagehot for Beginners: The Making of Lending of Last Resort Operations in the Mid-19th Century," *Economic History Review*, new ser. 65, pp. 580–608.

Bloomfield, Arthur (1959), *Monetary Policy under the International Gold Standard, 1880–1914*, New York: Federal Reserve Bank of New York.

———. (1963), "Short-Term Capital Movements under the Pre-1914 Gold Standard," *Princeton Studies in International Finance* 11, International Finance Section, Department of Economics, Princeton University, Princeton, NJ.

Blustein, Paul (2001), *The Chastening: Inside the Crisis That Rocked the Global Financial System and Humbled the IMF*, New York: Public Affairs Books.

Borchard, Edwin (1951), *State Insolvency and Foreign Bondholders: General Principles*, New Haven, CT: Yale University Press.

Bordo, Michael, and Finn Kydland (1996), "The Gold Standard as a Commitment Mechanism," in Tamim Bayoumi, Barry Eichengreen, and Mark Taylor (eds.), *Modern Perspectives on the Gold Standard*, Cambridge: Cambridge University Press, pp. 55–100.

Bordo, Michael, and Ronald MacDonald (2012), *Credibility and the International Monetary Regime: A Historical Perspective*, Cambridge: Cambridge University Press.

Bordo, Michael, and Peter Rousseau (2006), "Legal-Political Factors and the Historical Evolution of the Finance-Growth Link," *European Review of Economic History* 10, pp. 421–444.

Boyer-Xambeu, Marie-Thérèse , Ghislain Deleplace, and Lucien Gillard (1986), *Monnaie privée et pouvoir des princes. L'économie des relations monétaires à la Renaissance*, Paris: Presses de Sciences Po.

Braunstein, Yale, and Lawrence White (1985), "Setting Technical Compatibility Standards: An Economic Analysis," *Antitrust Bulletin* 30, pp. 337–355.

BRICS Post (2015), "China's Yuan 5th Most Used Payment Currency: SWIFT" (January 28), http://thebricspost.com/chinas-yuan-5th-most-used-payment-currency-swift/#.VdNwNZccBoF.

Briones, Ignacio, and André Villela (2006), "European Bank Penetration during the First Wave of Globalisation: Lessons from Brazil and Chile, 1878–1913," *European Review of Economic History* 10, pp. 329–359.

Broz, Lawrence (1997), *The International Origins of the Federal Reserve System*, Ithaca, NY: Cornell University Press.

———. (2012), "The Federal Reserve as a Global Lender of Last Resort, 2007–2010," unpublished manuscript, University of California, San Diego (December).

Burk, Kathleen, and Alec Cairncross (1992), *Goodbye, Great Britain: The 1976 IMF Crisis*, New Haven, CT: Yale University Press.

Burnham, Peter (2003), *Remaking the Postwar World Economy: ROBOT and British Economic Policy in the 1950s*, London: Palgrave Macmillan.

Caetano, José, and António Caleiro (2007), "Corruption and Foreign Direct Investment: What Kind of Relationship Is There?" in Raul Gupta and Santap Mishra (eds.), *Corruption: The Causes and Combating Strategies,* Delhi: Institute of Chartered Financial Analysts of India Books, pp. 56–72.

Cairncross, Alec, and Barry Eichengreen (1983), *Sterling in Decline: The Devaluations of 1931, 1949 and 1967*, Oxford: Blackwell.

Cargill, Thomas (2000), "What Caused Japan's Banking Crisis?" in Takeo Hoshi and Hugh Patrick (eds.), *Crisis and Change in the Japanese Financial System*, Dordrecht: Kluwer Academic, pp. 37–58.

Cassel, Gustav (1925), "The Restoration of Gold as a Universal Monetary Standard," in United States Senate, Commission of Gold and Silver Inquiry, John Parker Young (ed.), *European Currency and Finance*, Washington, DC: Government Printing Office, pp. 205–206.

Cassis, Youssef (2009), *Capitals of Capital: The Rise and Fall of International Financial Centres 1780–2009*, Cambridge: Cambridge University Press.

Castro, Conceicao, and Pedro Nunes (2013), "Does Corruption Inhibit Foreign Direct Investment?" *Revista de Ciencia Politica* 51, pp. 61–83.

Chandler, Lester Vernon (1958), *Benjamin Strong, Central Banker*, Washington, DC: Brookings Institution.

Chen, Hongyi, Wensheng Peng, and Chang Shu (2009), "The Potential of the Renminbi as an International Currency," unpublished manuscript, Hong Kong Institute for Monetary Research, Barclays Capital, and Hong Kong Monetary Authority (February).

Chernow, Ron (1993), *The Warburgs*, New York: Random House.

Chinn, Menzie, and Jeffrey Frankel (2007), "Will the Euro Eventually Surpass the Dollar as Leading International Currency?" in Richard Clarida (ed.), *G7 Current Account Imbalances and Adjustment*, Chicago: University of Chicago Press, pp. 283–338.

———. (2008), "Why the Euro Will Rival the Dollar," *International Finance* 11, pp. 49–73.

Chițu, Livia, Barry Eichengreen, and Arnaud Mehl (2014), "When Did the Dollar Overtake Sterling as the Leading International Currency? Evidence from the Bond Markets," *Journal of Development Economics* 111, pp. 225–245.

Choudhri, Ehsan, and Levis Kochin (1980), "The Exchange Rate and the International Transmission of Business Cycle Disturbances: Some Evidence from the Great Depression," *Journal of Money, Credit and Banking* 12, pp. 565–574.

Clapham, Henry (1944), *The Bank of England: A History*, 2 volumes, Cambridge: Cambridge University Press.

Clark, David (2003), "The Design of Open Systems," *IEEE Internet Computing* 7, pp. 86–95.

Clark, Gregory (1996), "The Political Foundations of Modern Economic Growth: England 1540–1800," *Journal of Interdisciplinary History* 26, pp. 563–588.

Clarke, Stephen V. O. (1967), *Central Bank Cooperation 1924–31*, New York: Federal Reserve Bank of New York.

Clarke, William (1965), *The City in the World Economy*, London: Institute of Economic Affairs.

Clavin, Patricia (2013), *Securing the World Economy: The Reinvention of the League of Nations, 1920–1946*, Oxford: Oxford University Press.

Clay, Henry (1957), *Lord Norman*, London: Macmillan.

Coeuré, Benoît (2015), "The International Role of the Euro: Concepts, Empirics and Prospects," Speech at Saint Joseph University, Beirut, October 3, 2015, https://www.ecb.europa.eu/press/key/date/2015/html/sp151002.en.html.

Cohen, Benjamin (1971), *The Future of Sterling as an International Currency*, New York: Macmillan and St. Martin's Press.

———. (2005), "Currency Choice in International Bond Issuance," *Bank for International Settlements Quarterly Review*, June, pp. 53–66.

———. (2015), *Currency Power: Understanding Monetary Rivalry*, Princeton, NJ: Princeton University Press.

Collins, Michael (1989), "The Banking Crisis of 1878," *Economic History Review*, new ser. 42, pp. 504–527.

Committee on Finance and Industry (1931), *Report*, London: HMSO.

Committee on the Global Financial System (2010), *Research on Global Financial Stability: The Use of BIS International Financial Statistics*, CGFS Papers 40 (June), Basel.

Conan, A. R. (1952), *The Sterling Area*, London: Macmillan.

Conant, Charles (1909), "The Gold Exchange Standard in the Light of Experience," *Economic Journal* 19, pp. 190–200.

———. (1910), *The National Bank of Belgium*, Washington, DC: National Monetary Commission.

Coste, Pierre (1932), *La lutte pour la suprématie. Les grands marchés financiers, Paris, Londres, New York*, Foreword by Pierre Quesnay, Paris: Payot.

Cottrell, Philip (2009), "London's First 'Big Bang'? Institutional Change in the City, 1855–1883," in Iain Fraser, Monika Fraser, Youssef Cassis, and Philip Cottrell (eds.), *The World of Private Banking*, London: Ashgate, pp. 61–98.

Crandall, Robert, and Kenneth Flamm (eds.) (1989), *Changing the Rules: Technological Change, International Competition and Regulation in Communications*, Washington, DC: Brookings Institution Press.

David, Paul (1985), "Clio and the Economics of QWERTY," *American Economic Review* 75, pp. 332–337.

———. (1986), "Narrow Windows, Blind Giants and Angry Orphans: The Dynamics of Systems Rivalries and Dilemmas of Technology Policy," Technology Innovation Project Working Paper 10 (March), Stanford, CA: Center for Economic Policy Research, Stanford University.

David, Paul, and Julie Bunn (1988), "The Economics of Gateway Technologies and Network Evolution: Lessons from Electricity Supply History," *Information Economics and Policy* 3, pp. 165–202.

David, Paul, and Shane Greenstein (1990), "The Economics of Compatibility Standards: An Introduction to Recent Research," *Economics of Innovation and New Technology* 1, pp. 3–41.

Davis, E. G. (1981)," "R.G. Hawtrey, 1879–1975," in D. P. O'Brien and John R. Presley (eds.), *Pioneers of Modern Economics in Britain*, Totowa, NJ: Barnes & Noble Books, pp. 203–233.

Day, A.C.L. (1954), *The Future of Sterling*, Oxford: Clarendon Press.

De Cecco, Marcello (1984), *The International Gold Standard: Money and Empire*, London: Frances Pinter.

De Roover, Raymond (1953), *L'évolution de la lettre de change: 14.–18. Siècles*, Paris: Colin.

Detken, Carsten, and Philipp Hartmann (2002), "Features of the Euro in International Financial Markets," *Economic Policy* 17, pp. 555–569.

Devereux, Michael, and Shouyong Shi (2013), "Vehicle Currency," *International Economic Review* 54, pp. 97–133.

De Vries, Casper (1988), "Theory and Relevance of Currency Substitution with Case Studies for Canada and the Netherlands Antilles," *Review of Economics and Statistics* 70, pp. 512–515.

Dominguez, Kathryn (1999), "The Role of the Yen," in Martin Feldstein (ed.), *International Capital Flows*, Chicago: University of Chicago Press, pp. 133–171.

Dominguez, Kathryn, Yuko Hashimoto, and Takatoshi Ito (2012), "International Reserves and the Global Financial Crisis," *Journal of International Economics* 88, pp. 388–406.

Eichengreen, Barry (1994), *International Monetary Arrangements for the Twenty-First Century*, Washington, DC: Brookings Institution.

———. (1998), "The Euro as a Reserve Currency," *Journal of the Japanese and International Economies* 12, pp. 483–506.

———. (2007), *Global Imbalances and the Lessons of Bretton Woods*, Cambridge, MA: MIT Press.

———. (2011), *Exorbitant Privilege: The Rise and Fall of the Dollar and the Future of the International Monetary System*, Oxford: Oxford University Press.

———. (2013), "Number One Country, Number One Currency?" *World Economy* 36, pp. 363–374.

Eichengreen, Barry, and Marc Flandreau (2009), "The Rise and Fall of the Dollar (Or When Did the Dollar Replace Sterling as the Leading Reserve Currency?)," *European Review of Economic History* 13, pp. 377–411.

———. (2010), "The Federal Reserve, the Bank of England, and the Rise of the Dollar as an International Currency, 1914–1939," *Open Economies Review* 23, pp. 57–87.

Eichengreen, Barry, and Ricardo Hausmann (2005), *Other People's Money: Debt Denomination and Financial Instability in Emerging Market Economies*, Chicago: University of Chicago Press.

Eichengreen, Barry, and Richard Portes (1990), "The Interwar Debt Crisis and Its Aftermath," *World Bank Research Observer* 5, pp. 69–94.

Eichengreen, Barry, Livia Chiţu, and Arnaud Mehl (2016) "Stability or Upheaval? The Currency Composition of International Reserves in the Long Run," *IMF Economic Review* 64, pp. 354–380.

Einzig, Paul (1931), *Behind the Scenes of International Finance*, London: Macmillan.

European Central Bank (1999), "The International Role of the Euro," *Monthly Bulletin*, August, pp. 31–54.

———. (various years), *The International Role of the Euro*, Germany: Frankfurt am Main.

Fan, Joseph, Randall Morck, Bernard Yeung, and Lixin Xu (2006), "Does 'Good Government' Draw Foreign Capital? Explaining China's Exceptional FDI Inflow," unpublished manuscript, Chinese University of Hong Kong (December).

Farhi, Emmanuel, and Matteo Maggiori (2016), "A Model of the International Monetary System," NBER Working Paper 22295 (December), Cambridge, MA: National Bureau of Economic Research.

Farrell, Joseph, and Paul Klemperer (2007), "Coordination and Lock-In: Competition with Switching Costs and Network Effects," *Handbook of Industrial Organization* 3, pp. 1967–2082.

Farrell, Joseph, and Garth Saloner (1986), "Installed Base and Compatibility: Innovation, Product Preannouncements, and Predation," *American Economic Review* 76, pp. 940–955.

Federal Reserve Board (1916), *Annual Report for 1915*, Washington, DC: Government Printing Office.

————. (1922), *Federal Reserve Bulletin*, Washington, DC: Government Printing Office.

————. (1928), *Federal Reserve Bulletin*, Washington, DC: Government Printing Office.

————. (1943), *Monetary Statistics of the United States*, Washington, DC: Board of Governors of the Federal Reserve System.

Feinstein, Charles (1972), *Statistical Tables of National Income, Expenditure and Output of the U.K. 1955–1965*, Cambridge: Cambridge University Press.

Feldstein, Martin (1997), "EMU and International Conflict," *Foreign Affairs* 76, pp. 60–73.

Fernandez, David (2015), "Beyond SDR: RMB as a Safe Asset," *Barclay's Emerging Markets Research* (May 15).

Fforde, John (1992), *The Bank of England and Public Policy 1941–1958*, Cambridge: Cambridge University Press.

Fink, Carole (1984), *The Genoa Conference: European Diplomacy, 1921–1922*, Chapel Hill: University of North Carolina Press.

Flandreau, Marc (ed.) (2003), *Money Doctors: The Experience of Financial Advising, 1850–2000*, New York: Routledge.

————. (2004), *The Glitter of Gold. France, Bimetallism, and the Emergence of the International Gold Standard, 1848–1873*, Oxford: Oxford University Press.

Flandreau, Marc, and Clemens Jobst (2005), "The Ties That Divide: A Network Analysis of the International Monetary System, 1890–1910," *Journal of Economic History* 65, pp. 977–1007.

————. (2009), "The Empirics of International Currencies: Network Externalities, History and Persistence," *Economic Journal* 119, pp. 643–664.

Flandreau, Marc, and Kim Oosterlinck (2012), "Was the Emergence of the International Gold Standard Expected? Evidence from Indian Government Securities," *Journal of Monetary Economics* 59, pp. 649–669.

Flandreau, Marc, and Nathan Sussman (2005), "Old Sins: Exchange Clauses and European Foreign Lending in the 19th Century," in Barry Eichengreen and Ricardo Hausman (eds.), *Other People's Money: Debt Denomination and Financial Instability in Emerging Market Economics*, Chicago: University of Chicago Press, pp. 154–189.

Flandreau, Marc, and Stefano Ugolini (2014), "The Crisis of 1866," in Nicholas Dimsdale and Anthony Hotson (eds.), *British Financial Crises since 1825*, Oxford: Oxford University Press, pp. 76–93.

Flandreau, Marc, Christophe Galimard, Clemens Jobst, and Pilar Nogués-Marco (2009), "Monetary Geography before the Industrial Revolution," *Cambridge Journal of Regions, Economy and Society* 2, pp. 149–171.

Foulke, Roy Anderson (1931), *The Commercial Paper Market*, New York: Bankers' Publishing.

Frankel, Jeffrey (1990), "And Now Won/Dollar Negotiations? Lessons from the Yen/Dollar Agreement of 1984," paper presented to the Institute for International Economics/Korea Development Institute Conference, Washington, DC (December 12).

————. (2011), "Historical Precedents for Internationalization of the RMB," Council on Foreign Relations Occasional Paper, New York: Council on Foreign Relations (November).

Fratzscher, Marcel, Arnaud Mehl, and Isabel Vansteenkiste (2011), "130 Years of Fiscal Vulnerabilities and Currency Crashes," *IMF Economic Review* 59, pp. 683–716.

Frenkel, Jacob (1978), "International Reserves: Pegged Exchange Rates and Managed Float," in Karl Brunner and Allan Meltzer (eds.), Public Policies in Open Economies, *Carnegie-Rochester Conference Series on Public Policy* 9, pp. 111–140.

Fukao, Mitsuhiro (1990), "Liberalization of Japan's Foreign Exchange Controls and Structural Changes in the Balance of Payments," *Bank of Japan Monetary and Economic Studies* 8, pp. 101–164.

Fukuda, Shin-Ichi, and Ji Cong (1994), "On the Choice of Invoice Currency by Japanese Exporters: The PTM Approach," *Journal of the Japanese and International Economies* 8, pp. 511–529.

Gallarotti, Giulio (1995), *The Anatomy of an International Monetary Regime: The Classical Gold Standard, 1880–1914*, New York: Oxford University Press.

Garber, Peter (1996), "The Use of the Yen as a Reserve Currency," *Monetary and Economic Studies*, Tokyo: Bank of Japan (December).

Gehlbach, Scott, and Philip Keefer (2009), "Investment without Democracy: Ruling-Party Institutionalization and Credit Commitment in Autocracies," unpublished manuscript, University of Wisconsin-Madison and World Bank (October).

Gilbert, Milton (1968), "The Gold-Dollar System: Conditions of Equilibrium and the Price of Gold," *Essays in International Finance* 70, International Finance Section, Department of Economics, Princeton University, Princeton, NJ.

Gimenez, Eduardo, and Maria Montero (2012), "The Great Depression in Spain," *Analyise Economica* 48, Servicio de Publicacions da Universidade de Santiago de Compostela.

Girma, Sourafel, and Anja Shortland (2007), "The Political Economy of Financial Development," *Oxford Economic Papers* 60, pp. 567–596.

Goldsmith, Raymond (1952), "The Growth of Reproducible Wealth of the United States of America from 1805 to 1950," in Simon Kuznets (ed.), *Income and Wealth of the United States: Trends and Structure*, Cambridge: Bowes & Bowes, pp. 244–328.

Goodhart, C.A.E. (1972), *The Business of Banking, 1891–1914*; London: Weidenfeld and Nicolson.

Gopinath, Gita (2015), "The International Price System," unpublished manuscript, Harvard University, Cambridge, MA (August).

Gourinchas, Pierre-Olivier, and Hélène Rey (2007), "From World Banker to World Venture Capitalist: U.S. External Adjustment and the Exorbitant Privilege," in Richard Clarida (ed.), *G7 Current Account Imbalances: Sustainability and Adjustment*, Chicago: University of Chicago Press, pp. 11–66.

Greenstein, Shane (1993), "Did Installed Base Give an Incumbent Any (Measurable) Advantages in Federal Computer Procurement?" *Rand Journal of Economics* 24, pp. 19–39.

Griliches, Zvi (1961), "A Note on the Serial Correlation Bias in Estimates of Distributed Lags," *Econometrica* 29, pp. 65–73.

Guaranty Trust Company of New York (1919), *Acceptances*, New York: Guaranty Trust Company.

Guinnane, Timothy (2002), "Delegated Monitors, Large and Small: Germany's Banking System, 1800–1914," *Journal of Economic Literature* 40, pp. 73–104.

Habib, Maurizio (2010), "Excess Returns on Net Foreign Assets—The Exorbitant Privilege in Global Perspective," ECB Working Paper 1158 (February), Frankfurt: European Central Bank.

Habib, Maurizio, and Mark Joy (2010), "Foreign Currency Bonds: Currency Choice and the Role of Uncovered and Covered Interest Parity," *Applied Financial Economics* 20, pp. 601–626.

Habib, Maurizio, and Leon Zurawicki (2002), "Corruption and Foreign Direct Investment," *Journal of International Business Studies* 33, pp. 291–307.

Han, K. (2006), "Corruption and Foreign Direct Investment," Paper presented at the annual meeting of the International Studies Association, San Diego.

Hatanaka, Michio (1974), "An Efficient Two-Step Estimator for the Dynamic Adjustment Model with Autoregressive Errors," *Journal of Econometrics* 2, pp. 199–220.

Hawtrey, Ralph (1922), "The Genoa Resolutions on Currency," *Economic Journal* 32, pp. 290–304.

Heller, Robert, and Mohsin Kahn (1978), "The Demand for International Reserves under Fixed and Floating Exchange Rates," *IMF Staff Papers* 25, pp. 623–649.

Henning, C. Randall (1994), *Currencies and Politics in the United States, Germany, and Japan*, Washington, DC: Institute for International Economics.

Horesh, Niv (2008), "'Many a Long Day': HSBC and Its Note Issue in Republican China," *Enterprise and Society* 9, pp. 6–43.

Horsefield, J. Keith (1969), *The International Monetary Fund, 1945–1965: Twenty Years of International Monetary Cooperation, Volume 1: Chronicle*, Washington, DC: International Monetary Fund.

Hoshi, Takeo, and Anil Kashyap (2000), "The Japanese Banking Crisis: Where Did It Come From and How Will It End?" *NBER Macroeconomics Annual* 14, pp. 129–212.

Howson, Susan (1980), "Sterling's Managed Float: The Operations of the Exchange Equalisation Account," *Princeton Studies in International Finance* 46, International Finance Section, Department of Economics, Princeton University, Princeton, NJ.

Huang, Yiping, Wang Daili, and Fan Gang (2014), "Paths to a Reserve Currency: Internationalization of RMB and its Implications," unpublished manuscript, National School of Development, Peking University and National Economic Research Institute, China Reform Foundation (March).

International Capital Market Association (2014), "The Current State and Future Evolution of the European Investment Grade Corporate Bond Secondary Market: Perspectives from the Market," Zurich: ICMA (November).

International Monetary Fund (2015), "Review of the Method of the Valuation of the SDR—Initial Considerations" (August 3), Washington, DC.

Ito, Hiro, and Menzie Chinn (2014), "The Rise of the 'Redback' and the People's Republic of China's Capital Account Liberalization: An Empirical Analysis of the Determinants of Invoicing Currencies," ADBI Working Paper 473 (April), Tokyo: Asian Development Bank Institute.

Ito, Takatoshi, and Michael Melvin (2001), "Japan's Big Bang and the Transformation of Financial Markets," in Magnes Blomstrom, Byron Gangnes, and Sumner La Croix (eds.), *Japan's New Economy: Continuity and Change in the Twenty-First Century*, New York: Oxford University Press, pp. 162–174.

Jacobs, Lawrence (1910), *Bank Acceptances*, 61st Congress, 2nd Session, Senate Doc. 569, Washington, DC: Government Printing Office.

James, John (1995), "The Rise and Fall of the Commercial Paper Market, 1900–1930," in Michael Bordo and Richard Sylla (eds.), *Anglo-American Financial Systems*, New York: Irwin, pp. 219–260.

Japanese Ministry of Finance (nd), "Chronology of the Internationalization of the Yen," http://www.mof.go.jp/english/about_mof/councils/customs_foreign _exchange/e1b064c1.htm (accessed August 31, 2016).

Jobst, Clemens (2009), "Market Leader: The Austro-Hungarian Bank and the Making of Foreign Exchange Intervention, 1896–1913," *European Review of Economic History* 13, pp. 287–318.

Jobst, Clemens, and Pilar Nogues-Marco (2012), "Commercial Finance in Europe, 1700–1815," in Gerard Caprio (ed.), *Handbook of Key Global Financial Markets, Institutions and Infrastructure*, London: Elsevier, pp. 95–105.

Juncker, Jean-Claude (2015), *Completing Europe's Economic and Monetary Union*, report prepared by Jean Claude Juncker in close cooperation with Donald Tusk, Jeroen Dijsselbloem, Mario Draghi, and Martin Schulz, http://ec.eu-ropa.eu/priorities/economic-monetary-union/docs/5-presidents-report _fr.pdf.

Kedia, Simi, and Abon Mozumdar (2003), "Foreign Currency-Denominated Debt: An Empirical Examination," *Journal of Business* 76, pp. 521–546.

Kemmerer, Edwin (1910), *Seasonal Variations in the Relative Demand for Money and Capital in the United States*, Washington, DC: National Monetary Commission.

———. (1944), *Gold and the Gold Standard: The Story of Gold Money Past, Present and Future*, New York: McGraw-Hill.

Kenen, Peter (1960), *British Monetary Policy and the Balance of Payments 1951–1957*, Cambridge, MA: Harvard University Press.

Kennedy, Paul M. (1987), *The Rise and Fall of the Great Powers: Economic Change and Military Conflict from 1500 to 2000*, New York: Random House.

Keynes, John Maynard (1913), *Indian Currency and Finance*, London: Macmillan.

———. (1930), *A Treatise on Money*, 2 volumes, London: Macmillan.

Kindleberger, Charles (1970), *Power and Money: The Politics of International Economics and the Economics of International Politics*, New York: Basic Books.

———. (1973), *The World in Depression, 1929–1939*, Berkeley: University of California Press.

———. (1988), *The International Economic Order: Essays on Financial Crisis and International Public Goods*, Cambridge, MA: MIT Press.

King, Frank (1989), *History of the Hongkong and Shanghai Banking Corporation, Vol. 2, The Hongkong Bank in the Period of Imperialism and War, 1895–1918,* Cambridge: Cambridge University Press.

King, Robert, and Ross Levine (1993), "Finance and Growth: Schumpeter Might Be Right," *Quarterly Journal of Economics* 108, pp. 717–737.

King, W.T.C. (1936), *History of the London Discount Market,* London: Routledge and Sons.

Kirschner, Jonathan (1995), *Currency and Coercion: The Political Economy of International Monetary Power,* Princeton, NJ: Princeton University Press.

Kirshner, Orin (ed.) (1996), *The Bretton Woods-GATT System: Retrospect and Prospect after Fifty Years,* Armonk, NY: M. E. Sharpe.

Kniffin, W. H., Jr. (1920), *Commercial Paper, Acceptances, and the Analysis of Credit Statements: Practical Treatise on Commercial Paper, with Particular Reference to the Processes by Which the Credit Risk Is Determined where Such Instruments Are Purchased as a Bank Investment,* second edition, New York: Bankers Publishing.

Kroszner, Randall S. (1999), "Is It Better to Forgive Than to Receive? An Empirical Analysis of the Impact of Debt Repudiation," revised research at the George J. Stigler Center for the Study of the Economy and the State at the University of Chicago Graduate School of Business.

Krugman, Paul (1980), "Vehicle Currencies and the Structure of International Exchange," *Journal of Money, Credit and Banking* 12, pp. 513–526.

———. (1984), "The International Role of the Dollar: Theory and Prospect," in John Bilson and Richard Marston (eds.), *Exchange Rate Theory and Practice,* Chicago: University of Chicago Press, pp. 261–278.

Kubelec, Chris, and Filipa Sá (2012), "The Geographical Composition of National External Balance Sheets: 1980–2005," *International Journal of Central Banking* 8, pp. 143–189.

Lewis, Cleona (1938), *America's Stake in International Investments,* Washington, DC: Brookings Institution.

Li, David, and Linlin Liu (2008), "RMB Internationalization: An Empirical Analysis," *Journal of Financial Research* 11, pp. 1–16.

Liebowitz S. J., and Stephen E. Margolis (1990), "The Fable of the Keys," *Journal of Law and Economics* 33, pp. 1–25.

Lindert, Peter (1969), "Key Currencies and Gold, 1900–1913," *Princeton Studies in International Finance* 24, International Finance Section, Department of Economics, Princeton University, Princeton, NJ.

Liviatan, Nissan (1963), "Consistent Estimation of Distributed Lags," *International Economic Review* 4, pp. 44–52.

Lovell, Michael (1957), "The Role of the Bank of England as Lender of Last Resort in the Crises of the Eighteenth Century," *Explorations in Entrepreneurial History* 9, pp. 8–21.

Maddison, Angus (1982), *Phases of Capitalist Development,* New York: Oxford University Press.

———. (2010), "Statistics on World Population, GDP and Per Capita GDP, 1–2008 AD," unpublished manuscript, University of Groningen.

Martin, Andrew, and George Ross (2004), *Euros and Europeans: Monetary Integration and the European Model of Society*, Cambridge: Cambridge University Press.

Matsuyama, Kiminori, Nobuhiro Kiyotaki, and Akihiko Matsui (1993), "Toward a Theory of International Currency," *Review of Economic Studies* 60, pp. 283–307.

Mauro, Paulo (1995), "Corruption and Growth," *Quarterly Journal of Economics* 110, pp. 681–712.

McBrady, Matthew, and Michael Schill (2007), "Foreign Currency-Denominated Borrowing in the Absence of Operating Incentive," *Journal of Financial Economics* 86, pp. 145–177.

McGuire, Martin, and Mancur Olson, Jr. (1996), "The Economics of Autocracy and Majority Rule: The Invisible Hand and the Use of Force," *Journal of Economic Literature* 34, pp. 72–96.

McKinnon, Ronald (1996), *The Rules of the Game: International Money and Exchange Rates*, Cambridge, MA: MIT Press.

———. (2001), "Optimum Currency Areas and the European Experience," unpublished manuscript, Stanford University, Stanford, CA (October).

———. (2010), "Rehabilitating the Unloved Dollar Standard," *Asian-Pacific Economic Literature* 24, pp. 1–18.

Mehl, Arnaud (2015), "L'euro sur la scène internationale après la crise financière et celle de la dette, " *Revue d'Economie Financière* 119, pp. 55–68.

Mehrling, Perry (2010), *The New Lombard Street: How the Fed Became the Dealer of Last Resort*, Princeton, NJ: Princeton University Press.

Meissner, Christopher (2005), "A New World Order: Explaining the International Diffusion of the Gold Standard 1870–1913," *Journal of International Economics* 66, pp. 385–406.

Metzler, Mark (2006), *Lever of Empire: The International Gold Standard and the Crisis of Liberalism in Prewar Japan*, Berkeley: University of California Press.

Ministry of Finance (1999), "Internationalization of the Yen for the 21st Century: Japan's Response to Changes in Global Economic and Financial Environments," Tokyo: Ministry of Finance (20 April).

Mintz, Ilse (1951), *Deterioration in the Quality of Foreign Bonds Issued in the United States, 1920–1930*, New York: National Bureau of Economic Research.

Mitchell, Brian R. (1998a), *International Historical Statistics, Europe, 1750–1993*, fourth edition, London: Palgrave Macmillan.

———. (1998b), *International Historical Statistics, Africa, Asia & Oceania, 1750–1993*, fourth edition, London: Palgrave Macmillan.

———. (1998c), *International Historical Statistics, the Americas, 1750–1993*, fourth edition, Amherst, NY: Prometheus Books.

Mitchener, Kris James, and Marc Weidenmier (2005), "Empire, Public Goods and the Roosevelt Corollary," *Journal of Economic History* 65, pp. 658–692.

Moggridge, Donald (1969), *The Return to Gold 1925: The Formulation of Economic Policy and Its Critics*, Cambridge: Cambridge University Press.

———. (1971), "British Controls on Long-Term Capital Movements, 1924–31," in Donald McCloskey (ed.), *Essays on a Mature Economy: Britain Since 1840*, Princeton, NJ: Princeton University Press, pp. 113–138.

Moreno, Ramon (1996), "Will the Yen Replace the Dollar?" *Economic Letter* 1996–30 (October 18), San Francisco: Federal Reserve Bank of San Francisco.

Moulton, Harold, and Leo Pasvolsky (1926), *World War Debt Settlements*, New York: Macmillan.

Myers, Margaret (1936), *Paris as a Financial Center*, New York: Columbia University Press.

Naughton, Barry (2011), "Inside and Outside: The Modernized Hierarchy That Runs China," unpublished manuscript, University of California at San Diego (November).

Neal, Larry (1990), *The Rise of Financial Capitalism: International Capital Markets in the Age of Reason*, Cambridge: Cambridge University Press.

North, Douglass, and Barry Weingast (1989), "Constitutions and Commitment: The Evolution of Institutions Governing Public Choice in 17th Century England," *Journal of Economic History* 49, pp. 802–832.

Nurkse, Ragnar (1944), *International Currency Experience*, Geneva: League of Nations.

Obstfeld, Maurice (2013), "The International Monetary System: Living with Asymmetry," in Robert Feenstra and Alan Taylor (eds.), *Globalization in an Age of Crisis: Multilateral Economic Cooperation in the Twenty-First Century*, Chicago: University of Chicago Press, pp. 301–342.

Obstfeld, Maurice, and Kenneth Rogoff (2011), "Global Imbalances and the Financial Crisis: Products of Common Causes," in Reuven Glick and Mark Spiegel (eds.), *Asia and the Global Financial Crisis*, San Francisco: Federal Reserve Bank of San Francisco, pp. 131–172.

O'Driscoll, Gerald (2011), "The Federal Reserve's Covert Bailout of Europe," *Wall Street Journal* (December 28), p. 15.

Ogawa, Eiji (2000), "The Japanese Yen as an International Currency," paper prepared for the KIEP/NEAEF Conference on Regional Financial Arrangements in East Asia, Honolulu, Hawaii (August 10–11).

Oneal, John (1994), "The Affinity of Foreign Investors for Authoritarian Regimes," *Political Research Quarterly* 47, pp. 565–588.

Ouyang, Alice, and Jie Li (2013), "Too Big to Change: The Stabilizing Force of Reserve Currency Preferences in the International Monetary System," *Emerging Markets Finance and Trade* 49, pp. 120–133.

Packer, Frank, and Elizabeth Reynolds (1997), "The Samurai Bond Market," *Current Issues in Economics and Finance* 3, New York: Federal Reserve Bank of New York (June).

Papaioannou, Elias, and Richard Portes (2008), "The International Role of the Euro: A Status Report," *European Economy-Economic Papers* 317, Directorate of General Economic and Monetary Affairs, European Commission.

Park, Yung Chul (2011), "The Role of Macroprudential Policy for Financial Stability in East Asia's Emerging Economies," in Masahiro Kawai and Eswar Prasad (eds.), *Asian Perspectives on Financial Sector Reforms and Regulation*, Washington, DC: Brookings Institution, pp. 138–163.

Parrini, Carl (1969), *Heir to Empire: U.S. Financial Diplomacy, 1916–1923*, Pittsburgh, PA: University of Pittsburgh Press.

Patrick, Hugh (1998), "The Causes of Japan's Financial Crisis," Paper prepared for the Conference on Financial Reform in Japan and Australia, Canberra: Australian National University (August 24).

Patterson, Robert H. (1870), "On Our Home Monetary Drains, and the Crisis of 1866," *Journal of the Statistical Society of London* 33, pp. 216–242.

Petrescu, Nicholas (1920), "The International Financial Conference at Brussels," *Bankers Magazine* 101, pp. 979–987.

Phelps, Clyde William (1927), *The Foreign Expansion of American Banks: American Branch Banking Abroad*, New York: Ronald Press.

Pittaluga, Giovanni, and Elena Seghezza (2016), "How Japan Remained on the Gold Standard Despite Unsustainable External Debt," *Explorations in Economic History* 59, pp. 40–54.

Portes, Richard, and Hélène Rey (1998), "The Emergence of the Euro as an International Currency," *Economic Policy* 26, pp. 307–343.

Quinn, Dennis, and A. Maria Toyoda (2008), "Does Capital Account Liberalization Lead to Growth?" *Review of Financial Studies* 21, pp. 1403–1449.

Quintyn, Marc, and Genevieve Verdier (2010), "Mother, Can I Trust the Government? Sustained Financial Deepening–A Political Institutions View," IMF Working Paper 10/210 (September), Washington, DC: International Monetary Fund.

Rajan, Raghuram, and Luigi Zingales (2003), "The Great Reversals: The Politics of Financial Development in the Twentieth Century," *Journal of Financial Economics* 69, pp. 5–50.

Reinhart, Carmen (2010), "This Time Is Different Chartbook: Country Histories on Debt, Default, and Financial Crises," NBER Working Paper 15815 (March), Cambridge, MA: National Bureau of Economic Research.

Reinhart, Carmen, and Kenneth Rogoff (2008), "Is the 2007 U.S. Subprime Crisis So Different? An International Historical Comparison," *American Economic Review* 98, pp. 339–344.

———. (2009a), "The Aftermath of Financial Crises," *American Economic Review* 99, pp. 466–472.

———. (2009b), *This Time Is Different: Eight Centuries of Financial Folly*, Princeton, NJ: Princeton University Press.

———. (2010), "Growth in a Time of Debt," *American Economic Review* 100, pp. 573–578.

Rey, Hélène (2001), "International Trade and Currency Exchange," *Review of Economic Studies* 68, pp. 443–464.

Roodman, David (2009), "A Note on the Theme of Too Many Instruments," *Oxford Bulletin of Economics and Statistics* 71, pp. 135–158.

Rose, Andrew, and Mark Spiegel (2004), "A Gravity Model of Sovereign Lending, Trade, Default and Credit," *IMF Staff Papers* 51, pp. 50–63.

Sachs, Jeffrey (1985), "The Dollar and the Policy Mix: 1985," *Brookings Papers on Economic Activity* 16, pp. 117–185.

Santarosa, Veronica (2015), "Financing Long-Distance Trade without Banks: The Joint Liability Rule and Bills of Exchange in 18th-Century France," *Journal of Economic History* 75, pp. 690–719.

Santos Silva, Joao, and Silvana Tenreyro (2006), "The Log of Gravity," *Review of Economics and Statistics* 88, pp. 641–658.

Sargent, Thomas (1983), "Stopping Moderate Inflations: The Methods of Poincaré and Thatcher," in Rudiger Dornbusch and M. H. Simonsen (eds.), *Inflation, Debt and Indexation*, Cambridge, MA: MIT Press, pp. 54–98.

Sato, Kiyotaka (1999), "The International Use of the Japanese Yen: The Case of Japan's Trade with East Asia," *World Economy* 22, pp. 453–608.

Sayers, Richard S. (1936), *Bank of England Operations 1890–1914*, London: P. S. King & Son.

———. (1976), *The Bank of England 1891–1944*, Cambridge: Cambridge University Press.

Scammel, William (1968), *The London Discount Market*, New York: St. Martin's Press.

Schenk, Catherine (2010), *The Decline of Sterling: Managing the Retreat of an International Currency 1945–1992*, Cambridge: Cambridge University Press.

Schiltz, Michael (2012), "Money on the Road to Empire: Japan's Adoption of Gold Monometallism, 1873–97," *Economic History Review* 65, pp. 1147–1168.

Schuker, Stephen (2003), "Money Doctors between the Wars: The Competition between Central Banks, Private Financial Advisors, and Multilateral Agencies 1919–39," in Marc Flandreau (ed.), *Money Doctors: The Experience of International Financial Advising 1850–2000*, London: Routledge, pp. 49–77.

Schularick, Moritz, and Alan Taylor (2012), "Credit Booms Gone Bust: Monetary Policy, Leverage Cycles, and Financial Crises, 1870–2008," *American Economic Review* 102, pp. 1029–1061.

Schultz, Kenneth, and Barry Weingast (2003), "The Democratic Advantage: Institutional Foundations of Financial Power in International Competitition," *International Organization* 57, pp.3–42.

Shannon, H. A. (1952), "The Modern Colonial Sterling Exchange Standard," *IMF Staff Papers* 2, pp. 318–362.

Shonfield, Andrew (1958), *British Economic Policy since the War*, London: Penguin.

Shy, Oz (2010), "A Short Survey of Network Economics," unpublished paper, Federal Reserve Bank of Boston (March).

Siepmann, H. A. (1920), "The International Financial Conference at Brussels," *Economic Journal* 30, pp. 130–159.

Smethurst, Richard (2007), *From Foot Soldier to Finance Minister: Takahashi Korekiyo, Japan's Keynes*, Cambridge, MA: Harvard University Asia Center.

Stasavage, David (2002), "Credible Commitment in Early Modern Europe: North and Weingast Revisited," *Journal of Law, Economics and Organization* 18, pp. 156–187.

———. (2007), "Partisan Politics and Public Debt: The Importance of Whig Supremacy for Britain's Financial Revolution," *European Review of Economic History* 11, pp. 132–139.

Strange, Susan (1971), *Sterling and British Policy*, London: Oxford University Press.

———. (1988), *States and Markets*, London: Pinter.

Subacchi, Paola (2013), "Expanding Beyond Borders: The Yen and the Yuan," ADBI Working Paper 450 (December), Mandaluyong, Philippines: Asian Development Bank Institute.

Subramanian, Arvind (2011), *Eclipse: Living in the Shadow of China's Economic Dominance*, Washington, DC: Peterson Institute of International Economics.

Subramanian, Arvind, and Martin Kessler (2013), "The Renminbi Bloc Is Here: Asia Down, Rest of the World to Go?" Working Paper 12-19 revised (August), Washington, DC: Peterson Institute of International Economics.

Suzuki, Toshio (2012), "The Rise and Decline of the Oriental Bank Corporation, 1842–84," in Shizuya Nishimura, Toshio Suzuki, and Ranald Michie (eds.), *The Origins of International Banking in Asia: The Nineteenth and Twentieth Centuries*, Oxford: Oxford University Press, pp. 86–111.

SWIFT (Society for Worldwide Interbank Financial Telecommunication) (2015), "RMB Breaks into the Top Five as a World Payments Currency" (January 28), http://www.swift.com/about_swift/shownews?param_dcr=news.data/en /swift_com/2015/PR_RMB_into_the_top_five.xml.

Sylla, Richard (2005), "Political Economy of US Financial Development," unpublished manuscript, New York, New York University.

Taguchi, Hiroo (1994), "On the Internationalization of the Japanese Yen," in Takatoshi Ito and Anne Krueger (eds.), *Macroeconomic Linkage: Savings, Exchange Rates and Capital Flows*, Chicago: University of Chicago Press, pp. 335–357.

Takagi, Shinji (2011), "Internationalizing the Yen, 1984–2003: Unfinished Agenda or Mission Impossible?" *BIS Papers* 75, Basel: Bank for International Settlements.

Takeda, Masahiko, and Philip Turner (1992), "The Liberalization of Japan's Financial Markets: Some Major Themes," *Economic Papers* 34, Basel: Bank for International Settlements.

Tavlas, George (1991), "On the International Use of Currencies: The Case of the Deutsche Mark," *Essays in International Finance* 181 (March), International Finance Section, Department of Economics, Princeton University, Princeton, NJ.

Tavlas, George, and Yuzuru Ozeki (1991), "The Japanese Yen as an International Currency," IMF Working Paper 91/2 (January), Washington, DC: International Monetary Fund.

Thornton, Henry (1802), *An Inquiry into the Nature and Effects of the Paper Credit of Great Britain*, edited with an Introduction by F. A. von Hayek, 1939, New York: Rinehart & Co.

Traynor, Dean (1949), *International Monetary and Financial Conferences in the Interwar Period*, Washington, DC: Catholic University of America Press.

Triffin, Robert (1960), *Gold and the Dollar Crisis: The Future of Convertibility*, New Haven, CT: Yale University Press.

———. (1964), "The Evolution of the International Monetary System: Historical Reappraisal and Future Perspectives," *Princeton Studies in International Finance* 12, International Finance Section, Department of Economics, Princeton University, Princeton, NJ.

Truman, Edwin, and Anna Wong (2006), "The Case for an International Reserve Diversification Standard," Working Paper 06-2 (May), Washington, DC: Peterson Institute for International Economics.

Truptil, Roger (1936), *British Banks and the London Money Market*, London: Jonathan Cape.

Ugolini, Stefano (2011), "Foreign Exchange Reserve Management in the 19th Century: The National Bank of Belgium in the 1850s," Working Paper 2010/22, Norges Bank Bicentenary Project, Oslo: Norges Bank.

———. (2012), "The Origins of Foreign Exchange Policy: The National Bank of Belgium and the Quest for Monetary Independence in the 1850s," *European Review of Economic History* 16, pp. 51–73.

———. (2013), "The Bank of England as the World Gold Market-Maker during the Classical Gold Standard Era, 1889–1910," in Sandra Bott (ed.), *The Global Gold Market and the International System from the Late Nineteenth Century until Today: Actors, Networks, Power*, Basingstoke, UK: Palgrave Macmillan, pp. 64–87.

———. (2016), "Liquidity Management and Central Bank Strength: Bank of England Operations Reloaded, 1889–1910," Working Paper 10, Oslo: Norges Bank.

United Nations (1948), *Public Debt, 1914–1946*, Department of Economic Affairs, Lake Success, New York: United Nations.

United States Bureau of the Census (1975), *Historical Statistics of the United States: Colonial Times to 1970, Bicentennial Edition*, Washington, DC: Government Printing Office.

Usher, Abbott (1914), "The Origin of the Bill of Exchange," *Journal of Political Economy* 22, pp. 566–576.

———. (1934), "The Origins of Banking: The Primitive Bank of Deposit 1200–1600," *Economic History Review* 4, pp. 399–428.

Vigreux, Pierre-Benjamin (1932), *Le crédit par acceptation: Paris centre financier*, with a Foreword by J. Velay. Paris: Librairie des Sciences Politiques et Sociales.

Warburg, Paul (1910), *The Discount System in Europe*, Washington, DC: National Monetary Commission.

——. (1930), *The Federal Reserve System*, 2 volumes, New York: Macmillan.

Wei, Shang-jin (2000), "How Taxing Is Corruption on International Investors?" *Review of Economics and Statistics* 82, pp. 1–11.

Weingast, Barry (1995), "The Economic Role of Political Institutions: Market Preserving Federalism and Economic Development," *Journal of Law, Economics and Organization* 11, pp. 1–31.

West, Joel (2007), "The Economic Realities of Open Standards: Black, White and Many Shades of Gray," in Shane Greenstein and Victor Stango (eds.), *Standards and Public Policy*, Cambridge: Cambridge University Press, pp. 87–122.

White, Harry Dexter (1933), *The French International Accounts 1880–1913*, Cambridge, MA: Harvard University Press.

Williams, David (1968), "The Evolution of the Sterling System," in C. R. Whittlesey and J.S.G. Wilson (eds.), *Essays in Money and Banking*, Oxford: Oxford University Press, pp. 266–297.

Williamson, John (2012), "Currencies of Power and the Power of Currencies: The Geo-Politics of Currencies, Reserves and the Global Financial System," unpublished manuscript, Washington, DC: International Institute for Strategic Studies.

Wilson, William (2015), "Washington, China, and the Rise of the Renminbi: Are the Dollar's Days as the Global Reserve Currency Numbered?" Special Report 171 (June 17), Washington, DC: Heritage Foundation.

Winkler, Max (1933), *Foreign Bonds, an Autopsy: A Study of Defaults and Repudiations of Government Obligations*, Philadelphia: Roland Swain.

Wong, Anna (2007), "Measurement and Inference in International Reserve Diversification," Working Paper 07-6 (July), Washington, DC: Institute for International Economics.

Wood, Elmer (1939), *English Theories of Central Banking Control, 1819–1858*, Cambridge, MA: Harvard University Press.

World Bank (2013), *Capital for the Future: Saving and Investment in an Interdependent World*, Washington, DC: World Bank.

Yang, Benhua (2007), "Autocracy, Democracy and FDI Inflows to Developing Countries," *International Economic Journal* 21, pp. 419–439.

Zhou, Ruilin (1997), "Currency Exchange in a Random Search Model," *Review of Economic Studies* 64, pp. 289–310.

acceptances. *See* trade acceptances
Agadir Crisis and foreign reserves, 29
Anglo-American Loan, 153
arbitrage trading, 177
Asian financial crisis, 164, 167–168
Asian Monetary Fund, 168, 221n21
Association of South East Asian Nations, 182

Bank of England, 8
    and Bank Charter Act of 1844, 16
    and Genoa Resolutions, 37–39
    and influence on international finance, 2
    as provider of emergency liquidity, 23
    and rivalry with Federal Reserve Bank
        of New York, 40–41
    and Treasury bills and bonds, 23
Bank of France, 25–26
    and liquidation of sterling reserves,
        49–53
    See also French banking system;
        French franc
Bank of Japan, 28–29, 163–169
Baring Crisis, 23–26
Big Bang
    Japanese financial, 167
    London's First Big Bang, 22, 129
bills of exchange, 17–29
bimetallism, 20
Boer War and effect on foreign reserves, 27
Bretton Woods-GATT System, 2
Brexit, 177
British banking system, 22, 58–81
    dominance in trade acceptances, 61–63
    merchant banks, 33, 61–62, 71
    See also Bank of England
Brussels International Financial Conference,
    36, 206n14. *See also* foreign exchange
    reserves
Bundesbank, 129, 173

Cassel, Gustav, 36, 38
central banking, 30–41
    and China onshore foreign exchange
        market, 184
    and currency swap lines, 184–186, 198
    and gold standard, 20–21
    and Genoa Resolutions, 36–40,
        206n19, 207n22
    and sterling holdings, 145–157
    See also individual bank names
Chiang Mai Initiative, 164, 168–169, 185
Chiang Mai Initiative Multilateralization
    (CMIM), 185
China, 3, 14, 118, 134, 161, 181–194
    anticorruption campaign in, 194
    cross-border transactions of, 182–186
        (*see also* renminbi)
    and disclosure of foreign exchange
        reserve holdings, 178
    and influence on international finance, 3
    and need for financial deepening,
        186–190
    and response to market volatility,
        188–189
    and status in world financial system,
        182–186
    stock market transparency in, 189–190
China Securities Regulatory
    Commission, 189
Chinese renminbi, 3–15, 56, 81, 107, 134, 168,
    169, 175, 181–194, 196. *See also* renminbi
Commonwealth
    members of, 84–115, 146–152
corruption, control of for attracting foreign
    investment, 193–194
Council on Foreign Exchange and Other
    Transactions, 162, 168
cross-border
    lending, 84, 179

cross-border (*Continued*)
    transactions, 5, 13, 116, 161, 172, 181, 182,
      186, 195, 197, 199
currency
    gold-based and silver-based, 16–29
    roles of, 4
currency composition
    of foreign exchange reserves, 6, 16–57,
      116–144, 196
    of international public debt, 84, 115
      (*see also* international public debt)
Currency Composition of Official Foreign
    Exchange Reserves data base (COFFER),
    6, 118, 202n17
currency swap lines, 184–186, 198. *See also*
    central banking
current account convertibility
    Great Britain's restoration of, 153–154
    restoration in Japan, 160

de Cecco, Marcello, 11, 27, 29, 203n26,
    204n23, 205n33
De Roover, Raymond, 17, 203n3
Deutsche Bank, 26, 33, 72, 201n21
deutschemark, 118, 119, 120, 124, 129, 132, 138,
    139, 155, 170, 173, 176, 196, 214n1, 216n19
dollar
    and competition from euro, 170–180
    and competition from renminbi,
      181–194
    as dominant currency, 3–6, 41, 43,
      52–56, 60, 97, 146, 172
    as invoicing currency in trade, 58–83
    overtaking sterling as leading reserve
      currency, 43, 50, 57, 93, 94, 106,
      118, 156
    rise of the, 60, 63, 93, 100, 104
    and sterling duopoly, 44, 94
    and use in international financial
      transactions, 84–115
    Yen-Dollar Agreement, 163
dollar acceptance market, 33–35, 61–69,
    79–81, 104, 206n5. *See* trade acceptances
Dollar Area, 148–151, 219n5, 219n12
dollar standard, 3, 147

ECB. *See* European Central Bank
economic dominance, economictheories of, 3
economic theories of international
    currencies, conventional and
    new views, 3–11, 14, 19, 24, 47, 56,
    57, 60, 84, 89, 127, 202n19

euro
    as competitor to dollar, 170–180
    and development as an international
      currency, 170–180
    neutrality position of ECB, 173, 222n13
    regional use of, 171, 178
    and sovereign debt crisis, 171, 175, 176
Euro area, 14, 170–180, 185, 186, 221n1,
    222n16, 223n22
euro crisis, 120, 178
euro-denominated bonds, 174, 176, 177
European Central Bank, 172–179, 185,
    213n12, 222n13
European Currency Unit (ECU), 118–120, 176
European Payments Union (EPU), 154
European Union, efforts to complete
    economic and monetary union, 107,
    179–180
European Union, Five Presidents'
    Report, 179
Exchange Equalisation Account, 147
exorbitant privilege, 13, 173

Federal Reserve Act, 30, 63, 65, 92, 206n5,
    209n11, 211n26
Federal Reserve Bank of New York
    and Genoa Conference, 40, 153
    and rivalry with Bank of England, 41
Federal Reserve System
    creation of, 32
    and Genoa Resolutions, 39
    and influence on international
      finance, 3
    and interest rate cuts during global
      financial crisis, 176
    and trade acceptances, 67–70
financial "Big Bang", Japanese, 167.
    See also Big Bang
financial centers, rise of, 17–21
Financial Convention at the Genoa
    Conference, 36. *See also* foreign
    exchange reserves
financial deepening, 103–107, 112, 191,
    213n25, 214n33, 224n20
financial development, 85, 93, 100, 106,
    112–184, 186, 190–193, 217n36, 224n22
financial liberalization, 162, 167, 221n8
financial openness, 131, 135, 217n34
financial repression, 159–160
financial technology, 5, 117, 195
Flandreau, Marc, 10, 19, 24, 25, 65, 72,
    101, 196, 203n24

foreign direct investment (FDI), 141, 161, 185, 194

Foreign Exchange Law, 161

foreign exchange markets
    development of, 17–20
    and electronic platforms, 9
    and the influence of empires and
        alliances, 26–29

foreign exchange market turnover, 171, 176, 177

foreign exchange reserves
    Brussels International Financial
        Conference, 36, 206n14
    dollar-sterling duopoly, 44, 94
    Financial Convention at the Genoa
        Conference, 36
    multiple currencies in, 9, 10, 24–26,
        203n23
    non-disclosed, 118, 178
    origins and history of, 20–29
    sterling decline in, 149–156
    volume data, 42–47
    See also currency composition

foreign public debt. *See* international
    public debt

French banking system
    and effort to restore franc as leading
        reserve currency, 50
    growth of, 25

French franc, 6, 7, 24, 44, 48, 54, 56, 86, 89,
    97, 118–120, 124, 176. 178, 195, 196, 207n3,
    211n3, 213n15

gateway technologies, 8, 9

Genoa Conference, 14, 36
    and Genoa Resolutions on Finance, 37
    and implementation of resolutions,
        40–41

Gensaki market, 161

German banking system, 19, 25, 71, 201n21,
    211n24
    growth of, 25
    and provision of trade credits, 71

Gilbert, Milton, 3

Glorious Revolution, 192

gold bullion standard, 21, 204n10, 204n11

gold-dollar system, 3

gold exchange standard, 15, 21, 27, 29, 32,
    37–41, 52, 57, 204n11, 205n24, 205n29,
    205n3

gold export embargo, 53

gold, in international public debt, 86–87

Gold Note Act of 1898, 27. *See also* India,
    connections with British banking

gold standard, 2, 15, 16–57, 69, 86, 87, 94,
    200, 202n14, 204n21, 206n12, 208n11,
    208n19, 212n5, 214n34
    and central banking, 20–21
    collapse of, 35
    and Genoa Conference, 36–40
    and pound sterling, 21–24, 35–38

Gold Standard Reserve, 27. *See also* India,
    connections with British banking

Great Britain
    and British India, 27 (*see also* India,
        connections with British banking)
    and colonial trade, 2
    and dominance of international
        finance, 1–41
    and Genoa Resolutions, 38
    and gold convertibility, 22, 35
    and post-World War II decline,
        145–157
    and seizure of Anglo-Austria Bank, 71
    and technological leadership, 1–2
    See also Bank of England

Great Depression, 11, 50, 67, 78, 105, 114

Hawtrey, Ralph, 37–39

hegemon, 1–3, 202n15

IMF. *See* International Monetary Fund
    (IMF)

India, connections with British banking,
    27–28, 213n15

India Office, 27

inertia, in the use of international currency,
    5, 8, 10, 43, 60, 85, 97, 100–115, 121–133,
    144, 156, 157, 165, 214n33

installed base, 5

international bond markets, 84–115

international currency
    benefits, 13, 173–174
    multiple, benefits and costs of, 12–13,
        197–199 (*see also* international
        monetary system: multipolar/
        unipolar, benefits and costs of)
    role in trade, 58–84, 182–183
    roles, 4
    theories, conventional and new
        views, 3–11
    See also currency composition: of
        foreign exchange reserves;
        names of individual currencies

international currency status
competition for, 24, 47, 64, 84,
116–144, 202n19
and inertia, 5, 8, 43, 60, 85, 106,
133, 156, 165
and persistence, 5, 8, 10, 14, 15, 56,
57, 60, 80, 81, 122, 123, 133, 156,
202n14, 216n23
regaining leadership in, 50, 52, 91
International Monetary Fund (IMF), 6, 7,
117, 119, 120–124, 131, 135, 140, 153, 155,
156, 158, 160, 168, 175, 178, 180, 196,
202n17, 213n12, 214n2, 215n11, 215n13,
216n26, 217n37, 220n22, 225n8. *See also*
Currency Composition of Official
Foreign Exchange Reserves
data base (COFFER)
international monetary system
model of, 10, 202n15, 226n9
multipolar/unipolar, benefits
and costs of, 12–13, 197–199
theories of, 1–15
international public debt
currency composition of, 88–97
and gold, 86
regional distribution of, 80–91
and war-related debts, 87, 89
international trade, role of currencies
in financing, 58–83

Japan, 2
deregulation of financial markets
in, 167
financial crisis in, 165
financial liberalization in, 162, 163 (*see
also* yen: internationalization of)
and high inflation, 160, 161
and post-World War II financial
system, 159–161
rapid economic growth of, 158
repurchase agreements in, 161
Japanese financial "Big Bang", 167. *See also*
Big Bang
Jekyll Island, 13, 32–34, 205n4. *See also*
Federal Reserve System

Kemmerer, Edwin, 32, 41, 204n11, 205n24,
205n3, 207n28
Keynes, John Maynard, 22, 35, 201n5,
205n24, 205n26, 205n27
Kindleberger, Charles, 1, 11, 201n3, 202n12,
224n14

Latin America, liquidation of sterling
reserves, 54
League of Nations and Genoa Conference,
36, 37, 40
lender of last resort, 22, 23, 186, 198
Lindert, Peter, 6, 7, 16, 24, 44, 196,
202n16, 205n33
lock-in, 5, 10, 12, 122, 203n25
"lost decade," 165, 166. *See* Japan: financial
crisis in

Maastricht Treaty, 172
Maddison, Angus, 1, 122, 201n2, 213n23, 220n1
McKinnon, Ronald, 3, 201n6, 222n18
Mitterrand, François, 172
monetary dominance, economic
theories of, 3
monopoly of international currency
status, 4, 6, 10, 12, 16, 19, 20, 24, 56,
57, 127, 171, 203n1
multiple international currencies, 8, 11,
13, 15, 84, 171, 196, 197, 199. *See also*
international currency

National Banking Act, 31, 62, 159
National Bank of Belgium, 16, 21
natural monopoly of reserve
currencies, 4, 6, 10, 12, 19, 20, 24,
56, 57, 127, 171.
See also reserve currencies
network economics, 4–14
network externalities, and international
currency status, 3, 18, 99, 106, 107, 122
network increasing returns, 4, 8, 9,
11, 14, 25, 44, 56, 57, 59, 80, 117, 127
New View. *See* economic theories of
international currencies, conventional
and new views
Nurkse, Ragnar, 42, 44, 47, 207n25,
207n2, 207n7

oil-price shock period, 160
Open Market Investment Committee,
67, 210n19
open systems, 8, 10, 127
Ottawa Economic Conference, 147
Outer Sterling Area, 146–150. *See also*
Sterling Area

Paper Currency Reserves, 27
People's Bank of China (PBOC)
and currency swap lines, 185

as regulator of twenty-first century
global economy, 3
persistence, in the use of international
currency. *See* international currency
status: and persistence
political stability, importance of for foreign
investing, 147, 193–194, 224n22
pound sterling. *See* sterling
Presidency Banks, 27, 205n25

Qualified Domestic Institutional Investors
(QDII), 184
Qualified Foreign Institutional Investors
(QFII), 183

Raj's cash balances, 27
Reichsbank, 26, 33, 200
renminbi, 3, 4, 6, 14, 56, 81, 107, 134, 168,
169, 175, 181–194, 196, 223n2, 223n4,
223n11, 223n13
clearing banks for, 184, 185
and dominance of twenty-first century
global economy, 3, 4, 6, 14, 56
internationalization of, 181–194
use of in trade, 182
renminbi-denominated bonds, 183, 184
reserve currencies
and composition of , 6, 14, 42–57,
116–144, 196
as natural monopoly (*see* monopoly of
international currency status)
sterling-dollar duopoly, 44, 94
Roosevelt, Franklin Delano, 53, 70
Russia, 19, 21, 25, 28, 90, 223n11, 223n12

safe haven, 199, 222n14
seigniorage, 27, 173, 174
Shanghai Composite index, 188
Shanghai-Hong Kong Stock Connect, 184
Silk Road Initiative, 186, 223n13
Single European Market, 171, 222n9
Snyder, John Wesley, 153
sovereign debt crisis of 2009, 171, 175, 176
sterling
and departure from gold standard, 42–57
as dominant reserve currency, 2, 4, 5,
11, 21–29
and end as leading reserve currency,
42–57, 145–157
as first global currency, 2, 4, 5, 11, 21–29
and recovery as leading reserve
currency, 52, 91–92

and role in gold standard, 21–24
and U.S. dollar duopoly, 44, 94
and use in international financial
transactions, 145–157
Sterling Area, 8, 43, 46, 52–57, 145–157
composition of, 46, 148
motivations for joining, 146–147
See also Outer Sterling Area
sterling balances, 14, 52, 54, 56, 149–157,
220n22
stock market capitalization, 142, 188,
217n36, 217n38
Suez Canal Zone, 155, 156
swap lines. *See* currency swap lines
Swiss franc, 44, 45, 48, 86, 118–124, 199,
207n3, 222n14, 223n8, 223n9

technology gap, 1
Tokyo Stock Exchange, 163, 165, 166
trade acceptances, 33–35, 61–69, 79–81,
104, 206n5
decline of market in, 34–35
dominance of London banks in, 61–63
Federal Reserve's involvement in, 67–70
Japan's use of, 163
rise of U.S. market in, 63–70
supply of, 60–63
and use in Latin American and
Asian trade, 34
trade credit
London as center for, 5
Transferable Accounts, 150
transparency, importance of for foreign
investing, 188–191
Triffin Dilemma, 12, 197, 225n3
Triffin, Robert, 42, 43, 47, 52, 122, 127,
203n29

United States, 2, 3, 6, 12, 13, 14, 24, 28,
32–41, 44, 54, 58–79, 90, 91, 100, 101,
114, 115, 123–129, 148, 150–160, 162–176,
185–199, 202n14, 206n10, 207n7, 208n19,
209n2, 210n14, 212n10, 213n14, 214n31,
214n32, 219n14, 221n6, 222n9, 225n2
banking and international operations,
31–32, 60–63
and Bretton-Woods-GATT System, 2
and dominance of international
finance, 2
and Genoa Resolutions, 36–41
and gold standard, 35
U.S. dollar. *See* dollar

view. *See also* international currency: theories, conventional and new views

Warburg, Paul, 33, 61, 205n4, 206n6, 209n7
Wilson, Harold, 156
Wilson, Woodrow, 206n12
World War I and effect on international
finance, 34–35

yen, 14, 29, 118–124, 139–141, 144, 158–169,
181, 184, 196, 215n7, 221n6, 221n7, 221n15,
223n8
and Council on Foreign Exchange and
Other Transactions, 162–168
internationalization of, 162–165. *See
also* Japan: financial crisis in
Yen-Dollar Agreement, 163

A NOTE ON THE TYPE

This book has been composed in Adobe Text and Gotham.
Adobe Text, designed by Robert Slimbach for Adobe,
bridges the gap between fifteenth- and sixteenth-century
calligraphic and eighteenth-century Modern styles.
Gotham, inspired by New York street signs, was designed
by Tobias Frere-Jones for Hoefler & Co.

CPSIA information can be obtained
at www.ICGtesting.com
Printed in the USA
JSHW081201280223
38319JS00004B/254